A JOURNEY TO THE
CENTER OF THE MIND

BOOK I:

The Coming-of-Age Years
(Mid-1950s to mid-1970s)

The journey begins...

AN FBI CRIMINAL PROFILER'S
CANDID MEMOIR

By

James R. Fitzgerald
Supervisory Special Agent (Ret.)
Federal Bureau of Investigation
Criminal Profiler/Forensic Linguist

∞ INFINITY
PUBLISHING

Copyright © 2014 by James R. Fitzgerald

ISBN 978-1-4958-0195-2 Hardcover
ISBN 978-1-4958-0237-9 Paperback
ISBN 978-1-4958-0238-6 eBook

Printed in the United States of America

Published August 2014

INFINITY PUBLISHING
1094 New DeHaven Street, Suite 100
West Conshohocken, PA 19428-2713
Toll-free (877) BUY BOOK
Local Phone (610) 941-9999
Fax (610) 941-9959
Info@buybooksontheweb.com
www.buybooksontheweb.com

DEDICATED TO:

Wally and Alma (My Parents)

Cass, Alma, and Marilyn (My Sisters)

Sean, Dan, and Ryan (My Sons)

…without whom, to a person, this book would have never been written, nor a fulfilling life led.

Title concept thanks to…

Jules Verne
From his 1864 novel,
Voyage au centre de la Terre
aka,
A Journey to the Center of the Earth

and

The Amboy Dukes
(Specifically Ted Nugent, Steve Farmer)
From their 1968 record album and single,
Journey to the Center of the Mind

Acknowledgements

Where do I start in acknowledging the people who helped form my story, my book, not to mention my life itself? I suppose at the very beginning....

In what I would call a "no-brainer," I will first and foremost acknowledge my parents, Wally and Alma, for providing me with what I would best describe as a very "normal" childhood and upbringing. I was definitely a surprise to them, born 12 years after my next oldest sibling. Plus, being a boy after three girls had to add to the challenge of a later-in-life child for them. But, they succeeded nonetheless, and with all four of us. The foundation they laid for me allowed me to grow up in a world where I only had to worry about, well, growing up. I wouldn't be the person I am without the two of them leading by example, staying out of the way when they should have, but most importantly being there when I needed them. I only wish they were still with us now.

I'm also very appreciative of growing up with three great older (but never old) sisters, Cass, Alma, and Marilyn. When as a 5-year-old I was building roads and bridges on the living room floor of our Philadelphia rowhome with books and blocks, it was they individually and collectively who would tell me that when I go to college I should study to become an engineer. I would ask them, "Why do I have to go to college? And, what's an engineer?" They would simply respond "You WILL go to college, Jimmy, and an engineer is a person who designs roads and bridges." I would argue that I didn't want to "design" them, I wanted to "build" them. I eventually figured it out, with their help, even if I didn't become an engineer. They were the first ones to encourage me to go to college way back then, even when none of them chose to do so themselves. Those seeds planted about attaining a college degree stayed with me since my earliest years and I'm proud to say I was the first in my extended family to become a college graduate. This eventually led to other career opportunities and accomplishments, many to be written of in this series of books. Along with my parents, I thank Cass, Alma, and Marilyn for this early academic direction. I only wish Marilyn was still with us now, too.

Sean, Dan, and Ryan, are my three sons. Although not directly referenced in *A Journey to the Center of the Mind, Book I*, obviously because they hadn't been born yet, I found myself thinking of my future kids often, even as a boy and young man. Since predominantly female babies seemed to run in my family, it was a surprise to me when each turned out to be a boy, including the last one, Ryan, who came along 11 years after Dan, 14 years after Sean. I did my best to pay-it-forward to them for how my parents raised me. That is, to later be the best parent I could be in leading by example and even letting them fall sometimes, but always trying to be there to pick them up. They would each ask me about my life growing up in the "olden days."

I'd tell them some of my stories and they said I should write it all down sometime. So, a big part of the reason I wrote this book was because of them, and the grandchildren and great-grandchildren I've yet to meet.

To a few people not a part of my bloodline...

I'd be remiss if I didn't thank Kena Childers, who is a fellow employee at The Academy Group, Inc. She did a great job of proofreading, formatting, and offering other suggestions for my book. She did it all with a brand new baby needing her full-time attention at the same time. She was definitely multitasking, but still took care of my book very well, and I have no doubt her little boy, too.

Angelo Cataldi, Philadelphia sports radio host extraordinaire, and a friend, provided me a literary shot in the arm when I needed it most. As any author will attest, writing can be an onerous task and sometimes right in the middle of a chapter, a paragraph, or even a sentence, frustration kicks in and you wonder where it's all going, what it all means, and you question the meaning and value of what's already written and what's about to be written. But, after Angelo read an early version of my book (which a mutual friend provided to him without me even knowing about it), he raved about it for days and weeks afterwards and strongly encouraged me to keep writing and complete the task at hand. So, I did, and here is the finished product. Again Angelo, much appreciation and thanks here for the positive and inspiring words when I needed them most.

Last, but certainly not least, I'd like to extend my warmest gratitude to Natalie Schilling, my partner and friend, for her guidance through this book writing process. I first met her in the early 2000s when she was my academic advisor and professor at Georgetown University Graduate School where I was working on my master's in linguistics. Who ever knew she would later serve as, among many other things, my muse in the writing of *A Journey to the Center of the Mind*? In fact it was Natalie, while on a mid-summer walk on the beach in Sea Isle City, New Jersey, who originally suggested the title. That, plus emulating her as she wrote her own successful book(s), provided the ongoing impetus to finish my own book(s). Thank you for everything, Natalie, and not just the muse part.

Table of Contents

Prologue

It was in the spring of the year, mid-morning, sunny and warmish outside. I seem to recall that I didn't need an overcoat or heavy jacket then. I was merely putting on my basic uniform of the day. The same one I wore many times back then.

I slowly started to don that uniform and equipment, which I had laid out neatly on the chair the night before. Then, to my surprise, before even beginning my daily "tour-of-duty," I heard the scream. It sounded like that of a young girl, and she was crying loudly and repeatedly. It was somewhat muffled, but not too far from my present location. She sounded as if she were in fear for her life. I knew I had to get to her and help her.

I continued the process of putting on my equipment when the screaming intensified. I was usually very methodical in strapping on my holster, inserting my guns into the holsters (yes, I actually carried two guns at the time), placing the handcuffs into their leather holder, putting on my hat, and positioning my badge where everyone would see it. But this time, with the girl's shrieks getting louder and more frequent, I knew I had to hurry. I didn't even have time to check my image in the mirror before I exited the building in an attempt to rescue the screaming girl from whatever it was that was causing her this distress.

After all, I was a "lawman" and I had a life to save.

Make that, an Old West lawman. Well, sort of. At least that's what I was pretending to be. You see, I really didn't live in the West, old or new. I lived in a rowhome in the Olney section of Philadelphia, Pennsylvania. It wasn't even *West* Philadelphia. Instead it was closer to Northeast Philadelphia. I was about five years old at the time of this incident, the first recollected undertaking in my then make-believe career in law enforcement. Oh, and the word "Lawman" was printed on my slightly tarnished tin badge, over the then most commonly used version of my name, "Jimmy."

I recall it was a few months prior that my father bought the badge for me when we were at, of all places, the then-annual Philadelphia Boat Show. (Although my dad really liked boats, and the water, unfortunately my family could never afford to own one. Nevertheless, he still attended the show every few years and brought me along too.) I can still picture the vendor meticulously personalizing the badge for me by engraving my name in cursive onto it with some sort of a special electronic tool that made lots of noise. The end result was a shiny tin star with "Lawman Jimmy" on it. Could it get any better than that?

I never forgot that my father gave me my first ever badge, albeit a pretend one. I would one day give back to him a badge, not made of tin, but a real one, and it would stay with him forever. He "deputized" me, sort of, as a little kid with that engraved tin badge. In my own way, years later, I returned the favor to him. He would watch over me as I wore that pretend badge, and no doubt later when I wore a real one.

But back to Lawman Jimmy, in my mind, that first badge made me official. I was actually a retro-lawman in that I was dressed in my best store-bought cowboy outfit. And while the days of the Wild West were long over, their scripted re-creation was still very popular on TV and at the movies. My guns and handcuffs were, of course, toys, although pretty authentic looking toys.

The year would have been about 1959 that my first "arrest" attempt was made. As I ran out the front door of my house, jumped on my small red bike (not a horse), and rode around the corner and up the nearby alley, I quickly found the screaming girl. She too was about five years old. Her name eludes me after all these years, but I could see that she was being tormented and teased relentlessly by who turned out to be her older brother and two or three of his friends. I sped to her side, purposefully jumped off my still moving bike, and told her I was here to save her.

She looked at me quizzically at first, as did the older boys, and then responded to my rescue attempt half-laughingly and half-dismissively by saying, "Go home, Jimmy Fitzgerald. I don't need your help! And you're not a real cowboy anyway!"

The brother and his friends collectively laughed out loud, forgetting momentarily their teasing of the girl. I asked her hesitatingly and with clearly less urgency than before if she was sure she didn't need my assistance. She emphatically said "No, go home, Jimmy!" as she then gleefully strode off with her brothers and his pals, seemingly her new best friends.

Upon hearing that from her, I shrugged my shoulders, re-mounted my horse, I mean bike, and rode off dejectedly into the sunset. Well, actually, it was closer to noon, and it was back to my just-around-the-corner rowhome. I realized then that I now had no one to save, arrest, or even pretend-shoot. At least not that day.

Didn't they see my badge? Didn't they notice what I was wearing? Didn't they know who I was? Or at least who I was pretending to be?

This never seemed to happen on TV.

This episode of childhood innocence would be an interesting prelude to my future involvement in family disputes and intimate-partner assaults at a time when I would wear an actual lawman uniform and badge and would carry real guns. Yes, guns as in more than one. In the real world of law enforcement, as a uniformed police officer, I always carried a hidden .38 caliber Colt Detective Special as my ballistic back-up. It was carried in my right-side ankle holster, along with my very visible police issued Smith & Wesson .357 Magnum on the left hand side (yes, I'm a leftie) of my waist holster.

As that real police officer many years later, I would respond to a number of calls and complaints from wives or girlfriends having been assaulted by their male partners. In more instances than I care to recall, upon arrival at their residences the women would again tell me, in so many words, to "go home." They'd inform me of this even as their eyes were freshly blackened or their teeth newly punched out. They loved their men, they somewhat unconvincingly told me as they watched their usually drunk and non-compliant guys being handcuffed. And, they were sticking by them, even if they had called the police just ten minutes or so before, screaming over the phone to the dispatcher that their man was trying to kill them. Now, they wanted me out of the place where just a few punches, pushes, or kicks ago, they had requested my presence.

So, yes, whereas in the early days of my career as a uniformed police officer, I was often told to "Go home, Officer Fitzgerald!" other times going home wasn't an option. This would become even more true years later as I moved from police officer to FBI profiler, where it became my job not only to catch bad guys in the act but to track them down both after and, ideally, before they committed their next acts of violence. To go inside their minds much as I once tried to get inside my own mind as a law enforcement officer, first make-believe and then real, to figure out why people who seemingly needed my help would turn me away, and how I could help them despite the resistance of victim, perpetrator, or both.

But I'm getting just a bit ahead of myself here....

How did I get from my Philadelphia neighborhood playacting a lawman to becoming a real one? Especially given that I wasn't even born into a law enforcement-oriented family. There were a few military veterans among my relations and only one relative, through a distant-cousin's marriage, who had ever worn a police uniform. Yet, that one law enforcement officer in my family did play a brief yet very important role in my life one hot summer night during my teenage years when it was me who needed help from someone else carrying a badge, and yes, a real one.

My law enforcement career started officially, though somewhat unceremoniously, as a 22-year-old Pennsylvania State University graduate with a degree in what was then called "Law Enforcement and Corrections." My first adult job was that of store detective at a large downtown Philadelphia department store. Then, 14 months later, I became a street cop in a mid-sized suburban Philadelphia police department, eventually attaining the rank of detective and then sergeant. Eleven years after entering the police profession, I became an FBI agent, with a first assignment to New York City. Seven years later, I was promoted to supervisor and criminal profiler, later adding the title of forensic linguist (one who analyzes language evidence) to my curriculum vitae.

In travelling this path, during the course of my innumerable tours of duty, I've experienced firsthand the beauty of live birth and the ugliness of sudden, violent death. I've been involved in fistfights, knife fights, shootouts, foot chases, car chases, minor and major investigations, and minor and major arrests, all in the course of a 31-year law enforcement career. I've laughed uncontrollably out loud at the end of some work shifts, yet could be emotionally traumatized at the end of others. I made great friends, and I lost great friends within my chosen profession. In the latter instances, I would often reflect on the concept of fate, since I had often been doing the same jobs as my friends and colleagues when they met their untimely and violent deaths. I just happened to be in different places, at different times, and just happened to be spared.

On occasion, in my early law enforcement career, I endured the painful drudgery of a job that was going nowhere, mired in paperwork and politics that did nothing to advance the cause of justice, or me. At other times, in my later career, I felt like I was at the very top of my profession, holding one of the most important positions anywhere in my field.

Looking back, I've arguably held one of the least esteemed positions (at least for a few months) in the law enforcement profession and later one of the most esteemed. Each of these stages of my life, as well as many phases before and after, taught me something about myself and about other people, about the good and bad in all of us, both within the law enforcement community and outside of it.

Each person, each incident, each gain, each loss, each success, each failure (and yes, there were a few of those), whether or not I realized it at the time, when added to my earlier personal life experiences, became for me foundational blocks in the building of my career – and the building of my person. The experiences and skills I gained both inside and outside of law enforcement led me to help solve major crimes and put some really bad guys in prison for a really long time and also sometimes ensured my very survival on the streets. But more importantly, they made me the person I am today, yes professionally, but also personally.

Now, several years into retirement, it's time to tell my story.

A Journey to the Center of the Mind (JCM) is actually comprised of three separate volumes. They are Book I, Book II, and Book III.

In JCM Book I, starting in the mid-1950s and going through the mid-1970s, my personal journey begins. It is focused chiefly on my youthful life experiences, accomplishments, and a few glaring mistakes (with some flash-forwards from later in life), and how I survived them (mostly) in one piece, mentally and physically. I'll share many events of my personal life, from grade school through college, with friends, my sometimes tenuous involvement with law enforcement before I was even engaged in that career, at my first real job (sort of) in the criminal justice system, and the effect of both the good and the bad experiences, and good and bad people I met, during this time. Sometimes the interconnections between my personal and later professional life will be seen as being clear and direct. At other times, the impact of my personal experiences, interests, feelings, and beliefs was less direct but still influenced my subsequent career-related decisions, both on a moment-to-moment and long-term basis, and thus ultimately shaped some quite important career outcomes as well. It culminates with my admission to and graduation from the Pennsylvania State Police Academy in Hershey, PA.

In JCM Book II, beginning in 1976 and ending in 1987, the journey continues with my official entry into the law enforcement profession as my eventual 11-year career as a patrolman, plainclothes officer, detective, and sergeant, at the Bensalem (Pennsylvania) Police Department, will be recounted in some detail. The police work, the personalities, the politics, and the prosecutions (sometimes all being intertwined), along with some very bizarre and interesting people I met, as well as some very bizarre and interesting situations I experienced, will be elaborated upon here as I make my way through a transitional time in U.S. history, and not just in the general culture, but in the law enforcement profession as well. Oh, and my own personal and professional transitions will become rather obvious too.

In JCM Book III, starting in 1987 at the FBI Academy in Quantico, Virginia, through my first assignment to New York City, to my promotion which brought me back to the FBI Academy in 1995, completes my law enforcement journey as I become an FBI special agent, criminal profiler, and later forensic linguist, all the while investigating some of the biggest cases of the 1990s and early 2000s. These cases include Unabom, the Jon Benet Ramsey homicide, Anthrax, the Washington, DC Sniper...just to name a few. It concludes with my retirement in 2007, although in the Epilogue, I'll discuss my work on the television series *Criminal Minds* and *Killer Profile*, plus some interesting and headline-grabbing cases I worked as a consultant with my Virginia-based company, The Academy Group, Inc.

In each of these books, I'll give an account of some truly great people I've encountered in my life, some perhaps not-so-great, and some of truly questionable character, integrity, and motivation, all while attempting to capture the times and places in which I lived and worked. Some of these people, whether I realized it right away or discovered it gradually, through careful, initially amateur profiling at the time, turned out to be downright evil. Criminals, victims, witnesses, wannabe-cops, groupies, and yes, even a few law enforcement officers, fall into the above categories, some where you would expect them to, and others into quite unexpected categorizations. And, while I'm at it, the reader will learn about my early mistakes and lapses in judgment too. I hold nothing back here, whether to my detriment or not.

Lastly, life has definitely not "concluded" for me in any way, shape, or form. I'm a still very active criminal profiler, forensic linguist, adjunct faculty member at Hofstra University and The Richard Stockton College of New Jersey, frequent guest lecturer at Georgetown University and other institutions of higher learning (both in the U.S. and internationally), *Criminal Minds* technical advisor, co-host and executive producer of my own television series, *Killer Profile*, and a writer.

This book (along with Book II and Book III) invites you to join me as I chart the sometimes smooth, sometimes rocky journey of my life's course – the one I chose or somehow fell into, or both – and the one which ultimately led to me becoming pretty darn good at what it is I decided I wanted to do, that is, become a law enforcement professional, criminal profiler, and forensic linguist.

Oh, and I hope a decent human being, too.

Author's note: Everything written in this book happened just as it's related by me, or at least as accurately as my still pretty good memory allows. However, for what should be obvious reasons, some names have been omitted altogether, other first names or job titles changed, or specific places, businesses, etc., remain unmentioned. This was done to protect the innocent, the guilty, and/or those people who fall somewhere in between. If it's a person's full name, or an identified business, school, or the like, it's the real deal.

Lastly, any opinions offered in this book are mine, and not that of the FBI's.

"It is always wise to look ahead,
but difficult to look further than you can see."

Sir Winston Churchill
British soldier, politician, historian, statesman
1874 – 1965

Chapter One

My earliest childhood memory is a brief but very specific one. It could have led to a crime or to a violent or tragic end but fortunately, for me, it didn't. It's interwoven with some very vague visual and other sensory recollections and later reinforced with various familial verbalized versions of the event.

That earliest memory is of me walking by myself in the woods, observing train tracks through the trees ahead of me, becoming instantly fascinated by them and continuing towards them on my unplanned and unchartered solo trek. I hear and then watch a train speed by, becoming even more excited at what I'm experiencing in the scene unfolding before me. Then, I'm suddenly being grabbed from behind and picked up by a large, sweaty black man.

I can still almost smell this man's perspiration on him. While I visually and aromatically recall the above series of brief but interconnected events relatively well, it's the facts regarding that day that I subsequently learned which pieced the complete story together for me.

It was sometime in the summer of 1956 when my then 15-year-old sister Marilyn, the youngest of my three sisters (I was born later in life to my parents), along with one of her girlfriends, decided to take her little brother Jimmy, then all of three years old, to Fisher Park, located about four blocks from where we lived. Fisher Park was then and is now what would be called an inner-city or urban park, encompassing around 23 acres, or six-to-eight city blocks, albeit irregular shaped city blocks, bordered on three sides by neighborhood streets, and on part of the west side by railroad tracks. There were and are trails throughout, but also semi-large sections of wooded areas that would not necessarily be visible from any of the walking trails or the other people-user sections, such as playgrounds, tennis courts, etc.

On this day, our mom and dad apparently gave their permission to Marilyn to take me to the little playground embedded inside the park. So off we went, on foot, for what should have been a lovely afternoon. My mom was home that day, doing her everyday housework. My dad was outside of the house, on a ladder, doing some painting. Luckily, about one hour later when Marilyn came home with her news, he didn't fall off that ladder.

Of course, I wasn't there, but I was told years later that when Marilyn walked home, by herself, and first told my dad that...gulp...she lost little Jimmy in the park, he let out a stream of ladder-top invectives that, I would learn later on certain occasions, few could successfully replicate. Never the four-letter kind, mind you, but invoking the name of the Lord Almighty in repetitive fashion, with multiple versions of "damn" and "hell" thrown in for good (or bad) measure, was our dad's verbal trademark when he was truly upset.

Within minutes, both my parents reportedly jumped into the family car. With a crying Marilyn in the back seat, a semi-hysterical mom in the front passenger seat, and a very mission-oriented dad behind the wheel, they hastily drove the short distance to the park, got out of the car, and walked to the last place Marilyn told them she had seen me. Her girlfriend was still there and told my parents that she had continued looking for me and calling my name in the immediate area, but to no avail. Little Jimmy was nowhere to be found.

Exactly what happened next remains unclear after all this time, but I was eventually turned over by the man who found this free-roaming toddler to the Philadelphia Park Police. Somehow my parents found the Park Police officer, or he found them, and I was returned safely and unharmed to them. My whole time out-of-pocket (a term later learned while in the FBI, meaning "unseen" or "unobserved") that afternoon was probably no more than 45 minutes. Long enough, though, for some bad things to have happened to a wandering three-year old....

Interestingly, I don't remember at all being scared or frightened during my "nature walk" that afternoon. I suppose it was my first ever taste of complete freedom in my young life. It occurred in this not-so-small urban park, with no parents, guardians, or older siblings around me, and I seem to have enjoyed every minute of it. And, what little boy wouldn't be attracted to railroad tracks? Geez, my dad would put up our Lionel train set every Christmas season in our basement. Here was the real thing, and LOOK, there goes a choo-choo train now. Let's have my little feet take me over there, closer to those tracks, look for the next train, get closer, and...whoa, what the...who's this big, burly man wrapping his arms around me and carrying me over his shoulder?

He certainly doesn't look like my parents or anyone I know. He's wearing some sort of a uniform. He's sweaty. Where is he taking me?

Within a few minutes, I was back with my parents and sister and all was well. Not that I ever knew that things were not well, but they were now, for sure.

I suppose if there's one specific morale or life-lesson to be learned from this tale, it's to not lose a small child anywhere, much less in wooded areas near railroad tracks. These types of occurrences happen frequently to parents and caregivers with their small kids. Fortunately, in the vast majority of times, they are resolved as in what happened to me, that is, child found, no harm and no foul. It's the rare cases in which a child is never found, or found abused, injured or dead, from his/her own misdoings or that of an opportunistic individual who is at the right place at the right time (for him), that result in the tragic outcomes and generate the morbid headlines.

In my future law enforcement career, I would investigate numerous missing child scenarios. Some just minutes after they occurred, some years afterwards. Some children were found very quickly, some were found dead or never found at all. I was very lucky that day in 1956. A good man found me and did the right thing before other bad things could have happened to me, such as being hit by a train or being found by one of those opportunistic individuals whom we now called pedophiles.

By the way, the man who found me worked for the railroad. I believe he simply found me, turned me over to the Park Police, and went back to his job. My family never got his name or had a chance to thank him. Who knows what would have happened to me that day if not for this railroad employee's alertness and actions.

Lastly, as it relates to this story, my sister Marilyn never again lost me, or any of her own four children with whom she was blessed later in her life.

Like many of life's difficult lessons, as I was to later learn, experiencing them just one time was usually enough to remember forever and avoid replication. For most people, that is.

As I got a bit older, and when I wasn't lost, I suppose I wasn't too different from most boys my age in the late 1950s. I was part of the first generation to be raised on that new-fangled in-the-home entertainment device known as television. TV back then during primetime was chock full of various cowboy shows and many young boys in the U.S. wanted to be like the lead characters, the ever-present good guys.

I did my best to emulate U.S. Marshall Matt Dillon of *Gunsmoke* and other lead characters at the time or those who came a bit later. TV shows such as *Wagon Train, Cheyenne, Lawman, The Rifleman,* and *Bronco*, to name a few, were weekly staples of mine. I eventually figured out that many of the characters portrayed in these shows were not portraying actual lawmen, but that didn't matter to my five-to-six year old television viewing mind. They were still "good guys" doing their best in the Old West to resolve issues usually involving money, women, land, cattle, Indians (before they were referred to as Native-Americans), or some combination of the above. Yes, there was usually some level of gunplay necessitated in order to resolve these issues. Episodes of these various shows almost always portrayed someone being shot, maybe even killed. But, in the end, justice was rendered. The guest "bad guy" du jour would ultimately wind up dead, run out of town, or in jail. Problem fixed forever; usually as a result of someone getting a good whooping, being shot, being incarcerated, or being hanged, because of the actions, direct or indirect, of the lead good-guy character.

It seemed most of my young peers watched these shows too, at least the ones that were over by 9:00PM. The violence portrayed was not graphic or necessarily gratuitous. These were Western-based morality plays, each story with clear beginnings, middles, and usually happy endings, all in 45 minutes or so total, some at 22 minutes or so total, minus commercials. But they did depict violence, no question about it, and sometimes as the solution to one or more problems.

Looking back, I believe the violence was outweighed by the shows' endings in which "good" always prevailed. The anti-hero character-type had not quite been portrayed yet on U.S. television, at least not with any regularity, and at least not before 9:00PM. The good guys were generally good, and the bad guys were generally bad. It was pretty easy to delineate the two. In real life, as I was to find out much later, it wasn't always that simple.

Back to my early upbringing, and my family, I can still vividly recall watching TV, sitting alongside of, or on the floor in front of, my stay-at-home mom, Alma (nee Kennard), and my dad, Wally, a Philadelphia Gas Works employee, in the living room of our home near the intersection of 3rd St.

and Nedro Ave., in the Olney section of Philadelphia. My sisters, Cass, Alma, and Marilyn, were there sometimes too, although they were 16, 14, and 12 years, respectively, older than me. At that time, they were less concerned with fictional TV cowboy shows than other aspects of being late-teens or early 20-somethings in the latter days of the 1950s.

Interestingly, my dad was born in 1904 in Philadelphia on Elfreth's Alley. This is a small street in the Olde City part of downtown Philadelphia, not too far from the Betsy Ross house, she of early U.S. flag sewing fame. Baby Wallace was born in the bedroom of his parents' house there. Hospital births to most were yet a few decades off. My dad was the youngest of 11 children to Jeremiah and Catherine (nee Wallace, and my dad so named) Fitzgerald. He was one of a set of twins, but his brother died shortly after birth. Children dying at or shortly after delivery were not uncommon then.

When young Wally and his family lived there, Elfreth's Alley was by no means an upscale location. In fact, it was quite the opposite as it was comprised of clearly working-class inhabitants living in the rather small and then rundown older rowhomes on this one block-long street. My dad's parents eventually moved the family from Elfreth's Alley to another somewhat newer Philadelphia neighborhood. Nonetheless, my father travelled through his early adulthood being a bit insecure of the fact that he was born on that particular economically challenged street in that neighborhood.

All that changed, however, in the late 1930s. As highway and building expansion was taking place in downtown Philadelphia, Elfreth's Alley and the homes on it were set to be demolished. However, various local historians and city-planners realized that the 32 homes on the block were, in fact, located on one of the oldest continually inhabited residential streets in the U.S. The street itself dated back to 1702. So, the move was made to preserve the street and repair some of the old houses. Over the years, that goal was met and now the street is officially recognized as a National Historic Landmark.

I'm proud to visit the Alley frequently and walk by the house in which my dad was born. In fact, on the anniversary of Wally's 100th birthday, my sisters Cass and Alma (Marilyn could not get off from work), my youngest son, and I, all spent a few minutes in front of his former home commemorating his birth, with lunch at a nearby restaurant afterwards. It was a fitting way to celebrate his birthday, although unfortunately, Wally was no longer with us at the time.

My mom was born in Beverly, New Jersey, and she moved with her family to Philadelphia when she was very young. She grew up on Ashdale Street near 5th Street, just about a mile away from our later home in Olney. Interestingly, my mom and I were the only ones in our family who were lefthanders. Growing up, I was freely allowed to enjoy my left-handedness, but her story from childhood was quite different. In or about 1920, when she started first grade at the Incarnation Catholic School, located just a few hundred yards from her home, upon noticing little Alma's propensity for left-handedness, the nun would literally tie her left hand to the side of her desk so she was then forced to learn penmanship with her right hand. It worked as far as the nuns were concerned. Throughout her life, she did practically everything left-handed, except write. Fortunately, the hand-tying of lefties died off by the time I entered first grade.

In the early 1930s, Wally met Alma when she was a cashier in the S.S. Kresge Five and Ten Cent Store, near 5th St. and Olney Ave. After a while they dated, then got married, and honeymooned in beautiful Atlantic City, New Jersey. Oh, and after three daughters, I was born about 23 years later.

Back to my own rowhome, and growing up in Olney in the 1950s, I was "all boy," as my parents and sisters often told me later, and that included wearing toy guns and badges and playing cowboy characters with my friends. However, I did have other activities at the time. I didn't just watch TV, of course. That alone, to the exclusion of other healthy activities, would not have been permitted by my parents. And, with only three channels to choose from then, there were virtually no interesting shows on during the day anyway, at least not for kids.

During the daylight hours, unless I was in school, I spent most of my free time outdoors, riding my bike around the block or up the nearby alley, playing stickball in the driveway near my house, engaging in hide-and-seek-like games with friends at twilight, and similar such activities. I got to know every nook and cranny, front yard and backyard, of the approximately 70 rowhomes on my semi-trapezoidal-shaped city block, each with its own family and their own lives. There were also three retail stores of various sorts on my block, including a drugstore/pharmacy, located about 100 feet due north of my front door.

Philadelphia is known as a city of neighborhoods. My neighborhood, Olney, was at the time a working class neighborhood located in the lower northeast section of the city. Its then residents were mostly of German and Irish ancestry. It is believed my paternal great-grandparents came to the U.S. and Philadelphia sometime during or soon after the Irish potato famine in the 1850s. My maternal grandmother was born in the Alsace-Lorraine area of France/Germany, depending on which country claimed the region in the late 1880s.

I recall a number of my neighbors and friends' parents speaking with German accents or Irish brogues. And, if not their parents, it was their grandparents who spoke those dialects or other languages, perhaps not speaking English at all. If they were not German-American or Irish-American, it would have been Italian-American or Polish-American residents in Olney at the time. The neighborhood was diverse, but clearly only Euro-centered diversity represented my Olney neighborhood at the time.

There were lots and lots of people crammed into this loosely defined neighborhood of just a few square miles. As it's all we knew at the time, this populous area was not a problem to us kids in any way, shape, or form. It simply was what it was and we made our daily way through these somewhat crowded everyday conditions. To add to the congestion, there weren't too many open fields in Olney.

Besides Fishers Park, if open spaces were to be found, they were supermarket parking lots or schoolyards, both covered in asphalt, not grass or dirt. Mostly, my neighborhood was just row after row of attached houses with a few larger single homes sprinkled throughout and with a major traffic way, 5th Street, between Grange and Duncannon Aves., serving as the main retail shopping district there.

My dad's parents bought our house when it was brand new in 1930. The city's population was increasing and the new home building, mostly all rowhomes, was expanding from the downtown area in concentric circles outward. When my dad married my mom in the mid-1930s, they moved in with my paternal grandparents (whom I never met) and eventually attained full ownership of the house after they died.

The 3rd St. house was in my family for 60 years, until it was eventually sold in 1990 to a relatively newly arrived Vietnamese-American family. Yes, non-European ethnic diversification finally came to Olney, it just took a while.

Being born pretty much the middle of the Baby Boomer Generation (1946-1964), there were young boys and girls just about everywhere one would look in Olney. One's best friends, at least at a young age, were mostly geographically derived as they rarely lived more than a few hundred feet away, with some even much closer.

At six or seven years of age, I probably had about six friends, all boys, all within my general age bracket, and all within a literal baseball throw of my front or back door. Of course, there were girls in the neighborhood, but I wasn't too concerned with them at this stage of development (except for perhaps that occasional lawman "rescue" attempt).

They seemed to do their things, and we boys did ours, and we rarely co-mingled outside of school.

Interestingly, one's friends in Philadelphia at that time would be further delineated by what school system they attended. I would eventually attend St. Helena School, a Catholic grade school run by the Archdiocese of Philadelphia. Non-Catholic friends of mine, in my immediate neighborhood, would attend Lowell School, a nearby public grade school.

When generically referring to these friends who didn't go to our Catholic school, we just naturally called them "Publics." It wasn't a derisive term in any way. It simply served to better describe someone to you.

I can still vividly recall youthful conversations that went something like, "Hey Fitzie, you know Billy, the new kid over on Fourth St?"

"No, I haven't met him."

"Yeah, he's a Public, he just moved here. He has a really fast black bike."

"Oh...okay."

It was during this time frame, with me around the age of six or seven and a first grader at St. Helena School that my first memories of real-life crimes entered into my consciousness. One, in retrospect, while affecting me directly, was very minor. The other, even though it didn't directly affect me, was much more serious. The former confounded me for a few days, yet the memories clearly linger. The latter had me asking questions of my parents and others for years, make that decades, to come.

Chapter Two

I mentioned previously that I enjoyed riding my bike as a child. My first two-wheeled bike was a red 20" Rollfast. I loved that bike. I rode it around my block, on the sidewalk, practically every day that weather would permit. Sometimes I would ride it to a nearby friend's house or simply ride for the sake of riding. Sometimes I was by myself, sometimes with others.

I can still picture the two retrofitted multicolored streamers hanging from both ends of my handlebars that flew in the wind as I picked up speed. The faster I pedaled the closer to horizontal they would become. I also remember fastening baseball cards with my mom's clothespins to the front and rear wheel frames of the bike. When the bike's spokes hit them, they made the neatest sound as I sped along the narrow sidewalks and the somewhat wider alley that cut the block in half. Faster speeds were met with an increasingly louder rat-a-tat-tat sound. Acceleration was clearly rewarded with heightened visual and audible effects, both for me the rider and anyone who was within ear and eye-view of this red, two-wheeled blur.

However, at this early age, even with my brightly colored and noisy bike, I wasn't allowed to cross three of the four streets which encompassed my particular city block. I could only carefully ride my bike on Calvert St., because it was a small less travelled street bordering the south side of my block. My dad also rented a garage there, one of about ten which were right across the street from the end of our shared driveway.

When back in my house for lunch, dinner, or for a break, I would almost always simply park my bike on the sidewalk directly in front of my house. I would just prop it up on its kickstand, not locked to anything, and there it would wait for my return. I had no bike lock, as it was never even thought of at the time by me. After all, who would steal a little kid's bike?

Well, one summer evening I walked out the front door, I believe after dinner, and my red bike was not there. I hesitated for a minute on the top step of the house, looked up and down the street, I'm sure figuratively as well as literally scratching my head, and went back inside and told my parents of my dilemma. They asked me several times whether I had left it somewhere else, maybe even in our small, fenced-in backyard, or in the driveway where my dad often parked the family car. I told them no, I had left it out front.

As it was very unlikely that a friend would have simply borrowed my bike, it was then determined that my bike had been stolen. I was apparently the victim of a crime, my first, at barely seven years of age.

Needless to say, I took this theft, this crime, very personally. I couldn't understand why someone would take another person's property, much less a kid's bike, much less MY bike. My parents didn't have the disposable income to simply go out and buy me a new bike that next day. They probably would have eventually, but I simply knew it wouldn't be right away. That night, my dad and I drove around in the family car looking for my bike. I walked around the block and up the alley looking for my two-wheeled friend the next day, and so did my mom on her almost daily walk to the local supermarket. No luck.

I recall that I was truly upset that first night and again on the following day. I'm sure I still managed to sleep that night, but remember waking up angry and frustrated the next morning. Was it all a dream? No, I realized shortly after awakening, I was still without my favorite, my only bike. Why didn't I put it in my backyard instead of the front of the house? Why didn't I hear the sound of the baseball cards as the bike was being ridden away? Who would do this to me?

Nonetheless, it finally set in. My bike wasn't lost. It wasn't misplaced. It was stolen. Someone else had it. Would I ever get it back? I wasn't sure, but I soon became determined to try.

I slowly came up with an idea. I'm not sure from where it originated. All those cowboy TV shows I was watching? I doubt it. Maybe an occasional police show my parents watched? I'm not sure. But, I somehow decided I would launch my own investigation. I had to, as no one else would do it for me. My parents were helpful, but busy, and they said it would be no use to call the Philadelphia Police Department, as it just wasn't important enough of a crime for them to investigate. I didn't quite understand this notion, but I reluctantly went along with them. I really had no choice.

My investigative plan then somehow came together. I asked, searched for, and then found a recent photograph of me and my bike. There was just one photo of it in the whole family album. It was of me on my bike on my way to the annual 4th of July parade, which marched north on 5th Street in my neighborhood every year on that date. Anyone could join in, and I did so the preceding summer. Luckily, the distinctive multi-colored streamers were on the bike at the time of the photo. I was granted permission to remove the photo from the album to make a very amateur "stolen" poster for my missing bike.

With my mom's help, the poster listed from where it was stolen, when, who to contact, and a phone number. As this was well before readily available photocopy machines or other easy ways to duplicate photographs or documents, there was only one version of it. This was my only chance to show people the poster with my stolen bike and ask them questions about it. The investigation now started in earnest.

What I planned to do then was what, in later years, when working truly serious crimes, would be called a "neighborhood canvass." That is, an interview of every person in every residence surrounding a crime scene. Usually, in an actual violent crime investigation, it would be a team of investigators going door-to-door to as many houses, apartments, trailers, whatever, as necessary, asking informational questions of the occupants as to what they saw, who they saw, who lives where, etc. Perhaps it would even include showing photographs of a missing child, an automobile, or maybe a composite artist's rendition of someone. It can entail several residences or hundreds of residences, over several hours, several days or several weeks. Not surprisingly, many a serious crime is solved by utilizing this old-fashioned gumshoe methodology.

Back to my 1960 bike theft investigation, the following evening after my bike had been stolen, I started going door-to-door up and down my block of 3rd Street. Each neighbor to whom I showed my little wanted poster responded in the negative. One of them was old Mrs. Levinson, a widow who lived two doors away. Like the rest, she could provide no positive information to me during my "canvass." I went to bed that night disillusioned, for the second night in a row. Not only was my bike missing, but my investigation into its theft was going nowhere. I must have gone to about 20 neighbors' houses that evening with nothing to show for it.

On day three of the great stolen bike caper, I continued to be dejected. I wasn't sure what else to do about it. I was slowly growing accustomed to the fact that I may be bike-less for the foreseeable future. But later that afternoon, of all people, the Widow Levinson called me over as I walked down the driveway past her small backyard garden. While dutifully watering her plants, she asked me if she could again see the poster of the missing bike. I ran back to my house and retrieved it and showed it to her yet again. She studied it for a minute or so, adjusting her glasses and holding it first closer and then farther away from her eyes as she was examining it.

I was bursting with anticipation as to what Mrs. Levinson knew. C'mon, tell me, if you know something! Did you see my bike or not? I thought these things to myself, but didn't dare say them out loud to her.

After a minute or so, Mrs. Levinson then told me that she thought she saw a bike that maybe looked like mine in the small overgrown grass lot next to the Acme (pronounced "ak-a-me" by her and many old-time Philadelphians) Supermarket. She said she wasn't a hundred percent positive, but it sure did look like it. I thanked her and ran from her backyard to my house. I remember asking my mom to please walk me to the Acme based on what Mrs. Levinson had just told me. To my mom's credit, she soon dropped whatever it was she was doing at the time and we walked the three or so blocks to the intersection of Mascher St. and Grange Ave. to look for it. I think she had to buy milk or some other grocery products anyway.

We hastily undertook the several-block walk and after a bit of searching of the grassy lot, sure enough there was my bike lying on its side, in the two-to-three foot high weeds. Although I was told by my dad to never lay my bike on its side for fear of scratching it, it was seemingly in the same condition that I had left it in front of my house three nights ago. The baseball cards were missing though.

Geez, was my bike stolen just for the baseball cards? Probably not, but it was strange that they were missing. Unless, the thief was even a bit criminally sophisticated and knew that the noise that they made would attract attention to him. So, for that reason, he pocketed or discarded them before riding off on it that night. Of course, I wasn't thinking in these specific terms back then, but much later in life and in my career, that's how I would have assessed it.

My "investigation" more-or-less ended at the recovery scene. My dad heard the news when he got home from work that night, and the next day he bought me a bike lock. I would never again leave my bike unattended without locking it. It was the first key I would ever carry. And, I never left it on the sidewalk in front of my 3rd Street home again. From then on, it was up the driveway and in my backyard to park it. Overnight, it was brought in through the backyard basement door, down the five steps to the basement, and stored safely therein.

I got my bike back, but the "crime" remains unsolved to this day. I have a gut feeling it will remain unsolved at this point. The emotions brought about by this material loss deeply affected me during those three days. I felt genuinely sad that I had one of my favorite toys and a functional piece of transportation equipment taken away from me. Not just a toy that I would put in a box and only play with sparingly, but one that I depended on almost daily for my ever-expanding travels as a young boy exploring my neighborhood. But, as noted, my sadness in short time turned to anger and frustration, then to an inspired dedication. I felt that if I was to have any chance of ever seeing that bike again, I would be the one that would have to find it. So, I devised a simple plan, and it worked. It got me my bike back.

Years later, as a police officer responding to calls of thefts and burglaries, some involving bikes, I felt genuine empathy for these victims. I always attempted to show some level of understanding toward them and their loss, whatever material possession it may have been. On occasion, but unfortunately not very often, my investigation would lead to the recovery of their stolen property. The look on the victims' faces upon its return was always very rewarding for me, even if a relatively rare occurrence.

Once, in the late 1970s, while working as a plainclothes officer in an unmarked police car, I broke up a bike-theft ring that had been plaguing a large shopping mall in my town on a regular basis. Luckily (for the bikes' owners, not for the thieves), I came upon the heist early one evening. The bikes were locked on an outside bike rack right outside the mall's movie theater. The owners of the bikes obviously did everything correct here, as they were, in fact, secured with locks. But, a determined thief will find ways around these security measures if he is motivated enough.

I continued to watch the nervous but committed two thieves in their pickup truck at a distance, over the course of about 20 minutes, through my mini-binoculars. They drove around and visually checked and re-checked that they were in the clear, or so they believed. I thought they may be on the prowl to steal a car, or commit a purse-snatch, as both were known to happen at this mall, the former with some frequency, the latter not so often. These type crimes, and drug sales, were the primary reasons my plainclothes squad was frequently assigned there. But, instead, I was to learn it was two-wheeled vehicles these criminals had in mind.

The two thieves eventually double-parked the truck near the bike racks and exited it. They brought with them their tools, cleverly hidden in a large shopping bag from one of the stores at the mall. They shifted their heads and darted their eyes back and forth the whole time while walking toward the bikes and before cutting the locks with the head shifting and eye darting continuing while casually rolling the bikes from the rack to their truck. I learned in this part of my law enforcement career, while watching them close-up through binoculars, that criminals' eyes, like predators on the Serengeti, are always very active and focused on their immediate horizon before, during, and a short while after committing a crime. It was a sure clue and giveaway to me that a crime was about to occur as they were either searching for victims or for police. These two were no different.

The visually aware thieves then threw the several relatively high-value bikes into the bed of their truck, covering them with a tarp. They then drove off, leaving the shopping mall parking lot, still looking around the whole time.

In my unmarked, non-police looking car, I followed them, radioing to nearby marked patrol cars as soon as I witnessed the crime and the direction of their egress. The thieves were aware shortly thereafter that someone was following them. They had no idea who I was as I had not yet deployed the portable revolving-red flashing light on my car's rooftop. They proceeded to drive faster and faster and a short, moderate-speed car chase ensued into the adjacent town.

The thieves were eventually pulled over with the assistance of a marked patrol unit a few miles from the scene of the theft. I jumped out, identified myself, and with the uniformed police officers, placed them under arrest. I eventually returned the bikes to their rightful owners that night, who, upon exiting the mall, called the police department to report their bikes having been stolen.

The thieves eventually admitted to having stolen at least a dozen other bikes from the same mall over the prior few months. They had a "fence" (someone who buys stolen goods) who would buy them for about $50 each. However, I never could make a case on their fence. There just wasn't enough evidence to fully identify him and arrest and prosecute him or recover the other stolen bikes.

In a small way, this relatively minor arrest proved to be very satisfying to me as a young police officer. Obviously, I knew this ring was not connected in any way to the theft of my bike over 20 years earlier, but it was rewarding, nonetheless. The theft of my own bike as a young boy stayed with me all those years. And, as I am still an avid bicyclist, I haven't lost the wind-blown feeling that riding a two wheeled, self-propelled transportation device can provide; presently minus the streamers and baseball cards. I always lock the bike too when I park it and even have a picture of my bike and its serial number recorded in my cell phone, just in case. As of this writing, I've never lost another bike.

Another, vastly more serious crime, also still unsolved, one in which I played no direct role but that affected me personally as a young boy, was that of the infamous "Boy in the Box" case in Philadelphia.

In 1957, a blonde haired boy, estimated to be between four and six years of age, right around my own age at the time, was found in a box, dumped like trash, in the Fox Chase neighborhood of Philadelphia. He was murdered with evidence of severe blunt trauma found on his body. As the crow flies, the body disposal site was probably about four miles from my house in Olney, although several neighborhoods away.

Even in the late 1950s, well before the mass media explosion, this case was covered extensively in the Philadelphia area, and then for years afterwards. I remember watching the 6 o'clock local news, which was on virtually every night in my house, and asking my parents about this crime.

Why was a boy in a box? How did he get there? What does "homicide" mean? Who are and where are his mommy and daddy? Why does he look "funny" in the picture they keep showing? (It was an actual photograph of the dead boy, with the help of some natural-coloring makeup, showcased throughout the media in an attempt to identify him.)

My parents couldn't supply me with answers that made any sense to my young mind. Quite frankly, there were few answers that made sense, and not many that the Philadelphia Police Department ever managed to answer, despite an intensive, decades-long determined effort on the part of that agency, other agencies, and numerous individual investigators. To this day, the boy and his murderer(s) have never been identified.

This was a case that I followed off-and-on for practically all of my life, even as a young adult and well before I entered the ranks of law enforcement. Reading of this case in the newspapers, and the extensive investigative efforts put into it, was an education in and of itself for me. I wondered, even in my early teens, on the tenth anniversary of the boy's body being found, and the local media coverage which ensued around that time, how would I have handled the investigation and how would I have tried to solve this boy's homicide.

I wasn't overly interested in specifics of his death or the explicit details of the crime scene. (Some serial offenders I later interviewed were, in fact, interested in these types of facts relating to murders and other violent crimes that they followed in the media in their youths. They weren't interested in how to solve the crime though, as was I, but more how to get away with it.)

That of which I did find myself curious regarded the behavior exhibited by those who would commit such a crime. What were the parents, one or both, or whoever killed the boy, thinking when they did this? What actions did they take before and after disposing of the boy's body?

I probably wasn't consciously using the word "behavior" in thinking about the killer or killers' possible actions, but even in my youthfulness, I wondered what made them, or other offenders like them, do something so abhorrent. And, could one somehow identify that behavior to solve or prevent these types of crimes?

The Boy in the Box case remains, to this day, the most publicized unsolved case in Philadelphia history. It has been highlighted on various local and national TV shows, and in other media accounts, over the many years since it occurred. Every decade or so, on the anniversary of the boy's discovery, the case tends to be revisited in a public forum.

The Vidocq Society, a quasi-secret association of crime-solving experts in the Philadelphia area, of which I am now proudly a member, brought their unique and comprehensive talents to this case many years ago and provided the equivalent of a cold-case review for the Philadelphia police. I have discussed this matter with several members of the Society who investigated this case over the years and I have informally offered some advice of my own based on my now many years of criminal investigative and profiling experience. Yet, it remains unsolved.

On February 25, 2012, I attended a brief ceremony, sponsored by the Vidocq Society, at the Ivy Hill Cemetery in Philadelphia. It was the 55th anniversary, to the day, of the young boy's lifeless body being discovered. He was interred to this location in 1998, from a Potter's Field in another area of Philadelphia. In attendance this day were various members of the Society, including Bill Kelly, one of the original Philadelphia Police Department investigators on the case. It was the first time I had actually talked to him, although I had known of him and had seen him at the monthly Vidocq crime-solving luncheons. His wife, two of his children, and one of his grandchildren were there with him that day, assisting him in walking, even with his cane, the short distance from his car to the gravesite. They knew what this five-and-a-half decade investigation meant to the now aged and physically (but not mentally) diminished patriarch of their family.

Bill Kelly said a few moving words at the gravesite in honor of the unknown boy. So did Bill Fleischer, one of the Vidocq Society's founding members. Fleischer was instrumental in the acquisition of this new and certainly more desirous final resting place for the boy. It's on prime property at the cemetery, adjacent to its main entrance.

The black granite headstone on the anonymous boy's grave reads "America's Unknown Child." It's a testament not just to this little unknown boy but to all the other unknown, abused, and forgotten children who came before and after him, and invariably, those yet to be born.

Perhaps before the 60th anniversary of this horrific crime, in February, 2017, the boy can finally be identified and a name put on his headstone. Equally important would be identifying who killed him, and determining if he was their only victim.

Bill Kelly died in March of 2014. May he rest in peace.

(The Vidocq Society maintains a website for information solely dedicated to this still unsolved case. It's www.americasunknownchild.net. Anyone with tips regarding this matter is strongly encouraged to access it. It's never too late.)

Chapter Three

Besides the two aforementioned crimes, albeit the former being a very minor one, my Philly neighborhood and the immediate surrounding neighborhoods in the early 1960s were relatively low-crime areas. But, Olney could still be a somewhat tough neighborhood at times. Yes, my neighborhood seemed to have its share of bullies. You're about to meet one of mine. My encounters with him ultimately changed my philosophy of life, even though my personal philosophical leanings were the last thing I was contemplating at the time. Then, regarding this bully, my youthful contemplations had more to do with avoiding bloody noses and black eyes.

I wasn't a small kid back then, and I don't think I was a kid that gave others an obvious reason to pick on me. (Not that anyone should be picked on for any reason, of course). But, with so many kids, I mean literally a hundred or more, all within the same basic age frames, living within a few square city blocks of each other, it must have at times either consciously or sub-consciously gotten too crowded for some or maybe boring for them. It was probably both.

There were no "turfs" or forbidden zones in any nearby area like there are today in some cities in which youth gangs have gained a foothold, but there were some kids who thought they could intimidate others if they came upon perceived weaker ones who happened to be away from the immediate area in which they lived. One of those kids was named Carl. I learned a life-long lesson from this bully but not without some bumps and bruises along the way. Ultimately, he may have learned a thing or two from me at the same time.

Carl was about two years older than me, around nine years of age to my seven, and he was bigger than me. He was known as the local tough kid. He didn't live on my block, but probably a few blocks away. In little-kid world in Olney, that was a long way from home. I'm not even sure when we first met, or how. He didn't go to my school (he was a "Public"), but somehow he would be in my neighborhood at times, passing through, walking somewhere, and our paths would invariably cross. I'm also not sure when we had our first confrontation, or exactly how it unfolded, but I can recall a few of them, at a few different times over the course of several months. He would see me and go out of his way, usually with one or two friends, to confront me and proceed to, well, beat the crap out of me.

Carl could be a scary guy. His reputation for beating up other kids and being a tough guy preceded him. We would meet up, inadvertently on my part to be sure, and he'd talk tough and challenge me at first, pushing me around at the same time, and then suddenly he'd sock me on the side of the head or in the belly with a quick punch. That would usually knock me down and he would then jump on top of me, pinning my shoulders and upper chest with his knees, and he would continue to torment me by punching me and slapping me in the face.

I don't think he ever bloodied anything other than my nose, but I was definitely sore and hurting, inside and out, each time.

And, I wouldn't fight back. After all, he was older than me, bigger than me, and a tough guy. What would happen if I did? Then, he'd really get mad and really hurt me, right? I seem to recall at least once or twice seeing Carl coming and then either hiding from him before he saw me, or actually running away from him. I wasn't proud of myself afterwards, but it at least meant that I wasn't going home bloodied that day. But, how long could I keep running away? That question was soon to be answered.

After what was probably my third or fourth confrontation with him in as many months, and getting beat up, yet again, I walked the few blocks home. Upon entering the front door my dad caught me crying. He saw that I was also a bit disheveled and scraped up. I reluctantly told him what happened and what had been happening over the last few months. For whatever reasons, I had not told him anything about Carl beforehand. Needless to say, he became concerned and did his best to comfort me. He never had this particular problem with my three older sisters. This was a first for him, as the parent of a young boy.

My dad had previously told me that he had boxed a bit in his youth, got into his own scrapes as a kid growing up in the Elfreth's Alley area, and learned to "handle himself" the hard way, that is, on the streets. He had won and lost some bouts, he said, but he never backed down from a fight. Later in life, he enjoyed *Friday Night Fights*, a weekly boxing program which was on TV at the time. I believe it was sponsored by the Gillette razor company. I would watch it with him too sometimes. Not my mom or sisters, though. They weren't boxing fans.

When he saw me crying after my most recently lost fight, or more correctly, uncontested beating, he pulled me aside that evening and told me, quite simply, that I had to fight back against this kid. I couldn't keep hiding, running away, or taking these beatings from him.

I recall saying something like, "But dad, he's tough, he's mean, he's bigger, and he knows how to fight."

My dad replied with something like, "Well, then we'll make you just a little bit tougher, meaner, and teach you how to fight."

"Uh...okay, I guess. Wait! Are you sure?"

So, down to the basement we went and Wally proceeded for the first time to teach me how to box. I was clumsy and no doubt did not possess the greatest form upon the initiation of this process. That was clear to even me.

During the course of this several nights of "training," my dad surprised me by telling me that I probably had one distinct advantage over this kid. I asked him what that could possibly be. He said, "You're left-handed, and it's likely he's right-handed."

I asked my dad what possible difference me being left-handed could make. He told me how right-handed boxers, or even street-fighters, don't like going up against left-handers. It was weak arm versus strong arm; it threw off their defense and, in turn, their punching ability. He then taught me along the way to fake it like I was a right-hander by pretending to throw a right-handed punch, have my opponent, most likely Carl, attempt to parry the blow, then slip in my hopefully more powerful left jab to the right side of his face. He also taught me to move around, duck, and not be hesitant to punch him in the "bread-basket," aka stomach.

We practiced these various maneuvers on an old throw-pillow and the open palm of my dad's hand a number of times, over a few nights, down in the basement. He had me convinced that this may just work. Besides slowly building my ability and confidence, he also taught me a trick. He said this wouldn't necessarily work with professionals in a boxing ring, but it should work on the streets.

My father told me to somehow find a way to distract my opponent and then throw my first left jab. Even just averting my eyes in some other direction behind him, while Carl was looking at me, would work in this type situation. I tried to remember all of this. We discussed this and did some more practice "sparring" a few times over the next week. He was on his knees and never actually hit me of course, but it was a good way to practice my newly acquired pugilistic talents. My dad told me to pretend that Carl's face was in the middle of the pillow. I did and that old pillow really took a beating. We had to sweep up the loose feathers after each training session.

Looking back, I recall that these practice sessions were always when my mom wasn't around. Was that a coincidence? Hardly.

This plan of my dad's would have to work, or I'd really be in trouble with Carl. And, the challenge was coming soon.

I should add here that my dad was not a ruffian, prone to violence, or one to get into skirmishes or to cause trouble. Yes, he could curse when upset, but at this stage of his life, he was in his mid-50s. If he had any of those ways about him in his youth, no doubt they were distant memories of his and those around him at this time. He was a gentleman; quiet and reserved. But, he had a sense of humor and an Irish temper (from him came my Irish half), and when pushed, he could let it fly. Never in a physical sense, mind you, around the family. But, based on what he told me, and showed me, I have no question that in his youth he used his fists to successfully resolve at least some of the problems he may have encountered.

I suppose my dad's advice in this instance, in and around 1960, seems somewhat anachronistic to those of us now living in the supposedly enlightened 21st Century. After all, shouldn't my parents have gone to Carl's parents' house and confront them? Perhaps the police should have been directly involved, or the school counselors notified (even though Carl and I went to different schools), and maybe even lawyers with briefcases taking their argument in front of some neighborhood civic board somewhere, and/or them filing lawsuits against everyone even remotely associated with Carl.

No, no, no, and no, because this wasn't the way it was back then. Those additional people weren't necessary or needed, at least not at this level, and certainly not in my neighborhood. People, even kids, tended to handle their own problems with their own devices. Sometimes, even with their fists.

As was inevitable, within a week or so, Carl and I crossed paths again. I can remember to this day, it was on the NW corner of 3rd St. and Grange Ave., probably about 150 yards from my house, but seemingly miles away from the safety and security that my home and family offered me. This show-down would occur on the lawn of a small, two-story, four unit, apartment building. I later delivered *The Evening Bulletin* newspaper to that same building where I would sit on the same front steps where the fight started, folding my papers on my way to deliver the news to the rest of my customers.

As it turned out, the news headline for Carl that evening wouldn't be a good one.

That afternoon, upon seeing Carl, I was scared, but this time I didn't run or hide from him. Carl and his buddies surrounded me, as had happened before when I saw him. I had two friends with me, but they stayed in the background. My friends were scared of these guys too.

Carl didn't waste any time. He led the taunts and started pushing me around. I took a few tempered pushes from him without doing anything back to him. As my dad had told me, I noticed Carl was telegraphing what he would do next. He was looking at his friends for reassurance and showing off to them at the same time as he was pushing me around.

When Carl put up his fist to get ready to hit me, I put up mine. I decided to try the trick my dad had suggested. So, I quickly glanced behind Carl at one of his friends and sort of winked at him and smiled at him. Carl must have wondered what I was doing or what his friend was doing and momentarily turned his head to see what may be happening behind him.

That was the diversionary tactic my dad talked about. It worked, and it was now or never. In the next split second, as Carl's right fist instinctively dropped, and he was slowly turning his head back toward me, I built up my courage and immediately hit him hard with a solid left hook to the right side of his face. He staggered backwards, but didn't go down. Instead, he shook his head as in disbelief and then came at me with a now really angry look on his face. I couldn't back off now. What did my dad tell me to do next? That's right, the phantom punch!

I faked a right jab, and when Carl went to block the punch that was never delivered, I hit him again with another left. He bent over a bit and by moving slightly alongside of him, I hit his mid-section with all my might with another left. His legs buckled and he fell down, gasping for air as my belly punch hit its mark. He was on his knees, so I pushed him backwards until he was flat on his back. I then jumped on him, and did the same to him that he had done to me all too many times in the past. I pinned his shoulders to the ground with my knees. I wouldn't let him up. Even though he was bigger than me, he didn't quite have the upper body strength to maneuver me off of him to get himself back up on his feet. Plus, I had hurt him. Maybe more than anyone else had done to him before, and in this, my first ever real boxing-style bout.

I kept Carl in that position for probably ten minutes, but as he was trying to punch me in the side a few times, I did the same to his face. These weren't pile drivers or haymakers, by any stretch of the imagination, but I know he felt them. I also noticed blood coming out of one of his nostrils. Now it was my turn to make him bleed. Finally, his buddies, whom to their credit did not attempt to help him by jumping in on the fight, perhaps due to no small part my friends also being there, said something like, "Hey Carl, the Fitzie kid beat you up…tell him he won this time and let's go."

Carl at first hesitated, but then reluctantly told me I won the fight. In hearing that, I agreed to let him up. My dad had also previously warned me not to take my eyes off of him, or anyone else with him, even after the fight was supposedly over. So, I got up slowly, one knee off each shoulder at a time, facing him and holding out my raised clenched fists in his direction while doing so. He got up next, gingerly, wiping the blood off of his face onto his sleeve and brushing the debris off his clothes. He looked at me, shook his head back and forth, and joined his buddies and walked away. I heard them teasing him as they walked away. He pushed one of them in defiance, but they kept walking. That's all I needed to see. I eventually put down my fists. I rejoined my very supportive and flattering buddies and walked in the opposite direction from Carl and his group.

Fight over. It was a TKO for the Fitzie kid.

I told my dad what happened later that night, and he was proud of me. My mom somehow heard the story, about my earlier basement lessons, and she was upset, asking my dad why he would teach me to be violent. The three of us talked it out, and I believe one of my sisters was later part of this conversation too. I was reminded by my dad and everyone else in the house that night, once again, to never start a fight. However, if so pushed, as I was literally in this situation numerous times, I was to react with enough, if not slightly more, of a physical response to overcome the threat.

I saw Carl again after that, as it was still our mutually shared neighborhood, but he never acknowledged my existence and he never attempted to fight me again. I apparently gave him a taste of his own medicine (and blood), and the dosage clearly worked. He remained a non-factor in my childhood from that point on.

Later in my youth, I would engage in other fist-fights, winning most and losing a few. The vast majority I didn't start. A few I'm ashamed to admit, I did, but there was always some reason. I swear....

My pacifist mom, years later, when I was probably about 16 years old, witnessed me in yet another street boxing match; this time, right outside our front door. On a spring afternoon, I was in the process of cutting the very small front lawn in front of my 3rd St. rowhome. While in the middle of this task, I was taunted by two brothers about my age who were walking southbound on the sidewalk on the other side of 3rd Street. I knew them from high school and previous mutual-tormenting incidents. One was a year older than me, one was a year younger. We verbally jousted across the street for a few minutes, but then it got serious. They dropped their book bags and challenged me to come over and fight them. So, I put down the push-mower and I graciously accepted their offer.

I crossed the street and immediately sought out the older, slightly bigger, of the brothers. He attempted a punch but missed and I landed the first punch of the fight. Then the younger brother punched me from behind. He did catch the side of my head by surprise, as my back was to him temporarily as we spun around. But, it didn't hurt me. I turned around and hit him squarely in the face.

I found myself out-boxing both of the brothers, but they still managed to land a few light blows upon me. As I learned that day, it's not easy fighting two guys at once. But, it didn't last that long as the "referee" suddenly showed up. And, she wasn't wearing a striped shirt, but instead an apron. It was my mom, who somehow saw round one of the fight and crossed the street pleading for me and them to stop fighting. We did, and it ended right there, with some continued jawing as they walked away. There was some bloodiness on their part, but no major wounds. They barely touched me. I figured that was it with them. But, it wasn't.

When the two brothers got home, I think around ten blocks from where I lived, they apparently told their mom what happened to them. (I knew of their mom. She usually walked them to and from high school, thus earning her sons the nickname, "The Mommy Boys.") She, not surprisingly, called the police and managed to have an officer sent to my house. This was the first time in my life that I ever dealt with a police officer in which I may have been in some degree of trouble. My mom was upset yet again that afternoon, as would be expected when a police officer comes to the front door and asks to talk to her about her son. Oh, and it was just my mom as my dad was at work.

The officer was very serious at first, asking us what happened a little while ago. But, before long, the officer eventually started lightening up, even trying his best to suppress a smile at times with my mom and me. He acted sort of surprised with the fact that the mother of the two boys who actually started the fight sent the police to the house of the one boy who had then physically gotten the better of them and whose own mom broke it up. The officer more-or-less took my side of the story into account and simply advised me upon leaving that I should avoid the "Mommy Boys" in the future. I did. I never fought the two brothers again. Some further verbal jousting in the confines of our high school hallways would take place, but that was it.

It surprised me a number of years later, when a New Agent Trainee at the FBI Academy, and when in the numerous hours of Defensive Tactics training, that a number of my male colleagues, usually the ones somewhat younger than me and who were not former police officers or military members, acknowledged that they had never been in a physical confrontation, that is, a fistfight, in their entire lives. Maybe they grew up in a more civilized time (I was about ten years older than many of my FBI Academy classmates), or at least in more civilized neighborhoods. Perhaps that's a good thing. I'm not sure though, especially as they were about to become FBI agents and would be arresting some bad men before long, who would not be taken without a fight.

My dad, and this series of incidents, taught me much more than the employment of Marquis of

Queensbury rules of boxing in certain situations and/or the necessity of always meeting force with force. Clearly, violence or the use of physicality is not usually the answer to life's problems. But, I did learn that day, at the NW corner of 3rd Street and Grange Avenue, I could not and would not run from any problem in the future. Even the very difficult problems, such as those that may be life or career threatening, had to be confronted head on. If not right at that moment, then it should be addressed very soon thereafter.

When faced with problematic issues in the future I would remind myself, once again, to fully assess the situation and to react accordingly. Sometimes, depending on the situation, the participants, and the environment, temporarily "retreating" was the appropriate reaction. There's nothing wrong with that strategy, if and when appropriate. If the latter option, I would step back from the situation, collect my thoughts, gather evidence and/or support, perhaps consult with others (as I did with my dad as a seven-year-old), develop my strategy, and then take it/him/her/them on at a time and place best suited for me, not necessarily when first confronted with the matter.

I wound up meeting a number of other "Carl" types in my adult life, and fortunately, in virtually every case, the results were similar. Some problems may have continued for a year or more, as sometimes that's how long my "strategy," whatever it may have been, would take to produce results. But, the Carls of the world, when eventually confronted on my terms, with rules that I established, perhaps by even using a distraction tactic or two similar to what my dad taught me, were generally rendered neutral, if not completely put out of their game when all was said and done.

Over time, I found that many a Carl-type tends to eventually implode by his or her own actions and personal shortcomings. When that's the case, it's just waiting them out sometimes. Physically pinning these types to the ground may not be necessary (or even legal), but their less-than-honorable outright or hidden agenda can be stymied nonetheless with the right plan of action. Carl learned that the hard way. So did a few others in my life, whether solely by my actions or combined with the actions of others. Many of these scenarios occurred behind the doors of my future police department. Several FBI agent co-workers learned some lessons the hard way too. They can all thank the young Carl, who got back what he used to dish out but then altered his behavior accordingly, at least around me.

Chapter Four

Before leaving this period of my life, two other major factors contributed to my personal development and how I would come to view the world as a maturing young man and eventually an adult. One was a "vacation" trip with my parents to a place very different than my Olney neighborhood. The other was a well-publicized murder. Make that two murders, one connected to the other. These experiences, while unrelated to each other, occurred about three months apart. Each affected me differently, yet profoundly for years to come.

By way of background, my dad had a lifelong lower back problem. He would sometimes be forced to miss weeks of work at a time because he simply could not get out of bed. He went to various doctors and clinics in the Philadelphia area, but none seemed to provide him the remedy to this recurring and debilitating problem. One of the doctors recommended surgery on his back. As is true today, back surgery is never guaranteed to be completely successful and was even less so back then. My dad had no assurances as to the outcome of any surgery options. In fact, he was told that sometimes back surgery can actually exacerbate the existing problem. My mom and my sisters and I were concerned about him. They debated aloud whether he should have the surgery or not.

In the meantime, my dad either read somewhere, a friend told him, or perhaps even one of his doctors told him, of a potential alternate treatment. It was one that did not require surgery, but was not without its own inconveniences and costs. The suggested remedy involved travelling a long distance from Philadelphia to a place none of us had ever visited in the past. That place was Hot Springs, Arkansas. And yes, the city was, in fact, named after the hot springs which poured forth from underground and were found to have therapeutic benefits to many who bathed in them. My dad learned that people would go there with various physical and medical ailments, including chronic back problems, sit in the hot spring spas for several hours over multiple days, and many would come away feeling much better and maybe even cured of their ailments. There were no guarantees here either for my dad, except it was not surgery and he was all but assured that he would not come away from the treatments feeling any worse.

After a few weeks of discussion, my dad figured, why not? If it didn't work, there was always surgery as the next step. The planning began for this trip and before long we were ready to go. As my sisters Cass and Alma were already married at this time, they weren't going with us. And, although still living at home, Marilyn, now 22 years old, was working full time and couldn't go with us.

Interestingly, no one in my immediate family at the time had ever been geographically further from Olney than the southern New Jersey seashore and the Pennsylvania Poconos, with the exception of a family road trip to Kansas City, Kansas, to visit my mom's brother George Kennard and his family in 1955. But, I don't remember it at all.

Nonetheless, with route-highlighted maps in hand, my parents and I left at 3:00AM on a Saturday morning in our family's black 1959 Ford Galaxy 500 to begin this three-week southern sojourn. It was early August, 1963. I was ten years old.

Growing up in late '50s and early '60s Olney, a then all-white community, I knew very little of the racial divide in this country and the civil unrest fomenting throughout. My dad would talk about some "colored neighborhoods" and "negroes" with whom he would come into contact through work. Some comments were positive, some quite frankly negative, but that was my only real exposure to any demographic class other than lower-to-middle income people with Western European backgrounds. There were no black kids in my large grade school and none anywhere in my crowded neighborhood.

When I would travel to downtown Philadelphia with my mom, always via the Philadelphia public transportation system, to shop at the large department stores and/or to take in a newly released matinee feature at one of the giant movie theaters, I would certainly come into contact with black people. But, I would have no interaction with any one of them, nor would my mom. This wasn't deliberate or planned, but just didn't seem to occur. In effect, race identification and assimilation was simply not a part of my life in the early '60s. I had virtually no comprehension of any racial issues nor did I know any people of color. It was something rarely discussed between my parents and me. Right or wrong, that's how it was at the time in my family. But, that all changed when we reached the deep south in the early 1960s. It was a wakeup call to me and no doubt to my parents too. This awareness may have been very slowly occurring throughout the rest of the U.S. However, travelling to this area in the summer of '63 most definitely expedited the process for my parents and me.

I'm not sure after all these years of the exact route we took in our long drive from Pennsylvania to Arkansas, but it seems by the second day of three days of driving, somewhere in one of the southern states, things had changed around us. People definitely talked differently, they dressed somewhat differently, and there were some odd signs that started popping up. I'm not referring to the seemingly ubiquitous roadside "Burma Shave" rhyming signs either. The odd signs I was starting to see weren't colorful or fancy like one would see advertising a product, place, or a service, but usually simply black and white (irony intended or not, I don't know), and mostly hand-printed.

I can still clearly recall seeing these signs. They read, "Colored" restrooms, "Colored Only" water fountains, and similarly so-delineated interior sections of diners and restaurants. In turn, we would also see the "White Only" signs too. The eating establishments were odd in that at most of them I saw no outside signs that forbade or restricted one group of people or another, but once inside, invariably, these facilities would have a smaller section roped off. It so happened that behind the ropes would be black patrons eating, with whites on the other side of the rope, usually closer to the door.

Guests to the eateries would both enter and exit from the same door, pay the checks at the same register, but the tables were set apart by a rope and/or a wide aisle.

While in Hot Springs, I recall asking my parents more than once why these "Colored Only" signs were needed. Why couldn't "colored people" (yes, undoubtedly, I used that term back then), pee, drink, and eat, where we did? My parents couldn't really provide an answer except to say, in so many words, "Things are different down here." They were right about that.

In the two weeks living in a nice, friendly motel in Hot Springs, with my dad hitting the spas almost every day, I managed to take in a few movies. There was a large theater in downtown Hot Springs that could be reached by a relatively short walk from the hotel. The marquis had the words "Air Conditioned" in lettering bigger than the names of the movies which were featured. As a relatively new feature to movie theaters, they made sure to advertise it accordingly. Especially, I suppose, in the hot southern states.

I recall gathering some other kids around my age who were staying at the motel, and I believe at least one local boy, and we together went to see *King Kong vs Godzilla* at the local theater one hot afternoon. On another evening, my parents and I went to see the movie *PT 109*, about President John F. Kennedy's experience in World War II. Both films had just recently been released in the theaters.

I recall on the evening visit to the theater commenting to my parents that we weren't seeing any blacks in the audience, nor did I notice any of those restrictive signs. I believe it was my mom who simply stated, "They probably have their own theater somewhere around here or maybe they're up in the balcony."

As usual, I asked her "Why?"

She repeated, again in so many words, "That's just the way it is here in the South."

Those two hot August weeks in Hot Springs, Arkansas, with part of a subsequent third week revisiting my uncle and his family in Kansas City, proved to be one of those learning experiences that could have never come from a book or from a television show or movie. I realized for the first time that there were people different than me, and different from Philadelphians and Olney-ites, in other parts of the country. I realized too some people seemingly had certain rights bestowed upon them while others were deprived of certain rights. On our long car ride back East, my parents and I agreed that it was not fair and something was amiss in this part of our country, this part of our culture.

I believe the three of us, that is, a 10-year-old kid and a set of older parents, came home from that trip with an altered and enhanced sense of understanding of this country, its history, and the people who inhabit it. Some things we observed were just not right and we agreed should be fixed. My parents and I would continue to discuss racial injustice in the subsequent years. Invariably, the discussion would be greatly influenced by what we saw in Arkansas during that steamy summer of '63. It also wasn't lost on my parents and me that my very life may have been saved by a black man in Fisher Park back when I was but three years of age.

Years later, as a very young uniformed police officer, I faced a form of discrimination for the first time in my life. Not "deep south" systemic and historical type racial discrimination as referenced from my 1963 trip there, but bothersome to me nonetheless. It was eye-opening, if not ear-opening, for me, too. It happened in one quick moment, but as it was the initial time this occurred to me, and being still a bit thin-skinned then, it was actually hurtful.

Quite simply, while standing at an intersection in full police uniform and directing traffic at the scene of an automobile accident, a car full of teenagers drove by and yelled out the window, "F**k you, you f**king pig!"

I was only on the job for a few months at the time and this was the first time I was aware that someone insulted me or challenged me not based on who I was, what I said, my beliefs, my actions, my personality, etc., but what I represented and essentially, what I looked like. That is, in my case, a uniformed police officer. While still directing cars around this accident scene, I found myself thinking that these kids didn't even know me. So, why did they yell that at me? Why are they judging me this way? I'm a decent guy, I'm fair to people, a recent college graduate, I've led a pretty good 23 years so far.

But then it hit me. Those kids were judging me in some ways no differently than others would judge a minority or a person of color, that is, based on what they look like, not who they are. And, once again, that wasn't right.

Let me restate emphatically here, I'm not comparing this traffic-directing scenario to the racial discord in the country in the past and the sufferings of generations due to the many injustices of some humans toward other humans. I clearly chose my profession and expected some of this type of abuse during the course of my career. Others don't choose their skin color or their socio-economic status or their gender or their sexual orientation. Nonetheless, it was a bit of a shocker that day and provided me with an even greater empathy toward minorities and people being judged by what they look like and/or what they ostensibly represent, as opposed to who they actually are as a person.

That time was far from the only time that I had nasty words yelled at me as a police officer, or even occasionally later as an FBI agent. I got used to it after a while. But, that early career experience of indiscriminate vitriol and fleeting hatred directed at me anonymously from that passing car reminded me of the plight of others and how bad it really was for years in this country. And, the signs were there, literally and figuratively, all over the place. It was just a matter of people reading them.

The other matter which proved to have a lasting effect on me, the rest of the country, and even the world, occurred just three months after my return from Arkansas. That was, of course, the assassination of President Kennedy in November of 1963, and the subsequent murder, on live TV, of his killer just two days later.

John F. Kennedy was very popular in my Olney neighborhood. As it was a majority Irish-Catholic neighborhood, and politically Democratic, he was strongly endorsed by most people I knew. As a very young boy, no older than seven, I remember observing the "Kennedy for President" signs in many windows of rowhomes as I would walk or bike my way along the sidewalks and streets. These particular signs were of red, white, and blue coloring with JFK's youngish, handsome face in the middle. The nuns in my school seemingly loved him too, and despite what's supposed to be a separation of church and state, encouraged us to encourage our parents to vote for him.

As my parents were registered Democrats, what some would now refer to as Old Democrats, they did, in fact, vote for Kennedy. They told me so when I asked. Although, they followed up their answers by mutually and politely telling me I should never ask someone for whom they voted. So, based on that admonition, I never did ask that question again of anyone, not even them. I could certainly guess though.

I should add that my family's admiration for JFK had nothing to do with his middle name being the same as our last name, either. I asked my parents if we were possibly related to him, even if just a little bit. They told me they were pretty sure there was no direct kinship.

Sometime in 1960, my mom and sister Alma, while walking along Olney Ave. near the Fifth St. shopping district about four blocks from our home, happened to come upon a slow-moving motorcade with then-candidate Kennedy. They saw him in person and he even waved from his convertible in their general direction. They were thrilled. This was the only president, or in this case, soon-to-be president, that my mom or sisters ever saw in person.

It took me until 2005 to actually be in the physical presence of a U.S. president. It was the dedication of the brand new FBI Laboratory on the FBI Academy grounds in Quantico, Virginia. President George W. Bush was there to cut the ribbon and give a speech outdoors on the expansive grounds adjacent to it. It was a great day for the state-of-the-art lab to be opened, although it bothered many of us FBI agents that we had to be gun-less on the grounds of our own training Academy. We were so ordered by the U.S. Secret Service who was overseeing the protection detail. We did, in fact, leave our guns in our respective offices that day. I understood where the Secret Service agents were coming from though. Just doing their jobs....

Kennedy was, of course, elected to the Presidency in November of 1960, but being as young as I was, after that I don't recall being too involved in political discussions about him. I'm sure what he did, or didn't do, while in office was the topic of conversation in my house on some evenings, but I simply don't recall the gist of any of these discussions. I do have a vague memory of the Cuban Missile Crisis, the nightly TV shows being interrupted because of this, and my parents telling me that the country was in very grave danger at the time. I remember that week the drills at school in which we students would have to hide under our desks in case we were attacked by the big, bad Soviet Union. But, the next thing I knew the crisis was over and things were seemingly back to normal.

On November 22, 1963, I was sitting in my fifth grade classroom at St. Helena School. My teacher that year was Miss Engel. It was after lunch and my class of around 70 students was well into our lesson plan of that afternoon. Around 1:45 that day, Mother Alma Joseph, our principal, did something she only normally did in the morning of each day. That is, she came onto the school's public announcement system. Upon hearing just a few initial words from her, I noticed her vocal patterns were different than in her usual morning announcements and prayers. We sat up and listened intently to the one tinny-sounding speaker on the wall in the front of our classroom. I think most of us knew in those first few seconds that something was inherently wrong.

Mother Superior started with: "Sisters, teachers, boys and girls, please excuse this interruption to your afternoon classes. I have some very sad news to give you. It just came over the radio that President Kennedy was shot this afternoon in Dallas, Texas. Please keep him, his family, and our country in your prayers."

Mother Superior may have then led us in the "Hail Mary" prayer after this brief announcement, but otherwise I think that's all she said then. It wasn't too long after that, perhaps around 2:00, when she came back on the PA and told us the President had died.

Miss Engel started crying after this second announcement, but shortly afterwards began to compose herself as she apparently realized she had to do so for the sake of her young charges. I don't think we went back to our lesson plan that day, whatever it was, but I really don't recall what we talked about after that initial announcement. About 20 minutes later, Mother came back on the PA and announced that the school was being dismissed about a half-hour early that day. As most moms were stay-at-home moms then, and we all walked home each day (no school buses were needed or provided at our school), it was really no big deal to let the school out early back then without any advance notice. So, dismissal was around 2:45 that day, instead of the usual 3:10, and home we walked on that chilly, overcast, ever-darkening November day.

On the way home, with my usual group of male friends, I remember it being a very somber ten minute walk. No joking around, pushing, teasing each other, or talking about mean teachers, "stupid" girls, "sissy" boys, or the like. It was an abrupt and immediate entry into the world of sudden death and national mourning for us. We said our good-byes as we reached our respective homes and just walked inside.

Upon opening my front door, I saw that my mom was crying. She had on the TV and it was non-stop coverage of what I then learned was the assassination of our president. Later, my dad and sister Marilyn came home from work, my then-married sisters Cass and Alma, and their respective husbands Bill and Jim, all stopped by for an unplanned and spontaneous familial support session. It was a very sad night for all of us. Undoubtedly, it was for the rest of the country and the world, too.

I would pepper my parents, sisters, and now two brothers-in-law, with questions that Friday night and over the weekend about the assassination. I questioned even more so as my regular TV viewing habits were completely thrown off as the three broadcast networks were nothing but non-stop black and white coverage of this national tragedy.

Why was the President killed? Who would do this? Who's this guy...Lee Harvey Oswald? Did he kill the Dallas police officer too? Years would go by before some of these questions could be answered to me and to a grieving nation. Some were answered to some level of satisfaction, others not so much.

Two days later, after coming home from Sunday Mass, in which the sermon was naturally dedicated to the death of our young Catholic president, and after eating a late breakfast, my parents again were watching the coverage of this matter. I recall being in the kitchen and hearing my dad all of a sudden excitingly yell out, "Jesus Christ, they just shot the guy!"

I ran into the living room to the TV and before long the rerun of Jack Ruby walking up and shooting Oswald in the chest was replayed again and again. Now, what the heck did THIS mean? Dad, mom, please help me understand here. Did I really just witness, even in rerun, the first actual murder ever carried live on TV?

Of course, those answers were not readily derived from my parents or others at that time. Suspicions still exist as to exactly what unfolded that day, before it and after it. The assassination became sort of the granddaddy of all national conspiracy theories that would originate over the next few decades. This one, like most of them, would be debunked, at least in my opinion.

Like other major criminal investigations at the time, the Kennedy assassination piqued my curiosity. I read every newspaper article I could back then, even as a 10-year-old. The fact that Kennedy's 1960 campaign was the only one that I remembered at the time, he being Irish Catholic, and having seen the movie *PT 109* just three months before, I took the matter somewhat personally.

I too had my conspiracy-related questions over the years, but it wasn't until I read Gerald Posner's non-fiction book *Case Closed*, published in 1993, that my opinion was solidified. As a criminal profiler and very experienced investigator by that time, upon reading his extensively researched and detailed book in the early 2000s, I became convinced that Oswald acted alone in killing President Kennedy.

Lastly, probably in 2006, I was interviewed by a retired FBI agent who was doing the routine five-year background check on me. This was a normal administrative action that every FBI employee undergoes every five years to make sure he or she is not involved in things which could be detrimental to the mission of the FBI. Issues like personal finances, travel, associations, national loyalty, drug usage, are all asked about, investigated, and sometimes even tested for, as in taking urine samples for drug tests. Upon talking to this retired agent, who was working part-time for the government doing these routine investigatory duties, he advised me that he actually worked the Kennedy assassination case. He was in another FBI division in another city in '63, but on the Saturday after the assassination he was deployed with many other FBI agents by J. Edgar Hoover to assist the Dallas FBI Division with their part of the investigation.

It was interesting to bridge that part of FBI history and speak with an agent who was actually feet-on-the-ground in Dallas at one of the most important times in one of the most important investigations in our country's history. He reminded me, ironically, that it was not a federal case back then. The FBI didn't even have legal jurisdiction over the assassination of our president. The Dallas PD was officially in charge of the murder of the U.S. president. That jurisdictional issue, of course, has since been changed. Not too long after the Kennedy assassination, Congress passed legislation making it a federal violation to assassinate a president of the U.S., not just a state violation. The FBI would then have jurisdiction for such crimes any time in the future.

And, for the record, there was no problem with my background investigation that year, just like every other time when so undertaken.

Chapter Five

As I grew older, maybe now 11 or 12, but while clearly still a kid, late spring, summer, and early fall afternoons and evenings in Olney, either after school or during summer vacation, would sometimes be spent sitting on my front porch with friends. There, besides just talking and literally watching the world go by the sidewalk and street in front of my house, we would also play various board and card games. My parents, as loving as they were, clearly were "old school" and believed that in daylight and decent weather kids and their friends should mostly stay and play outside. Also, there just wasn't that much room inside our house. While we had a basement in the house, it wasn't finished or furnished like some of my friends' basements, so if I had buddies come to the house, and it was anywhere above 55 degrees outside, we sat on the front porch. The sidewalk was only about ten feet below and out from where we sat, and the one-way (northbound) 3rd Street was only about six feet, the width of a parked car, past that. We didn't miss much that walked or drove in front of my house. While not enclosed, the porch was covered with a full roof, with our neighbor's enclosed porch forming a wall on the north side of it, and an open porch, like mine, on the south side of the house. Even most rainy days were fine for porch-sitting.

Occupying ourselves on the approximately 8-foot by 16-foot porch on some days worked for my friends, my parents, and me alike. There was actually somewhat a degree of privacy there, considering the fact that it was a rowhome, as the neighbors on the south side of the house rarely used their porch, except to ingress or egress through their front door. On my porch, with a couple very basic outdoor chairs, including a three-seat glider, which was heavier than any piece of furniture I've ever come across anywhere, and an awning to protect us from the hot afternoon sun and occasional rain, we would talk and play games for hours at a time. We would partake in day-long, even sometimes multi-day, games of Monopoly, Clue, Risk, chess, checkers, and other board games or card games. Obviously, this was long before the advent of video games.

The only interruptions that I recall to these lazy afternoon activities were either the onset of darkness, one of our parents telling us to come home (or in my case, inside the house) for lunch or dinner, and the yearly (at least) car accident up the street when someone would run the stop sign on Nedro Ave. and plow into another car going north on 3rd St. There were never any serious injuries involved; at least not any that I ever observed. That was a good thing. Oh, and I suppose the only other mid-day interruption would be when "Miss America" would walk by.

Miss America, the nickname my 11-12 year old friends and I gave her, was a woman, probably in her late 30s or early 40s, with long, flowing brown hair, who in nicer weather would take randomly scheduled walks along 3rd St. in nothing but a two-piece bikini and heels. I recall, even as a young boy and before those type things seemed to overtly interest me, that she was not an unattractive woman. She was sort of plain looking, but fit the bikini, or vice-versa, rather nicely. She was definitely an oddity who chose to dress, or more accurately, undress, as she did and then strut her stuff very slowly and nonchalantly along 3rd St.

Our bikini-clad occasional neighborhood visitor walked as if she was on a modeling runway, or on the stage at the Miss America Pageant in Atlantic City, with one high-heel shoe carefully placed in front of the other, for the whole length of the block. Cars, always with male drivers, if they spotted her in time from between the parked cars on both sides of 3rd St., would slow down and/or honk their horns and whistle or say things to her. But she maintained her poise, her pace, her gait, never looking at or responding to these lotharios who would attempt to interact with her, by whatever primitive audible means available to them.

On one or two occasions, my friends and I would bend down on my porch, sort of hiding from her behind the stone and concrete half-wall/railing, and teasingly wolf-whistle at her. She would not respond or even look over at us. She'd just keep walking, staring straight ahead. For whatever reason, we never bothered to follow her or find out where she lived. It wasn't our concern. Especially if someone was about to land their metallic token on Park Place and someone else had a hotel on it.

My mom, on one of these occasions upon hearing us whistling at Miss America, came out onto the porch and quietly but firmly told us to stop doing so. I responded with something like, "Why, Mom? She probably likes it."

Alma calmly replied that the woman was probably "not right" and we shouldn't be teasing her. We didn't really know what "not right" meant back then, but we understood that she was somehow not functioning as an everyday "normal" person. Ever obeying my mom (well, most of the time), we simply watched Miss America do her thing from that point on, without acknowledging her in any overt way. We'd whisper comments among ourselves and laugh, but nothing was articulated out loud for her to hear.

The 3rd St. Miss America walks were during the summers of '64 and '65. I don't know what ever happened to her or why she ever chose, in the first place, to walk along an urban residential street very provocatively in her bikini, or why or even when she eventually stopped doing so. She did this for just two summers that I recall and apparently retired her heels and bikini; at least on the streets of Olney.

Needless to say, my friends and I didn't just sit on the porch during our leisure time. There were summer activities at the Lowell School, at 5th St. and Nedro Ave. The Philadelphia public school system back then apparently had the finances to have a full staff of workers, mainly moonlighting public school teachers, who worked at the otherwise closed school for the summer. They would engage us kids in various organized games, contests, arts-and-crafts, and the like on a daily basis. The water sprinklers (there was no pool) were turned on at

3:00 every day. It was a fun place to go for us kids in our very crowded neighborhood. It would end every summer by the third week of August. Then, we were on our own until our respective schools opened.

If not on my porch or at Lowell schoolyard or riding bikes, my friends and I liked to play touch football and stickball in one of the parking lots or alleys in the area. In fact, it was while playing stickball that I probably came the closest to losing my life, or being seriously injured, at any time prior to my law enforcement career.

In the summertime in the alley across from my home (it was actually an L-shaped alley behind the houses on 3rd St., 4th St., and Nedro Ave.) we would often play a simple game of stickball, usually in the early evening as the sun was going down. We didn't always have regular baseball bats, so we would take our moms' old broom handles, saw them off, wrap masking tape around one end, and use them to hit Wiffle balls, pimple balls, and/or half balls, aka "halfsies." We'd run makeshift bases, albeit in a baseball diamond restricted by the dimensions of the narrow driveway, and play away, one team of boys against another, for hours at a time. Usually the game would be called for darkness and we'd all go home.

One evening, during a game, while waiting my turn to bat, I was sitting on the ground with my back leaning on a garage door that butted up to the alley in which we were playing. I was slightly in front of and off to the left of "home plate" and the right-handed batter, Steve Klarich. He was the older brother of my lifelong friend, Tim Klarich, who was my age. I was only casually paying attention to the game and the batter as I was looking up and talking to the boy who was standing next to me. After a few swings of his bat, resulting in foul balls or strikes, Steve swung hard at another pitch and missed the ball. He must have really been swinging hard because in doing so the bat inadvertently flew out of his hands. Like a horizontally spinning propeller blade, it flew at high speed and impaled in the garage door about four inches from my head. It went about a foot into the wooden panel and stuck in there on its own as if a hole had been drilled in the door and the bat forced straight into it. We sat in silence for a few seconds, then all of us let out various versions of, "Whoa! Did you see that!?"

We collectively laughed out loud, me somewhat nervously if I recall, but Steve eventually came over and removed the bat so we could resume the game. He said he was sorry too. He seemed to mean it. I told him it was okay. I'm fine. Nonetheless, I stood or sat behind him and the rest of the batters that evening. I think I may have struck out my next time at bat. I did hold onto the bat though.

No damage, right? Right.

Only kids could laugh when coming that close to serious injury or, gulp, much, much worse. Four inches closer, it would have been my head hit by the bat. There is little doubt that I would have lost an eye, all my teeth, broke a nose, or died, if that rapidly flying sawed-off broom handle had impaled me, instead of the garage door, at the speed it was going. But, as luck, great luck, would have it, it missed me – by those few inches.

Over the next few weeks, the homeowner apparently noticed the hole and patched it. I don't think he ever knew how the almost perfectly round hole wound up in one of the ground-level panels on his garage door. We never told him.

I took a walk in my old neighborhood in 2012. I went down the driveway where this incident occurred around 45+ years before. The same gray garage door is still there in one piece, albeit in bad need of a paint job. In the bottom panel remains the small wooden patch. Surely the present owner doesn't know just how close someone, specifically me, came to preventing that hole in his garage door. In retrospect, I'm very glad it was this garage door and not me that needed to be repaired afterwards.

While recounting my own near-death or near-very serious injury experiences from this time frame, it's only fair that I tell the story of when the situation was reversed and I put someone in jeopardy of losing their life or sustaining serious injury. It occurred during that same mid-1960s summer. It was also a flying wooden projectile, in this case, a model rocket that I had built and launched myself.

My cousin, Tom Collins (no relation to the drink), had gotten me interested in model rocketry around that same summer. We would build them from kits and launch them at one of the few open fields in Olney. Later that summer, while at a somewhat uncrowded southern New Jersey beach with my various aunts and their kids on a day trip, we launched a few rockets. They all worked fine and either descended into the surf of the Atlantic Ocean (as we aimed them in that direction) or gently floated down by their parachutes. The next launch of the day was of the biggest rocket in my "fleet." It was about 15 inches long with a pointy wooden nosecone. It had a parachute inside that was supposed to deploy by a secondary burst of the small solid fuel engine on the rocket's return to earth. On earlier "test flights," in a small open field in Olney, it clearly worked. However, for some reason, something went wrong on this flight.

After climbing to about 400 feet, the rocket plummeted back to earth as fast as gravity would allow it, the wooden nosecone with the parachute inside securely in place.

Houston, we have a problem!

My rocket crash landed on the boardwalk adjacent to the beach about 15 feet from a woman strolling with her small children. Much like the aforementioned bat sticking horizontally into the garage door earlier that summer, the pointy-nosed rocket, with nosecone and parachute clearly not deployed, stuck vertically, also like an arrow shot from a bow, downwards into the wooden boardwalk.

I recall leaving the beach with one of my other cousins, Bonnie Haeberle, running up to the boardwalk, and needing two hands to pull my parachute un-deployed, nose down, fins up rocket out of its resting place stuck perpendicularly in one of the boards. The woman glared at me and Bonnie, understandably, but never said a word. We ran just as fast as we could back to the beach, recovered rocket in hand.

Clearly, if that homemade model rocket had hit the woman or her kids, it would have been disastrous for them in terms of sustaining major injuries, or worse. But, as I was very lucky with the flying broomstick/bat incident earlier that summer, so were these people with my rocket. Needless to say, further planned launches for that day were scrubbed.

Despite its urban setting, my neighborhood actually had a wooded area in it, and we Olney kids could occasionally be woodsmen too. About five blocks in an easterly direction from where I lived was Tookany Creek Park. While miles long, Tookany Creek ("crick" as most Philadelphians would call such a thing), is a relatively narrow, elongated body of water, which runs a serpentine course with adjacent wooded areas on each side through the eastern portion of Philadelphia, starting in the faraway northern suburbs and ending in the Delaware River. It served my neighborhood friends and me as a nearby portal into the wild, or at least about as wild as a wooded area could be within the confines of the then fourth largest city in the U.S. With friends, I would probably spend a few afternoons there a month while between the ages of 9 and 12, pretty much year round. Some days my friends and I would pre-plan and pack lunches in our empty school bags. Back then, over-the-shoulder U.S. army-style bags were popular for boys to carry to school and, minus books, they sufficed for long hikes too. On those "expeditions," we'd sometimes spend the whole day in the woods.

On one, cold, wintertime Sunday afternoon, with I suppose nothing else to do that day, a trip to the woods was in order. While there and on the slightly sloping banks of the Tookany Creek, near the small waterfalls directly north of the Adams Ave. Bridge, I acted on a dare from one of my buddies. Never one back then to let a good dare go by, I stupidly agreed to attempt to walk on the frozen ice over what was, and still is, one of the deeper parts of the creek. It was not very thick ice as I was about to learn. After walking to near the center of the creek, about 15′ from the bank, I fell through. I found myself suddenly completely under the surface of the very cold water. When I first came up from the bottom, which I'm not sure I ever actually touched, I hit my head on the ice above me.

Fortunately for me, I didn't panic, as I had managed to suck in some air right before my head went beneath the surface. (I learned this trick body-surfing under the waves in the Atlantic Ocean on my family's occasional trips to the New Jersey seashore.) After what seemed like a few minutes but what was no doubt closer to a few seconds, in my heavy winter jacket, which was at this point starting to get water-logged, I managed to break through the ice above me and half-wade and half-crawl to shore and eventually climb up onto the creek bank. After nervously laughing about the incident with my friend, we then walked back home, me dripping cold water the whole time. He reminded me, somewhat sarcastically, that I did win the bet. There was no gloating though. Fully dressed and soaking wet, I didn't feel much like a winner right then and there.

I thought my parents would be really mad at me when I got home but they weren't. After telling them what happened, my mom hugged me, even while I was still dripping wet, and insisted that I take a hot bath. She told me that I was lucky to be alive. She and my dad further advised that I shouldn't attempt to walk on ice or take similarly dumb bets again. I wholeheartedly agreed with them on both and kept those promises.

A few decades later, usually during the summer months, more than a handful of people would drown at that same location when it became a city-sanctioned swimming hole. I did a thoughtless thing that wintry afternoon and was very fortunate to have survived it.

While the earlier referenced Miss America's neighborhood swimsuit-clad wanderings were odd, they were still mostly at a distance from me, at least from across a street, and with no personal interaction between the parties. My first actual up-close-and-personal experience with truly unusual and potentially criminal adult behavior occurred in the nearby Tookany woods when I was about 12 years old. That behavior was experienced as a result of finally meeting the man with the nickname, "Hackoff Harry." That was what the local kids called an adult male who would occasionally be seen walking through the aforementioned woods. Why that name? Well, this man liked strolling through the woods stark naked. And, he was reported by several of the neighborhood kids to occasionally be observed playing with himself ("hacking off?") while on these walks. I'm not sure where the "Harry" came from, but his occasional penchant for self-fondling apparently earned him the "Hackoff" part of his conveniently alliterative nickname.

Harry was nothing more than a rumor for my friends and me during this time frame, but other kids had sworn that they had seen this mystery man, in all his glory, as he strolled through the woods during warmer weather. What exactly he would do or say was unclear, and prone to many different variations, depending on the kid telling the story. And usually it was from what he had heard from someone else. My friends and I didn't dwell much on this urban legend. (Before, I believe, the term "urban legend" was probably even coined). He was our version of a non-furry Abominable Snowman or Bigfoot. Did he exist or not? Was he a threat or not? It didn't matter to us as we still went to the woods regularly just to escape into nature and have fun away from the hustle and bustle of our big-city environment.

As it turned out, it wasn't too long for me before the legend came true as one day my friends and I actually met Harry. He did exist literally, and somewhat scarily, in the flesh. It was way too much flesh, as I was about to find out.

I believe there were three of us together in the woods that day, me and two buddies, just hiking and looking to spend time there and off the streets. I seem to recall that it was a relatively warm mid-June day, possibly the afternoon of the last day of school, and because of that we were all in a very good mood. At some point, probably about 300 yards into the woods, well into the thick of it, we stopped along one of the trails and were sitting on a log in a small adjacent clearing, pretty much out of sight and sound of the bordering neighborhoods and any other human beings. Or so we thought.

I believe one of the three of us was using matches in an attempt to light a small fire to roast some marshmallows that we brought with us. There's nothing like city kids "roughing it" in the deep, dark woods. But our tranquility and semi-isolation were about to be violated, on multiple levels.

After hearing some leaves and twigs being stepped on behind us, we collectively looked over our shoulders to our lefts and rights. It wasn't that unusual to occasionally come across other kids in the woods also looking for the same urban escape as me and my friends that day. After all, the woods were not all that vast or expansive, there were only so many trails and clearings, and there were plenty of kids. But, as we soon learned, this wasn't just another kid walking toward us.

We could see that it was an adult male, probably in his 30s, slowly approaching our little campsite. It didn't take a future profiler and behavioral expert to figure out that this must be Harry, as he was completely naked, wearing only a hat and a pair of shoes of some sort. For me and my friends, seeing an adult at all in the Tookany woods was unusual enough. It being a naked adult male made it genuinely bizarre and pretty scary to us three pre-teens.

Harry had apparently seen us before we saw him, as he walked from behind over to us and immediately stopped at our location. He walked around us and was now standing almost directly in front of us while we attempted to heat our marshmallows over our little campfire. His arms were akimbo and he initially simply said "Hi" to us. We didn't look directly across at him as our sitting eye-levels would have had us staring directly at his exposed penis, which none of us (we later readily admitted) had any strong desire to observe close-up. Instead, we looked at each other for some sort of reassurance, collectively and non-verbally thinking in unison (we later concurred), "Is this really happening?"

I remember Harry then asking something like, "What are you boys doing?"

One of us (I don't recall if it was me or not) gave the kid-common response to that type question, "Uh, nothin'."

He then asked if we noticed that he was naked. We each mumbled something, but while looking at each other again for some hopeful reassurance, we didn't really answer him. His next statement surprised us even more, if that was possible. He said, to our astonishment and to no one in particular, "I'll bet my dick is bigger than yours."

Okay, this was getting way weird now.

I recall looking at one of my buddies and sort of smirking, but we didn't respond to this statement either. I didn't want Harry seeing me smirk though, so I did my best to hide it from him. After a few more now long-forgotten yet seemingly inane questions and comments from him, he said he was leaving and simply strode off further into the woods. For the record, he did not fondle himself while talking to us and he did not seem particularly excited in any physical way, shape, or form to be there with us. The same, I can assure the reader, applied to my friends and me.

We had no idea what this guy wanted from us. He never touched any of us nor asked us to remove our clothes or compare body parts or anything like that. (We would have definitely run away if these acts were so requested, or fought him off if force was attempted.) We all agreed later that day that we weren't REALLY scared of him during his visit, but I suppose we were still a bit overwhelmed by the encounter with him in all his...uh...nakedness. This was my first and only encounter with the once-rumored but now confirmed-to-exist Hackoff Harry. One time was plenty for me.

I never told my parents of this meeting in the woods with the naked man. Back in those days, at least with me and most of my buddies, those type anecdotes wouldn't be shared at home. I'm not sure why. Maybe we felt as if we had done something wrong, or had been somewhere that we shouldn't have been. That clearly wasn't the case. I remember later that week telling some older neighborhood boys of this encounter, to which they responded that they would have "beat the crap out of him" if they had seen him in the woods. I wasn't sure why they threatened to do that as he never did try to harm us. He was odd, surely. But, my parental up-bringing and my slowly developing adolescent mind figured that he shouldn't be the victim of un-necessary violence. Certainly not for what he did, and didn't do, to us.

I don't know what ever happened to Harry. I'm not sure if there were any other sightings of him in the woods and/or an eventual arrest of him, or if some older kids beat him up and he subsequently decided to forego his naked strolls, or what.

Was he an actual or potential child molester? Was he an actual or potential sexual predator? Or, was he just a naturalist, a practicing nudist? If just a naturalist, why so in this relatively small urban tract of land surrounded by residential neighbor-hoods? And, why did he reference his penis size to my young friends and me? That certainly changes the dynamics of his behavior, now looking back as an adult and a criminal profiler.

After all these years, I simply don't know the answers to any of these questions. (I've also always wondered where he hid his clothes during his na-ked jaunts, where he entered and exited the woods, etc.) I would need more information from additional verifiable incidents to truly assess Harry and his actions.

My encounter with this man, on that circa 1965 late-spring day, didn't alter or affect my life in any notable way. But it was clearly a mental reference point when, later in life, I was asked to provide assessments of individuals, usually men, engaging in what appeared to be unusual sexually oriented behavior. Some behavior was clearly criminal in nature. Other noted behavior, perhaps similar to Harry's, may have been odd, but was not necessarily a violation of the law.

While what Harry did may be considered suspicious and unusual, it is not necessarily suggestive of violent criminal behavior. (Yes, Indecent Exposure as per Pennsylvania criminal statutes, but that would be about it.) It could have been a precursor activity on his part to attempt to assault young boys, but, perhaps not. The actions we witnessed that day could have been the extent of his apparent need-driven behavior. That is, to walk naked through a wooded section of a large city and "shock" young kids, both visually and on occasion verbally. If that's all he ever did, that would be suggestive of him being an exhibitionist, yet pushing his luck, and the law, by doing so in a compressed, easily accessed, and relatively well-visited wooded location. However, commenting on his genitalia size and verbally comparing it to that of the young boys he happens to meet in the woods is certainly problematic behavior on his part and further suggestive of a diagnosable mental condition of some sort, not to mention further law breaking.

The separate sightings of both Miss America and Hackoff Harry were certainly interesting and memorable experiences in my early life. After the rendezvous with Harry, my friends and I would joke on occasion about somehow setting the two of them up on a "blind date." We wondered how that would work out. Probably not very well, we eventually agreed. Miss America would be over-dressed, for one thing.

MAY 1955

Two year-old Jimmy and his mom, Alma,
in front of 3rd St. house, 1955

L to r: Rich Davoli, Dieter Ballman, Jim Fitzgerald;
First Holy Communion, St. Helena School/Church, 1962
(Photo from Dieter Ballman Collection)

Jim Fitzgerald at "I.Q. Zoo,"
Hot Springs, Arkansas, 1963

Wally Fitzgerald in our row home basement
with one of my 1965 Christmas presents

The Evening and Sunday Bulletin

WITH AND MARKET STREETS   PHILADELPHIA PA 19101

December 22, 1965

James Fitzgerald
58   N. 3rd St.
Phila., Pa.

Dear Reader:

Lexicographers say the 45-letter medical term for a form of silicosis is now the longest word in the dictionary. It is pneumonoultramicroscopic-silicovolcanokoniosis. In recent years, long words such as antidisestablishmentarianism, electrophotom-icrographically and proantitransubstantiationist have made their appearance. For many years, the word dis-proportionableness was regarded as the longest of the English language.

Very truly yours,
ANSWERS TO QUERIES

IN PHILADELPHIA NEARLY EVERYBODY READS THE BULLETIN

1965 response letter from Philadelphia Evening Bulletin re "longest word in English language."

James Fitzgerald
"School Safety Patrol Award of Merit," 1967

Flying Bat Garage Door from Home Plate view;
Jim Fitzgerald was sitting on ground near bottom row
second panel from left (Photo, 2012)

Flying Bat Garage Door, close-up of lower panel
with former owner's "patch" (Photo, 2012)

Apartment building and front lawn,
3rd St. and Grange Ave., where 1961 showdown fight
with bully occurred (Photo, 2012)

Chapter Six

Looking back at my early years growing up in Olney, and despite the occasional interactions with almost naked or completely naked strangers, my upbringing and early life experiences were otherwise relatively unremarkable. When not in school, watching TV, riding my bike, playing games on my porch, engaging in sports, or roaming the not-so-deep inner-city woods near my house, I found myself reading books as often as possible.

My parents greatly encouraged reading. Neither of my parents was educated beyond high school, but they were nonetheless avid readers of books and newspapers and could be engaging conversationalists on many topics. My dad enjoyed books related to history, to include biographies and autobiographies. My mom was mostly a reader of fiction. She was also a big fan of newspaper crossword puzzles. She introduced me to the art of these particular word games early in life. This evolved to playing the board game Scrabble and later learning to do the daily newspaper Cryptograms, in which the words in long sentences/short paragraphs had to be alphabetically unscrambled in an attempt to make readable the usually clever quote or proverb. I got very good at each of the above as language and spelling (at least in English) came to me easily.

It, no doubt, laid the foundation for me to become a successful forensic linguist years later.

Regarding my early interest in language, and with no prodding from anyone around me, when I was twelve years old, I sat down and wrote a letter to the "Answers to Queries" column in the *Philadelphia Daily Bulletin* newspaper. I read it every day as the varied topic questions posed by readers were generally interesting and thought provoking. The answers provided by the newspaper staff were interesting and edifying too.

My language-oriented question to the "Queries" staff was a simple one. I asked in my carefully typewritten letter, "What is the longest word in the English language?" I was hoping the question and response would be published in the daily newspaper column. But, for whatever reason, it wasn't. Instead, about a month later a one-page typewritten letter was mailed to my house, addressed to me, and it contained the answer.

The letter was dated December 22, 1965, and it began,

"Lexicographers say the 45-letter medical term for a form of silicosis is now the longest word in the dictionary. It is pneumonoultramicroscopicsilicovolcanoconiosis."

It was simply signed, "Very truly yours, ANSWERS TO QUERIES."

I still didn't really understand what the word meant, nor did I really care, despite the additional very brief descriptive info. However, it was nice that the newspaper staff responded to my query. I had my answer and now I knew the word. To this day, I've never used that word in a spoken sentence. I never used that word in a written sentence either, well, until the inclusion of it in the above paragraph.

My dad, knowing the importance of speaking standard English, would challenge me directly when he knew I was pronouncing or using words in a non-standard manner. For one, as with many people in casual conversation, I had an early habit of "dropping" word endings. For example, I would say, "I'm goin' down Fis Street," meaning I'm proceeding to the main shopping district (Fifth Street) in my neighborhood.

My dad would simply state back to me, "Spell that!"

I'd retort, "Spell what?"

He'd respond, "Where you're go-ing," emphasizing the "-ing" in that word.

I'd then somewhat sarcastically and uber-emphatically pronounce the verb as "goinG." I'd then proceed to spell "F-i-f-t-h S-t-r-," at which point Wally would stop me. He'd then remind me that, in my rapid speaking style, I didn't pronounce the street as it was spelled. He was right. I substituted "Fis Street" for "Fifth Street," changing the "f" into an "s" and omitting the "-th" from my pronunciation. Again, such reduced features are not that uncommon as I'd learn later in my Georgetown University phonology courses. The tongue, when involved in speech, often follows the path of least resistance, especially when certain sounds or sound sequences are particularly difficult to pronounce, like the "-fth" sequence in "Fifth." It took a bit of tongue-related discipline on my part to pronounce the "-th" in "Fifth" before the "s" in "street," and as a child I was initially reluctant to do so, as all my buddies tended to talk the same way too. The same applies, of course, to pronouncing words ending in "-ing" in the standard way rather that as "-in."

My dad and I would go back and forth too about the pronunciations of "Acme" and "creek," when one of us would slip up and pronounce those words as did many other Philadelphians, that is, "ack-a-me" and "crick," respectively. Neither of us realized in those days that we Philadelphians pronounced the word "water" as "wooder." That's a southeastern Pennsylvania/southern New Jersey/Delaware pronunciation, whose origin is unknown. Years later, in my formal linguistic studies, I would learn about the distribution of this and many other regional pronunciations and lexical usages from around the U.S. And this knowledge would even help me solve crimes.

Having these nonstandard pronunciations and other vernacular language usages pointed out to me by my dad early on (never in public, I should add, but only when just the two of us), as well as by a few grade school and high school teachers, eventually paid off when later I would undergo job interviews, was asked to give speeches, and testify in court.

Later on, in my early 20s, just for fun, I'd sometimes "correct" my dad in the manner in which he would pronounce certain words. Two of those words were "exzilerator" for "accelerator," and "lozenger" for "lozenge." He'd always tell me he was appreciative of my language advisories to him, but rarely afterwards would he actually alter his pronunciations of those words. He was, as a matter of fact, pretty set in his ways in that regard.

There was one particular high school English teacher of mine who was also very fastidious about his students' speaking styles and lexical usages, and who would correct us in class when the various language miscues manifested themselves. I learned to appreciate those "corrections" too, as they were offered in the proper spirit by him. Years later, as a police officer, I came upon this same teacher in a rather compromising situation one night. As with my dad, just for fun, I actually "corrected" him for a language miscue of sorts while addressing the larger issue at hand. He appreciated it and what I did next for him that night, too.

When it came to reading, I certainly read the books assigned as homework in school. First of all, I usually wanted to do so. Secondly, the nuns would beat us if we didn't.

I also enjoyed the Marvel and DC comic books of the time and the "funnies" in the newspapers (as well as the news and sports, too, or at least some of it), but just as many of my readings back then were books of my choice. After hearing my parents talk for years of the "Crime of the Century," at least in their half of the 20th Century, which occurred to one of America's greatest heroes, Charles Lindbergh, I walked to the Olney Branch of the Philadelphia Library and borrowed a 1962 book entitled *Kidnap*, written by George Waller. It was in the "adult" section of the library, not the "children" section, where before then I had borrowed all my books.

Kidnap was a very detailed telling of the story of Charles Lindbergh and his wife, Anne Morrow, and the 1932 kidnapping and subsequent murder of their young son from their New Jersey home. The area of the kidnapping, in Hopewell, NJ, was only about 25 miles from my house, as that earlier referenced crow would fly. And, my parents were right. This was truly the "Crime of the Century" in its day, and reading about it some 30-plus years later utterly enthralled me.

Although I knew in advance of the eventual outcome, having heard it over the years from my parents, while reading the early chapters of the book I found myself asking similar questions to the Boy in the Box case, "Who would do something like this?" "Why?"

I wondered how the investigators would ever solve this crime. The biggest difference between this case and the case of the little boy in the box though was a ransom demand. It was a for-profit kidnapping, not just the killing and abandoning of a young child. This kidnapper/killer wanted money for the baby's safe return even though he (but no one else yet) knew his victim was already dead, having been killed most likely accidently during the abduction itself from the Lindbergh home.

I read the book and all my questions were answered as to how it was eventually solved. Upon being introduced to this very early well-written literary exposure of a major U.S. criminal investigation, and solved no less (Richard Bruno Hauptmann was eventually arrested, convicted, and executed for this crime), I began to think that working on a major investigation, helping to solve a major crime or crimes, was something that I would find truly rewarding.

I also found intriguing, for whatever reason at the time, the fact there was spoken and written language assessed in the Lindbergh kidnapping case.

Along with other investigative clues, this evidence eventually helped identify the kidnapper/killer. This taught me, very early on, that language evidence could be as important as any other types of forensic clues in an investigation.

I put this type of evidence to the test in the Unabom case decades later. I also now use the ransom letters from the Lindbergh case, as well as the writings of the Unabomber, along with other cases, when I'm teaching forensic linguistics in the U.S. and around the world. They are invaluable from a language-as-evidence perspective and serve as excellent teaching instruments.

Back at the time, I don't remember thinking to myself or telling anyone that I wanted to be a cop, a detective, an investigator, an FBI agent, or certainly a criminal profiler or forensic linguist. (Neither of the last two terms were even part of our lexicon in the mid-1960s.) But, I believe that the seeds of interest were planted in me by this book, this case, and the other criminal investigations to which I had been indirectly exposed over the years and would later read about in other books or in the newspapers.

As I was reading about these varied crimes, I would put myself in the shoes of the investigators. Mix in the "lawman" play-acting as a kid, some later cop-related TV shows, and perhaps it was a combination of all these factors that contributed to decisions to be made by me in the not-too-distant future which would lead me to be part of, if not instrumental in, the investigations of some of the most horrendous and publicized crimes of my generation.

My dad, apparently aware of my early interest in anything related to the field of true crime, told me when I was a bit older of a very famous defense attorney in Philadelphia named Chippy Patterson. He came to local prominence in the 1920s and 1930s. My dad said that in his own youth, during times when he was out of work during the Great Depression and/or had some free time on his hands, he would actually sit in the courtrooms in Philadelphia's City Hall and watch Chippy in action. He was, by all accounts, a very unconventional attorney, known to dress sloppily, at times act bizarre, carry all his legal files in one broken-down, oversized, over-stuffed briefcase, and yet someone who almost always found clever and ingenious ways to have his usually down-trodden clients acquitted of their criminal charges.

Again recognizing this interest of mine, my dad recommended a 1960 book to me. It was *The Worlds of Chippy Patterson,* by Arthur H. Lewis. It was well-written, very entertaining, informative, and insightful. I found myself, at times in my adult life in the criminal justice system, trying to think like Chippy and utilize maneuvers and methods sometimes "outside the box," yet all completely legal of course, to better investigate and further facilitate my cases through the court system. As an eventual law enforcement officer, I was on the prosecution side of the system, not the defense side like Chippy. And, I tended to dress a bit better than he reportedly did. (I have witnesses who will attest to that.).

As a practitioner in the criminal justice system, I don't believe I ever met a defense attorney, or any attorney, quite like Chippy Patterson. I have gone up against some very interesting ones, nonetheless. Some were brilliant, some far from brilliant, some bizarre, and some who were certainly not the best dressers or even seemingly daily bathers. However, as I matured and evolved within the legal system, I never saw defense attorneys as my enemy when taking an investigation, an arrest, a prosecution, through the adversarial process. To me, they served as my internal and external check-and-balance system in the case investigation, profile, linguistic analysis, or whatever it was to which I may be testifying. They had a job to do, a client to represent, and I had my job to do, that is, to represent the government (or a client, when later in life retired from law enforcement) and do so to the best of my ability.

There was only one time I was really "beat up" on the stand by a defense attorney. That happened the very first time I ever testified in open criminal court. It was a shoplifting case. It taught me yet another lesson that would last a lifetime. That caper, and the court case itself, are forthcoming.

My father would also relate to me in his later life that in the Depression-era 1930s, when he would be looking for work in the Philadelphia area, he would occasionally walk along the docks on the Delaware River. (Elfreth's Alley, where he was born, was not far from there.) While in that area, he recalled seeing numerous Japanese freighters, almost weekly, loading ton after ton of sheet metal, iron ore, steel, and similar type materials that they would buy in the U.S. and then return to their homeland. As an amateur historian and relatively well-read in that genre, even back then, he was sure that someday in the not too distant future the Japanese would be "shooting that scrap metal back at us." My mom later confirmed he did, in fact, say that to her in the '30s. He, along with others, was proven correct when on December, 7, 1941, the Japanese Imperial Forces attacked Pearl Harbor.

Part of his opinions regarding the potential Japanese aggression came from another man my dad greatly admired from afar. That was U.S. Army General Billy Mitchell. I recall engaging in conversations about him with my dad on occasions as I was growing up.

Gen. Mitchell, in the 1920s and 1930s, attempted to convince otherwise reluctant military leaders and politicians in Washington, D.C., that the next war would be waged, in no small part, in the air and a strong air force component to the military was paramount to the security of the U.S. As a result of Gen. Mitchell's politically unpopular actions and opinions, he was eventually subjected to a military court martial. In the long run, Gen. Mitchell and his reputation were vindicated. Air superiority during World War II was crucial to the defeat of the Axis powers, and it remains critical to any country's defense to this day. Gen. Mitchell was right, and the others who disagreed with him were clearly wrong.

I included the above examples of individuals of whom my dad spoke highly, such as Chippy Patterson and Gen. Billy Mitchell, and of his (my dad's) unschooled, yet ultimately accurate, historical observations predicting Japanese war time aggressions, as being indicative of the positive parental influences to which I was exposed while growing up. Along with others, my dad admired these two disparate men, who while outliers within their own professions, and to some degree even society, nonetheless undertook what they thought was right to accomplish their respective goals and objectives. He didn't want me, as a kid and certainly later in life, to be afraid to say or do what wasn't always popular, or say or do what was simply agreed upon by the crowd. He wanted me to enter into maturity knowing that if I clearly studied and researched an issue at hand, and/or had a well-thought out gut instinct about any matter of importance, I should freely express my true feelings and opinions and fight for them, even if not readily accepted initially by others.

My father added that, at the same time, I should never turn anyone away who is willing to offer me advice or an opinion about a matter of interest to me. I wouldn't necessarily have to take this person's advice or agree with his or her opinions, but I should always be willing to listen to them nonetheless. Even a seemingly ignorant person can teach others, sometimes, what they need to know about certain aspects of life. As he would quote to me, "Even a broken clock is right twice a day."

It wasn't always easy, I would later learn, to vent these sometimes unpopular opinions, but my dad did impart those valuable lessons to me, and they bore out for me in the future.

Many years later, during the DC Sniper case in 2002, when I was the first profiler/forensic linguist to suggest that there may be two snipers working in tandem and at that they were possibly African-American, I realized that I was the outlier in the room among my FBI and task force peers. But, my dad's insistence that I stick to my guns when I was pretty darn sure that I was right eventually paid off, in that case and others.

Lastly here in regards to Wally Fitzgerald's sort of philosophy of life, at least when it came to expressing words of wisdom to his four kids, it should be noted that he was not the particularly touchy/feely type. I don't remember him ever telling me he loved me or my sisters, but we all know he did. He saw his role as a father as being a positive role model, that is, living a good life, a balanced life, and conveying to his children that which he found interesting, insightful, and, most importantly, useful in life.

In terms of what's "useful" in life, my dad was a pragmatist, through and through, and not one focused on theories and hypotheses. At the same time, he admired the guy who was "different" and ultimately not afraid to be so. He respected the occasional person who would go out on a limb with an idea or a well-thought out opinion and who would be willing to sacrifice much to make his beliefs known and then undertake certain actions, even if not popular at the time. He stressed that people, and even entire countries, undertake certain actions for a reason. Those actions, and perhaps ongoing patterns before and after related to them, can prove very beneficial in trying to figure out exactly what it is they're doing, why, and what they may do next.

I modeled my profiling career on these tenets imparted upon me to a large degree by my dad.

Chapter Seven

As with everyone while growing up and experiencing life, my dad and mom weren't with me all the time. Their conversations with me only went so far. Much of life's other learning experiences, as with most of us, were gained on my own. That included those gained during my school years.

My grade school years were relatively noneventful. I attended all eight years at the same school, St. Helena School. I am a graduate of the class of 1967. At the time it was one of the largest grade schools in the city of Philadelphia. The student enrollment teetered around 1500, spread from first through eighth grade. From first through sixth grade for me, there were three classes in each grade. Our class size averaged 70 students. Finally, in seventh and eighth grades, another class was added and it went down to *only* 50+ students per class.

I still blame these class sizes on the reason that I've never been good at advanced math. Not an excuse, mind you, but the 70-to-1 student-to-teacher ratio certainly didn't help me in that subject area when I initially struggled and could have benefitted from additional teacher interaction. Fortunately, reading, spelling, history, geography, and other subjects came to me relatively easily.

I should add that I wasn't an angel while in grade school; in fact, far from it for a few of those years. It seems I would get in trouble of some sort a few times from fifth through seventh grades. Usually, it was as a result of me talking when I was not supposed to be talking. I could be the wise-guy, even class clown, as some would remind me later for at least a few of those grades, depending on the teacher. Punishment imposed by the teachers would include staying after school, being beaten, and being given repetitive writing assignments.

One of the latter assignments, in fifth grade, was the granddaddy of them all, at least to me. I was ordered to write, in one overnight period, 500 times, "I must not talk after the bell." Thank you Sister William Loretta. She wasn't even my teacher at the time, but didn't approve of me talking while standing in line in the schoolyard after the lunchtime bell rang. She didn't even know my name as she was a seventh grade teacher. Nevertheless, I spent a whole school night writing it, with a severely limp left hand to show for it afterwards. My parents knew about it (how could I hide handwriting 3500 separate words and going through three pencils), but back then they would never consider calling the convent to talk to Sister and complain about this worthless punishment.

Or, was it worthless? I know I didn't talk in line again for a long time after that writing assignment.

I later learned when given similar writing-for-punishment assignments, even in high school, the value of good old-fashioned carbon paper. A #2 pencil with a certain form of carbon paper (gray/black, not blue) with a blank page under it would cut the punishment writing assignment time and effort in half. I must have done a dozen such assignments that way during high school. One priest in particular would have the entire class write out the day's newspaper editorials five times if we were too rambunctious for him in class that day. At least in these written punishments we were learning of the various newspaper editors' opinions on certain matters. But Sister William Loretta's same-sentence-500-times assignment was clearly punishment for punishment's sake. Nothing externally learned in the process of doing that one.

Did I mention being beaten in grade school? Most of my trouble occurred in classes taught by the St. Joseph Order nuns, as opposed to the lay teachers. During the '60s, the faculty at St. Helena school was probably two-thirds nuns, with the remaining one-third being lay teachers. The nuns, at least some of the older ones, could be very strict, set in their ways, and tough as nails. I paid the price for their strictness and their set ways more times than I care to recall, as these ways included the liberal application of corporal punishment. Yes, as in slaps and wooden sticks to the head and to various body parts.

I remember having chalk and/or erasers thrown at me (both almost always finding their target, my head), my face slapped, getting yardsticks across my butt, and taking it on the knuckles with regular wooden rulers and for a whole school year one of those solid-wood, three-sided, foot-long engineering rulers. Each time I got a beating at school I would never tell my parents. If I had told them of these disciplinary tactics handed out by the nuns during the day, I'd be in even more trouble with them later that night. I preferred to keep my getting-into-trouble to no more than once per day, if at all possible.

During the first week of eighth grade, I was appointed to the St. Helena School Safety Patrol. With that, I was assigned my first "real" badge. It came with a white harness belt of some sort and I proudly wore both each day at lunchtime (as the vast majority of the students walked home for lunch) and after school, while I escorted one of five lines of hundreds of kids up the street from the school to the corner of 5th and Godfrey. There, the full-time school crossing guard took over. My "safety" responsibilities were then done for the day.

And, for the record, I never lost a kid during that whole year. That's an accomplishment of which I'm still proud.

While on the Safety Patrol in eighth grade, I had my first up-close-and-personal meeting ever with a police officer. He came to our building early in the school year one day to talk to us. He may have spoken to our whole class, too, but it seemed he was there to congratulate the safeties and tell us what an important job we were doing. He was a friendly, well-spoken, relatively young officer and was very engaging to my classmates and me. He represented the Philadelphia Police Department very well. Of course, he was in full uniform, to include his gun, and that didn't hurt his image and persona among us eighth grade boys.

(Girls weren't allowed to be safeties back then. Clearly a sexist attitude still existed during this time in regard to these types of positions and appointments. They couldn't be altar servers at Mass, either. That has all changed, fortunately.)

After the officer's talk, and when some of us safeties were helping him take whatever display items he had brought in with him back to his patrol car, the question all of us wanted answered was eventually asked of him. That is, "Hey Officer, did you ever shoot anyone?"

I don't think I asked it, but I'm not really sure after all these years who did. The officer's simple response was, "No."

We left it at that, with no follow up questions. I'm not sure what my fellow students and I would have followed up with if he had replied, "Yes."

Years later, I would be asked that same question many times as a uniformed police officer. And, it wasn't always a kid asking it. Sometimes, depending on who posed the question, and my mood at the time, I would reply with some level of sarcasm, "No, but the day (or night) is still young."

That's cop humor, whether others found it funny or not.

Looking back at my year in eighth grade, I'll never forget the date November 27, 1966. In the early morning hours of that day something tragic happened in my Olney neighborhood that was a true rarity, certainly during that timeframe. That is, a Philadelphia police officer was shot and seriously injured. This happened while he was responding to a botched robbery attempt. It occurred near the intersection of 5th St. and 66th Ave., only about four blocks from the location of my school, and perhaps ten blocks, or about a mile, from where I lived. I forget exactly how I first heard of this incident, whether from an early morning TV or radio news account, or my parents. At first, I didn't know the officer's name or the exact details of the crime.

Later that evening, upon learning from the TV news the shot officer's name and seeing his picture, I was somewhat relieved to learn that it was not the officer who had come to visit us only weeks before. It was gleaned from the news over the next 24 hours that the shooter, now under arrest, was a man named William Barnes. He had shot and paralyzed a rookie police officer named Walter Barclay, who was one of the responding officers to the robbery call.

I found myself very much distressed by this event. I'm not sure then why the shooting of the police officer bothered me as much as it did. As a young boy, being exposed to the media as I was in my home, I was certainly aware of other police officers in Philadelphia and its environs having been shot, and other violent crimes which had occurred that victimized the innocent or even perhaps the not-so-innocent among us. But, because this one occurred in my neighborhood, and/or perhaps because I had just met my first "real" police officer a month or so before, I was really bothered by it. This tragedy was to become even more personal to me by the next day, and I've regretted what I did on that day ever since.

On the next full day following the shooting, the buzz throughout St. Helena school and its students was that the shooter of the police officer was, in fact, the older brother of one of my fellow eighth graders, James Barnes. And, he happened to be in my homeroom that year. I wasn't that friendly with this particular student, as he had not been at the school as many years as me. But, I knew him and had known of him for a while, although we were never in the same class together before. As we were seated alphabetically, he sat about five seats in front of me in the first aisle of our eighth grade homeroom. He was noticeably quiet in school since the previous day.

At some point on that second day after the shooting, and on the same day that the information became known at school about the sibling connection between the shooter and my classmate, it happened. It was either at the change of classes, or on the regularly scheduled boys' lavatory run, that I found myself walking right up behind my fellow student Barnes, still in the classroom. Leaning towards him, speaking close to his left ear, I spontaneously stated, quietly and for only him to hear, four words.

Those words were simply, and sarcastically, "Hey Barnes, nice brother!"

That was it. That was all I said; four words. James slowly turned around and glanced back at me, perhaps in an attempt to confirm which one of his classmates just made this uncalled for remark, looked to his left, then to his right, and then just began walking forward to wherever it is we were going. We separated ahead somewhere and there was no further interaction. We never shared a word or activity between us again that school year. I don't remember seeing him much again after our class graduated. I believe he later went to a different high school than me.

A short time later, maybe even that night, I realized that what I said to my classmate that day was wrong. Yes, I still felt bad about the police officer,

but my fellow eighth grader was in no way responsible for what his older brother (by 18 years I later
learned) did to seriously injure the officer. I have no
doubt that he felt awful for a long time after this
tragic incident yet, to his credit, as far as I know, he
still managed to show up at school the days immediately afterward. In doing so, he certainly didn't
need me to say to him what I said.

No one ever corrected me or admonished me or
challenged me for what I said to James Barnes that
day. They didn't have to. Plus, no one but James
ever heard me say it. It was between him and me.
However, something in me realized shortly afterwards that I was out of line to have said what I did
to him. I learned a lesson that day, or shortly thereafter, and I have never forgotten it. Perhaps I was
maturing, at least to some degree. After the fact, I
suppose, in the case of this particular incident.

In 1991, while an FBI agent in New York City
assigned to the Bank Robbery Task Force, one of my
co-workers and friends, NYPD Det. Charlie
Jardines, was shot in Brooklyn after a short foot
chase of a suspect wanted for bank robbery. The
suspect was also shot at and wounded by Det.
Jardines. Charlie was seriously wounded and
rushed to the hospital. I was on another assignment
that day and not at the scene of the shooting. However, I responded to the area shortly after the shooting and was eventually assigned with another
NYPD detective to stay with the shooter in the hospital, who was in custody and being treated for his
bullet wound there. He had been arrested and was
initially in the same hospital as Charlie, who of
course also had a police/FBI detail guarding him.

While not violating any of the shooter's civil or criminal rights, during the course of several conversations with him that evening (which he initiated), I did manage to have a few choice words for him regarding his actions from earlier that day. The words I said were to the cop-shooter/bank robber himself, not to one of his family members. Unlike what I said decades before to the younger Barnes, I have no regret for the words directed at the shooter in the hospital that night. They were between him and me, and they were from the heart; especially as I knew Charlie was only a floor above me, in surgery, for the wounds suffered because of this felon.

Det. Jardines fully recovered from his injuries and a year or so later took a well-earned disability leave from the NYPD. He is now teaching school in New York City. The suspect also recovered and was eventually tried and convicted of bank robbery and attempted murder of a police officer.

A legally interesting, yet nonetheless sad, footnote to the 1966 shooting of the Philadelphia police officer surfaced in 2007 when former Officer Barclay, on full disability and confined to a wheelchair ever since the 1966 incident, died of a urinary infection. William Barnes had already served 16 years in prison for the attempted murder of Officer Barclay, and was freed, but still on parole in 2007. When Barclay died, 41 years after the shooting, the Philadelphia District Attorney's office re-charged Barnes, this time with second-degree murder. The DA's office maintained that the urinary infection and Barclay's subsequent death was a direct result of the shooting in 1966. Thus, Barnes was re-arrested, again placed in custody, and faced another trial stemming from that night four decades ago.

At the trial, the defense claimed that Barclay's death was not the result of the shooting, but instead because of three car accidents, two falls from his wheelchair, and neglect from caregivers. At the 2010 trial, Barnes was found not guilty of the murder. I believe the jury reached the proper verdict in this matter.

In May of 2014, after some 47 years, I located and reached out to my former St. Helena school classmate, Jim Barnes. After some catching-up on life, I reminded him of my thoughtless schoolroom comment I made to him regarding his brother back in 1966. Immediately afterwards I apologized to him. Jim accepted it unconditionally. I thanked him and we've maintained contact ever since.

Back to my grade school days, and on a much, much lighter note, during that same eighth grade year, I was to learn something about almost becoming a snitch or informant. Later in my professional life, it became very clear to me how valuable confidential informants, or snitches, can be. But, could I be turned into one at 13 years of age? And by a nun?

My eighth grade nun was a hardnosed, no-nonsense, quick-to-lose-her-temper woman of the habit. Her name was Sister Ruth Dolores. She was probably in her 50s, wasn't tall or heavyset, but she was mean and she could pack one heck of a punch or a slap. I never experienced one of them myself, but I saw her hit classmates of mine square in the face or in the belly numerous times. I observed her punches and slaps in real-time, my classmates' reactions, the eventual welts that would develop, and heard their tales of pain and discomfort afterwards. I sympathized with them for the physical damage she inflicted.

Sister Ruth didn't usually hit the female students, but she could make them cry like babies. On such an occasion, one of my eighth grade female classmates wore the slightest touch of makeup to the annual Sunday evening May Procession. While assembled in our classroom, before the procession around the school and into the church was to begin, Sister Ruth belittled her, an otherwise quiet and studious fellow student, in front of the whole class. With tissue paper, she forcibly and demonstrably wiped the smidgen of makeup off her crying face. It was not a good start for our class to what should have been an otherwise spiritual evening, especially with our parents waiting outside for us. It was much worse for the young girl who was publicly embarrassed in front of our whole class by our nun.

I think Sister Ruth is the one that finally taught me, through fear of getting seriously hurt by her left and right hand slaps and punches (she was noticeably ambidextrous in that regard), that I should learn to keep my mouth shut at times. I certainly did in her class. Maybe it was my reluctance to getting socked in the face, or maybe it was that thing called maturity once again slowly starting to set in, although very slowly by some accounts back then. Either way, I concentrated more on listening in class that year than talking.

Once, while in class, and obviously not that mature yet, I was passing around to my fellow students a short, non-class related "essay" that I had spent considerable time undertaking while at home. I had even typed it on my parents' old Underwood typewriter that, at the time, I was learning to use more and more, one finger-peck at a time.

In the clearly G-rated essay, I made fun of, in a light-hearted and whimsical way, one of my fellow male students. Sister Ruth saw it being passed around, with students giggling aloud upon reading it, and slowly walked over to my area of the classroom. She took the document from whoever had it at the time. She quickly figured out I was its author, and I was now awaiting the worst. She stayed right in the aisle, next to my desk, and read it to herself from beginning to end. I was never more nervous in a classroom than I was at this time, while she read my short story. I was awaiting a right or a left hook at any moment, maybe even both in rapid succession, as she was noted for her one-two combinations.

Sister Ruth eventually relaxed her arms, putting them to her side, turned on her heels and looked directly down at me. Instead of her belting me, to my great surprise, she smiled and started sort of half-laughing. She then handed the document back to me.

In doing so, she said to me, in effect, "Excellent writing style. It's humorous, Mr. Fitzgerald. You're good at this. But, put your skills to something more constructive. Understand!?"

I replied with the then oft heard classroom refrain, "Yes, Sister."

Sister Ruth seemed to like me after that. It didn't hurt that I was also a good student in her class and had relatively recently learned to stifle my over-the-top verbal expressiveness. It didn't hurt in a number of ways.

From all of the homework assignments ever given to me while in any class anywhere, I credit Sister Ruth Dolores and one of her assignments as being the oddest. It was one of the easiest, but at the same time confounding in its simplicity, meaning, and purpose.

One day, our homeroom nun simply asked the class out loud if anyone knew the shortest flight one could take from Philadelphia International Airport. Some guessed out loud (when called upon), but no one knew the answer for sure. She then assigned all of us, including other students who rotated through her classroom, over 200 in all, to find the answer. Why she would want to know this is unclear. But, as I didn't want to miss out on a rather easy homework assignment, I knew I would comply and do my best to get her that answer, and the added homework bonus points she was offering.

Later that evening, after dinner, I looked up in the Yellow Pages the phone number for the airport. I called the main number. A man answered and said "Philadelphia International Airport, may I help you?"

I simply said, in so many words, "Sir, can you please tell me the shortest flight someone can take from your airport?"

He stated back adamantly and angrily, "Jesus Christ! Another one! It's Newark! Tell her it's Newark, New Jersey, damn it!"

And, he hung up.

Apparently a pervious caller, perhaps dozens and dozens of them, told the poor guy that this was a homework assignment from our nun. At least he was a religious man in that he invoked the name of Christ in giving me his answer. That was reassuring.

Sister Ruth asked the class the next day if anyone had the answer for her regarding the airport/flight question. We all sort of answered simultaneously that it was Newark. She thanked us and we moved on to the regular lessons of the day.

Upon talking to my fellow students about their assignment of the day before, we pieced together the timeline and learned that the later in the day and evening that we called the airport, the more angry the guy became whose job it was to answer the phone. He probably received upwards of 200 calls that day and evening from the St. Helena School eighth graders, all asking him the same inane and innocuous question. To this day, the reason Sister Ruth gave us that assignment remains a mystery.

Later that year, Sister Ruth would recommend and nominate me to various positions and assignments within the classroom and the school. I know she gave me a good reference for high school, although I never actually saw them. But, it was toward the end of the school year, perhaps in May of '67, when she put me in a very strange situation, one of arguably a semi-sexual nature, which to the present time perplexes me even more than the shortest-flight-from-Philadelphia homework assignment.

On that day, right after we students returned from lunch and were just settling into our respective desks, Sister Ruth called my name and asked to see me in the hallway. This was never a good thing, at least in my personal eight year-long St. Helena school tenure. I obediently got up from my desk, adjusted my tie, pushed back my hair, and walked out the classroom door. She followed me closely and shut the door behind us, from the outside. It was completely empty in the darkened hallway, other than the two of us standing there. My back was against the wall, and she was now standing about a foot in front of me. As she was about four inches shorter than me, even with the nun's habit on her head, I found myself looking down at her. She was sort of crowding me, and I felt as if I was in a tight spot for some reason. It made me feel sort of claustrophobic, even with the empty hallway all around us.

With just the two of us outside the classroom, me standing with my back to the wall and her looking up very intently up at me, Sister Ruth cleared her throat and then said to me in a very serious tone, "Mr. Fitzgerald, I have a question for you and I want you to answer it with complete honestly. Do you understand?"

Naturally, in my all too well-rehearsed fashion, I responded, "Yes, Sister."

What choice did she give me? After all, I couldn't lie to a nun. Plus, she'd punch and/or slap me if she found out that I was in anyway less than truthful.

Sister Ruth then asked, very cautiously and very succinctly, the following question. "Do you know the meaning of 69?"

I was momentarily flabbergasted. Why would she be asking me this question? What does she know? What does she think I know? What has she heard? Geez, did someone set me up here?

She's not asking me if I know who may have left graffiti behind on a bathroom stall or a wall somewhere that may have incorporated that number. She wanted to know what the number actually meant. What do I tell her in this situation? After all, she's a...a...nun! I'm a kid! A Catholic school kid! I've got my whole life ahead of me here. 69? Geez...what am I supposed to tell her?

What seemed like eons in my young, just barely-teenaged mind probably lasted just a few moments from the figurative question mark of her semi-sexually oriented query to me and my not-quite-yet answer to her. In that immeasurable amount of time, I found myself weighing all my available options, each in split-second fashion.

I could advise her simply that it's the number that falls between 68 and 70, but I knew that was not what she wanted to hear, and would probably result in a flying fist to at least one side of my head.

If I tell her I knew what it meant, and I was not completely sure at the time that I DID know exactly what it meant, will that in and of itself get me in trouble?

If yes, will she think I had something to do with whatever and wherever this "bad" number had appeared? If yes, will she then want me to explain further what it means? How could I do that? She's a...a...nun!

What do I do?

At some point, I eventually cleared MY throat, perhaps more than once, no doubt in an effort to buy some time. I think I even slowly said, "Welllllll...." I believe I even added, "Uh, 69, right?" As if she would be asking me about 169, or 96, or any other number other than that particular one.

But, as my verbal stalling tactics were running out, I eventually responded to her in the safest and securest way I knew how at the time.

"No, Sister, I don't know what it means."

She glared at me for a few seconds, backed up a bit, came forward again, and asked me if I was sure.

I shrugged my shoulders and replied with the ever-predictable, "Yes, Sister."

She hesitated for a few more seconds, squinted her eyes a bit, pursed her lips, looked me up and down, and finally said I could go back into the classroom.

Of course I said, "Yes, Sister," and then walked back into the classroom. I never was so relieved to utter those two words.

This was the only time Sister Ruth asked me any question such as this one. It was the only time I had to lie to a nun about something I didn't know, or that I pretended I didn't know. Actually, I'm not sure what I did know that day about that number and/or its usage on the school premises some-where, only that I knew that I hadn't written it anywhere or used it in a sentence with anyone. Plus, when all was said and done, I didn't want to be a snitch for her and get someone else in trouble, although I knew nothing about whatever incident involving the number 69 may have occurred. No matter what, I just wasn't going to be her or anyone's snitch...or just as bad, maybe even worse, I wasn't talking about sexual things with a nun.

To this day, I still wonder what Sister Ruth would have said or done if I had responded in the affirmative to her question. Would there have been further questions? Would she have wanted details? Specifics? I don't know these answers.

Sister Ruth Dolores was a good teacher and a good nun. She was tough as nails, but could be fair. Well, to most of us, most of the time. I don't think she meant anything untoward by this question to me. Maybe her curiosity about the issue got to her, or maybe it was her curiosity as to what an almost 14-year-old boy may know about it. I doubt very much if there was any sexual agenda behind it. At least I don't think so.

About 15 years later, it was me who turned the tables and was asking sexually related questions to a member of a religious order; this time, it was a priest. It wasn't in the hallway of a school, either. It was late at night in the interview room of my police department. His sexual agenda, as it related to the two young boys I found him with, was very clear to me. I still wanted to hear his answers though. I eventually heard them. He was one of the first of many priests who had to answer these questions to law enforcement. I would be one of the first officers to bring a priest to justice for it.

More on this man and his crimes in Book II.

I graduated from St. Helena School, and on that night after the ceremony Sister Ruth gave me a firm handshake (with no further sexually oriented questions) and wished me luck at my new school. I thanked her, said goodbye, and never saw her again.

As the summer after eighth grade started, so did my first job. I was a paperboy for the now long-defunct *Philadelphia Evening Bulletin* newspaper. I delivered papers seven days a week, including Sunday mornings, throughout that summer and all of my freshman year in high school. My route was right in my own immediate neighborhood too, so that made it pretty easy.

This was probably the heyday of newspaper circulation, sales, and deliveries, certainly in the Philadelphia area. In my slice of Olney, I was one of approximately 40 other newspaper boys (no girls once again) who would walk to the branch office at Philip St. and Grange Ave., a small converted commercial store on the first floor of a rowhome which served as a starting point for the carriers to pick up our papers from the branch manager and deliver them accordingly. We'd turn our collection money into him too at the end of the week. I had about 70 dailies and about 45 Sundays.

It wasn't a bad route. It made me about $12 per week. That was pretty good for a 14 year-old in the late '60s. I would usually carry them in my old wooden wagon, with side bars, that my dad built from scratch years before. On certain days though, when it was known that the paper was to be thinner, I carried them over my shoulder, on my back, in the *Bulletin* provided newspaper bag. My dad would all but plead with me to use the wagon though, instead of straining my back. He did not want to see me go through life with the back problems that plagued him for many years. I listened to him, well, most of the time.

On Thursdays, we always had to "stuff" the papers. We paperboys hated that because it required an extra step in the delivery of the papers. There would be a supplement that was neighborhood-oriented (in my case to the Northeast Phila-delphia area) and that came in a separate bundle from the newspapers themselves. So, that supple-ment would be folded and "stuffed" into the front of the paper and delivered accordingly. I learned to fold a paper, "lock" it with or without the supple-ments, to the point that it would stay folded even after I threw it up by the door of the porch. No rub-ber bands for me except on the much thicker Sun-day editions, and the much dreaded Thanksgiving Day paper, the biggest of them all. Lots of advertis-ing on that day made for a very think newspaper as the retailers prepared for Black Friday, even before this big shoppers' day was called by that name.

My paper route was an interesting entrée for me into other peoples' homes and in doing so, their lives too. I would collect the money from my cus-tomers every Thursday and Friday afternoon or ear-ly evenings and sometimes Saturday. I would knock on the doors and ask for the .95 cents to $1.25 or so that they owed, the amount depending on whether they received a Sunday paper or not. After a few weeks on the job, my dad bought me one of those metallic coin changers that are carried on the front of a person's belt. It was designed so that coins could be inserted into the top penny, nickel, dime, or quarter slot, and also removed as change when needed by a thumb action near the bottom. It was convenient for collecting, but...well, not too cool on the streets. I stopped using it after a month or so and just carried all the loose coins in my some-times bulging pockets.

Some of my customers paid every week on time. Some gave me tips; some did not, ever. Others I had to keep revisiting over several weeks to get them to pay. Some I knew were hiding inside their homes when I knocked or rang the bell.

At least one woman liked to answer the door occasionally in negligee. She was an attractive 30-something and would be an eye-opener for this 14-year-old paperboy some Friday afternoons. I noticed she would only dress that way when her husband was not at home. If he was home, she would answer the door in her regular everyday clothes. You think it would be the opposite, or at least I did back then. I never could figure out the dynamics of that couple's situation, but as long as they paid on time, I was okay with it.

Oh, and her tips were nice too.

I kept the paperboy job for about 14 months, until August of '68. That's when high school football tryouts were scheduled. I turned the route over to one of my friend's younger brothers as he had been my substitute paperboy when I occasionally wasn't available. As it turned out, I quit my job too soon.

My new high school, only about eight blocks from my house, was Cardinal Dougherty High School, "CD" or "CDHS" for short. At the time, it was the largest Catholic high school in the U.S. During my four years there, the total enrollment was approximately 6,000 students. My graduating class, four years later in 1971, had around 1,400 students in it. It was a co-educational school, but then there was The Wall.

The large, three-story (plus basement) U-shaped building was divided into a boys' and girls' side, cut right in half at the bottom of the U. And, the twain never met. Well, not inside the building anyway. Before and after school, and during the occasional dances, it was okay to mingle with the opposite sex, but there was no interaction during school hours. It was boys on one side for all their classes and girls on the other for theirs. That finally changed a bit around my junior year. The Wall came down and we could then mingle after lunch, and certain courses such as Religion would on occasion be taught co-ed by my senior year. These rare classes were a strange experience after four years of not having girls in the classroom. It was a much welcome educational experience though.

At CD, the homeroom and class assignment was based on one's overall academic standing. The freshman boys' class ran from D1 through D20. D1 was ostensibly the smartest students and D20…let's just say they were NOT the smartest students. I was assigned to D3 my freshman year. Not bad, as I was pretty close to the top of the academic ladder among the CD freshman class. Along with my decent grades and entrance exam score, no doubt it was also the result of a good referral from Sister Ruth Dolores, despite me not answering her one, big question of me.

Unfortunately, I dropped to C6 (out of C1 through C20) my sophomore year. My freshman year algebra grades brought me down. Going backwards is never a good thing. It bothered me and my parents when we learned of the "demotion" by three rungs on the CD academic ladder. I made sure it would not happen again.

Starting my junior year, my high school went to tracks in each individual subject, and not just 1 – 20 based on academic standing. The rationale for the change was that it was less stigmatizing to the students in the upper teen classes and beyond. I suppose it made sense, to those who cared, anyway.

Outside of high school, my TV watching habits had shifted over the prior several years. There weren't as many Westerns on the daily schedule as years before and the ones that were on didn't overly interest me. While I enjoyed some rather silly half-hour sitcoms, there was no doubt that my favorite show at the time was on Tuesday nights at 10PM. It was not just my favorite show by the way, but much of the U.S. considered it one of their favorite shows too. Starting in seventh grade, I was granted special permission from my parents to stay up until 11 on that one school night just to watch it. I had to be done with my homework, have my bath, and be in my PJs before it even started though.

The show was *The Fugitive*, starring David Janssen.

The show told the story of Richard Kimball, a medical doctor from somewhere in the U.S. Midwest, who was wrongly accused and then unjustly arrested and convicted of killing his wife. He received the death penalty. He managed to escape on his way to prison as the result of a train wreck. The next four years of the series told his story of being on the run, generally in small towns around the U.S., having close calls with the police, and almost getting captured in each episode. He was pursued relentlessly by a determined police detective, Lt. Philip Gerard. Oh, and there was this one-armed man who really committed the murder. He showed up three or four times per season on different episodes. However, like Kimball just narrowly escaping Gerard (who was skeptical the one-armed man was the killer), this guy always managed to narrowly escape Kimball.

The final two episodes of *The Fugitive*, in late August of 1967, tied up all the loose ends. Kimball finally located and personally confronted the one-armed man, on an old wooden roller coaster of all places. Lt. Gerard was there as a witness, hears the confession, and it was all resolved. Case closed. Kimball was now a free man.

My appreciation of *The Fugitive*, and the plight of the truly innocent, was brought very close to home when it turns out a few years after that final episode that I was the one wrongly accused of several crimes. I was 16. The crimes: burglary and attempted rape. There was no one-armed man to blame in this case. Instead, it was a four-legged cat.

No, I couldn't or wouldn't possibly make that up. And, yes, I was 100% innocent.

Chapter Eight

The late 1960s for me, like most during their high school years, was a time of maturing, growing, and learning more and more about myself and others. Nationally and internationally, it was a turbulent time, as the civil rights movement was in full swing, the Vietnam War at its height, hippies, long hair, baby boomers coming of age, many turning to drugs, unbridled sex, the whole Woodstock mindset, etc.

Actually though, none of those issues seemed to directly affect me at this stage of life. Indirectly, there's no doubt that these evolving issues and the slowly imposing cultural shift did, in fact, influence me. It no doubt affected everyone coming of age during that decade. But, for me, it was still living in my same Olney neighborhood, with my parents, in a functional and loving home. It was just the three of us now as each of my sisters was married and living on their own. I was already an uncle to seven nieces and nephews. As for my everyday life, I was continuing to expand my interests and friendships along the way as they presented themselves, even during these otherwise turbulent times.

Among other interests at the time, I recall enjoying the first-run movie experience in downtown, aka Center City, Philadelphia. I recall seeing *The*

Graduate on Christmas night, 1967, with my good friend Tom Lubas and another friend. At 14 or so, we were the youngest there and dressed very casually while others, mostly couples, were attired in suits and dresses. I recall seeing *2001: A Space Odyssey*, sometime around then too, again with Tom, at another one of the now-extinct big movie houses in Center City.

In fact, it was at that theater that I met my first real-life celebrity. Of all people, it was Red Buttons, the character actor and veteran of many movies. I have no idea what he was doing in Philadelphia that night, but I eventually mustered up the courage to ask him, just before the lights dimmed and the curtain opened, to sign the back of my movie ticket stub. He did and I have his autograph to this day.

Besides Red Buttons, the only other celebrities I met during the next few years of my life, who were both local to Philadelphia, each had the same name. That was and they were, Jim O'Brien. They happened to be the only Jim O'Briens I ever met in my life.

The first Jim O'Brien was a local high school basketball phenom. He moved into my Olney neighborhood about halfway through his time at Roman Catholic High School, which was located in Center City, Philadelphia. He never transferred to my high school for his junior and senior years, despite the fact that where one went to an Archdiocesan grade or high school in Philadelphia back then was based on the geographical location of one's residence. He must have received a special dispensation. Being a multi-year All-Catholic point guard may have helped him receive that dispensation to stay at his school, instead of having to transfer to mine. This Jim O'Brien went on to play at St. Joseph's College (now University) and later coach various college and professional basketball teams, including our hometown Philadelphia 76ers during the early 2000s.

We weren't necessarily the best of friends nor did we really hang out together back in the day, but we did know each other. I recall giving him rides to St. Helena Church in my parents' car on occasion when I would see him on Sunday mornings walking north on 5th St. to Mass. I also played basketball with or against him every once in a while at Lowell schoolyard. He could spin circles around, jump over, and score at will on most of us on the court back then, but he was modest about it and an overall nice guy. I followed his career from afar over the next few decades. He's an Olney boy who did well, although having moved to the neighborhood a bit later in his teenage years.

The other celebrity Jim O'Brien will be discussed later, and more than once. Suffice it to say for now, after meeting him briefly in person a few times in my late teens in very friendly situations, he was the person who later provided me, while in adulthood, with some of the most devastating news of my life. And, he was on TV when he did it.

This latter painful anecdote will be related in Book II.

At this stage in life, in my mid-teens, basketball, in one form or another, became an almost daily past-time of mine. Playing it and following the Philadelphia 76ers and the local "Big Five" college basketball teams during their respective seasons were of great interest to my friends and me. Shooting hoops with friends at nearby Lowell schoolyard was a great way to keep fit and competitive at the same time.

Always looking for a basketball event, even during the off-season, my good friend since St. Helena School, Tom Lubas, an excellent basketball player at Cardinal Dougherty High School, invited me one summer evening along with his dad to attend a game of the newly formed Baker League. This was a league put together by iconic Philadelphia basketball legend Sonny Hill and was designed to help keep the players in shape during their off-season. The games would be held at various public playgrounds throughout Philadelphia.

We arrived at the game early that evening. We knew it would be fun to watch the players in their pre-game warm-ups. This particular playground had an indoor court which probably seated no more than 100 people. It was not air conditioned and I recall it being a hot and humid night. The players, I'm sure, were very aware of this too, especially once the game started. On the night we attended, among the other present or future NBA players there was Princeton University grad and New York Knick (and future U.S. Senator) Bill Bradley.

While watching all the players getting ready for the game, I happened to focus on Bill Bradley. He was doing his layups and the shoot-around right in front of where we were sitting, literally no more than 20 feet away. I recalled him taking his jump shots for a while, but then stopping and staring at the basket, shooting again, stopping, staring, taking some foul shots, and at one point even standing under the basket and jumping straight up to touch the rim itself. (He was tall enough at 6'5" and athletic enough to easily do so.) Neither Tom nor I was sure why he was undertaking these seemingly strange actions on the court. We just figured it was part of his ritual before each game. But, as we were to find out, it was something other than that.

After a few minutes of watching Bill do this, he went off the court and engaged one of the playground employees in discussion while pointing up to the backboard at the same time. The worker nodded his head and left the court area. A minute or two later he came back with a tall stepladder. He temporarily postponed the players' shoot-around at this end of the court and placed the ladder directly under the basket. He climbed the ladder and then pulled out a tape measure from his belt.

What the heck was this?

Bill Bradley then came over, took the tape from him, and placed the beginning of the tape itself flush to the floor. The guy on the ladder then held up his end of the tape measure, pulled it taut, and placed the tape directly on the basket's rim. He nodded his head down at Bill and I heard him say, "Yep, it's an inch plus off."

The worker got off the ladder, moved it a few feet behind the basket, climbed back up, and used some crank-like tool to move the backboard and rim either up or down, I forget in which vertical direction after all these years. He climbed down, remeasured it and it was apparently fine. He then halted the shoot-around at the other end of the court, measured that basket, and yelled to Bill, "This one's right at 10 feet."

Bill just waved his hand as if to say "Thanks," and he and the other players restarted their shoot-around. The game began a few minutes later. I don't recall who won, but know it was a great game and a great experience for my good friend Tom and me.

I'm not sure if what I saw that evening pre-game had an immediate effect on me or was something that came to me years later in retrospect. Obviously, watching these great basketball players do their magic on the court, and being this close up, was why I was there that night in the first place. But, at some point in my life, recalling that Baker League game and Bill Bradley's early-on powers of observation, his suspicion that something, somehow, someway, was amiss in his personal environment, and then not hesitating to react to it accordingly, figured later in to how my various cognitive evaluations of a situation would develop. It would either consciously or subconsciously manifest itself in my actions and reactions years later when situations in my own personal environment suggested that something was seemingly amiss.

What the future NBA Hall of Famer taught me that night, even if indirectly and not fully understood at that very moment, was to be ready to react accordingly to things that just don't seem right. That is, to say something, do something, leave a place, go to a place, warn someone, or whatever, if those internal warning signs start flashing and tell you to do so. If it doesn't feel right, in something as relatively minor as an athletic event, or in a potential life-threatening situation such as a "routine" car stop for a police officer, one shouldn't hesitate to react accordingly if something is amiss. I would adopt this "something doesn't seem quite right here" attitude for the rest of my working life and in my personal life too. Sometimes it amounted to nothing. That's okay, because other times I was spot-on.

This attitude probably saved my life numerous times in my later career. On at least one occasion, as a police officer, it involved a hidden sawed-off shotgun within inches of a subject's hand during a car stop. I knew something wasn't quite right, I "measured" things correctly that night, and I'm still here to talk (and write) about it.

This event will be further discussed in Book II.

My friend Tom Lubas went on to have a successful four year basketball career at Cardinal Dougherty High School and later at Philadelphia College of Textile and Science (now Philadelphia University). Years later, he turned to tennis and competed successfully in amateur championships in a few different states. However, in the early 1990s, he unknowingly contracted Lyme's Disease while living in the Philadelphia area. Shortly thereafter, he and his wife Sue moved to central Florida and when the symptoms started kicking in, the physicians there did not recognize that it could be, in fact, Lyme's. It went to Stage 3 before it was correctly diagnosed.

Needless to say, Tom is suffering today from a plethora of physical ailments. He's still a good friend. I visit him every year or two and talk to him every few weeks. Our mutual friends and I hope that he gets through this very difficult physiological problem.

Chapter Nine

Besides school, life in the late '60s for me wasn't all opening nights of major Hollywood movies, playing/watching basketball games, and associating with future pro basketball coaches. It was sometimes just hangin' on the corner with a friend or two. After that very positive eighth grade experience in which I met the Philadelphia police officer at my school, my next up-close-and-personal dealings with the police occurred about two and a half years later, on a street corner. It taught me a lot about how the criminal justice system works, about some good cops, some bad cops, and the potential importance of some fortunate familial connections on my part. There was only one police officer in the known history of my family up to that point, and he and his position proved very valuable to me one particular evening.

On a warm evening during the summer of 1969, I was walking around our immediate neighborhood with my good friend (and future Philadelphia police officer) Rob McCarthy. We were the same age and both about to enter our junior years at Cardinal Dougherty High School. It was about 8:00 and it was still light outside. I have no idea how or why we wound up at the intersection of 5th and Spencer

Streets. It was right across the street from Fisher's Park (where I went missing about 13 years before) and St. Helena School. I had probably gone to his house on 4th Street, and we together walked to that general area for one reason or another. Very likely, it was out of sheer boredom on a night when nothing else was going on. There was a movie theater very close to there, the Fern Rock Theater, and Rob's older brother, Bill (also a future Philadelphia police officer), worked there as an usher. He would sometimes sneak us in there through a side door to catch a flick. Maybe that's why we walked to that area. Either way, as it turned out, to be at that place at that time would prove fateful to me.

At that intersection, on the southeast corner, was a two-story brick building, connected to a row of stores along 5th Street. The corner establishment was a retail drug store called Modern Pharmacy. While standing on the double-wide sidewalk at that intersection, alongside the sole entrance to the store, probably just talking with Rob, something made me look up at the drug store sign. There, on the approximately 20' long metal "Modern Pharmacy" sign that was affixed to the 5th Street side of the building, between the first and second floors, was a cat. It sat seemingly motionless, without its head or tail moving at all, or at least from what we could observe from our vantage point.

The cat slowly aroused our curiosities, as opposed to the other way around, as is the mythical reputation of our feline friends. For no real reason, we started yelling at it and clapping our hands in attempts to figure out if it was even alive. But, the cat never moved, or at least not that we could see.

We thought this was really strange. How did the cat get up there? Was it stuck? Was it afraid to move? Was it even still alive? We simply couldn't tell in the now fading light of the evening. We actually considered spending a dime in a nearby phone booth to call the fire department. (Yes, payphone calls were still at 10 cents per call in the late '60s AND still in glass booths with folding doors.) Perhaps they could come and rescue it, as was sometimes seen on television. But instead, I decided to use the change in my pocket in another way.

To see if the cat was even still alive, Rob and I searched our respective pockets and found a few pennies. With them, we decided to lob them toward the cat. If it moved, and we could see if it was somehow stuck or trapped there, we would then consider calling the fire department or contacting someone in the building to come and help it down.

I want to emphasize that I was then and am now an animal lover. I would never do anything to harm an animal, including this seemingly-trapped, scared, or maybe even dead cat. We weren't attempting to injure it in any way, but simply to have our pennies gently come down on top of the cat and see if it would make any movement at all. IF we could get it to move, then we would consider our next step to help it get down.

So, we pitched a few pennies upward. None ever actually came down on the cat, but tended to hit the side of the upper part of the building, the sign, and possibly even a closed window which was right above the cat. Some lodged on the ledge, some bounced back to us on the sidewalk. However, shortly after our investment of about six cents worth of pennies between the two of us, all hell broke loose. Those tossed pennies quickly became the worst investment of my young life.

Rob and I were probably standing about 15 feet apart from one another alongside the drug store, in effect triangulating our upward penny tosses. It was only about a minute or so that we were throwing the pennies at...that darn cat. To this day, I'm not sure if the cat ever moved or not. In any event, in the next instant, Rob and I were about to move really, really, fast, like a couple of cats ourselves. That's when a heretofore unnoticed first floor recessed door flew open and a crazy man came charging out of it at full speed. He screamed, "I'll get you assholes!"

Upon yelling that and other words, this crazy man randomly turned to his left toward Rob and started running directly at him. Rob took off south on 5th St. Rob was (and still is) tall and long-legged. He was one of the fastest guys in our neighborhood. The man picked the wrong guy to chase. Off they went, south on 5th St., in front of the Fern Rock Theater, and toward Champlost Ave.

Derived undoubtedly from some sort of urban survival instinct, I chose to run in the opposite direction, north on 5th St. I'm not sure why I ran, as no one was chasing me, not to mention that neither Rob nor I had done anything wrong. Nonetheless, I ran and turned right onto Spencer St., and then immediately down an alley, behind the drug store. I remember going southbound through that alley, which was parallel to 5th St., continuing to run behind the Fern Rock Theater. I eventually slowed down a few short blocks from the scene of the penny throwing incident onto Champlost Ave. I figured if I was just walking, instead of running, no one would suspect anything.

Then I thought to myself, "Wait! Suspect me of what?"

I was lobbing pennies at a cat, to see if it was alive to possibly help it. Was that wrong? Who was this crazy guy who chased us, or at least Rob, anyway? I was about to find out the answers to all of these questions, and then some.

As soon as I slowed down in the alley and began walking onto the sidewalk near the intersection of 5th St. and Champlost Ave., I noticed a red Philadelphia Police Department "paddy wagon," aka police van, driving by very slowly.

(The PPD police vehicles' color scheme was changed from red to light blue in the early '70s. It was determined by various experts at the time that the color red on a police car was "psychologically inflammatory" at potential crisis situations. The color blue did not supposedly evoke the same emotion, so the color was eventually changed.)

Upon walking onto Champlost Ave., I noticed that the crazy running guy who charged at us out of the side doorway was somehow right there too, just coming around the corner on foot. I didn't see Rob anywhere. In those next few seconds, the crazy now-walking guy yelled to the police officers in the van, while pointing at me, "That's one of them!"

Upon apparently hearing this accusatory admonition, the officer in the passenger side of the van jumped out, ran over to where I was standing, and he and the crazy guy both grabbed me by my arms and pushed me down on the ground. The officer then handcuffed me behind my back, searched me, pulled me not so gently up to my feet, and started walking me over to the back of the van. Its doors were now open, apparently done so by the driver, and they ordered me, make that firmly escorted me, inside the van.

With one foot still on Champlost Ave. and the other up on the van floor, in a voice no doubt filled with great fear and trepidation, I mustered the courage to ask the cops, one on each arm, "What's going on here? Am I under arrest or something?"

The crazy, formerly running guy (finally having caught his breath), who I now noticed was wearing shorts, a t-shirt, and a pair of sneakers then said, "Yeah, you are! For attempted rape! Now shut up and get in the van! I'll see you over at the 35th District!"

I remember incredulously asking this guy, "WHAT are you talking about? Who are you?"

He blurted back, "You messed with the wrong person this time! I'm a cop and you're going to jail!"

The crazy guy/cop then told the other two police officers that he would go home, get changed, and meet them at the District to "file charges."

What the heck...?

In the back of the van, now en route from the 5th St. and Champlost Ave. "arrest" scene to Broad St. and Champlost Ave., the location of the 35th District Police District building (they call them police "districts" in Philadelphia, not "precincts"), the officers were talking to me through the little window between their seats and the back of the van. Fortunately, I was the only one "in custody" at the time. I wouldn't have wanted to be back there with any real criminals, that's for sure.

As the two officers told me during the ride, the crazy running-then-walking guy was an off-duty

Philadelphia police officer who lived in the apartment above the Modern Pharmacy. Apparently, as I was to learn, two nights ago while the officer was at work, sometime after midnight, someone allegedly tried to break into his apartment while his wife was there alone. So, two nights later, on this particular night, he's home, off-duty, he sees Rob and me lobbing pennies at a cat near his upstairs window, and here I am, under arrest for, gulp (make that multiple gulps), attempted burglary and rape.

Then I wondered, "Where was Rob?" Obviously, he made a clean getaway.

As I was further attempting to mentally synthesize this immediate emotional and informational overload, I repeated to myself, "A clean getaway?" I'm in the back of a paddy wagon in handcuffs. I'm only 16. I didn't do anything wrong. Geez, we were trying to help a cat, which may or may not have even been alive. That's it. I was nowhere near this guy's place two nights ago, and I never tried to rape anyone, anywhere, anytime, much less this crazy running guy/police officer's wife.

What's going to happen now? I've never been arrested before. This isn't how the system is supposed to work. Is it? This isn't what I've seen on TV or read about in books.

Is this how it started for Richard Kimball? It took him four years on the run to straighten out his legal problems. Where's my one-armed man?

I don't remember too well the specifics of the next sequence of events. Somehow, I was brought into a juvenile holding cell area at the 35th District. I gave some basic information to the officers from the van and then they turned me over to another officer. This officer, I believe a "juvenile officer," allowed me to call my parents.

I wasn't sure what would happen next, but I made the call. It was about 9:15PM at this point. My mom answered and I told her where I was. They asked me why I was there. In earshot of the processing officer I clearly told her, "I was throwing pennies at a cat."

I don't recall what she said next, but within about 45 minutes, both my parents showed up at the police station.

After sitting handcuffed to a chair for what seemed like forever, I was eventually un-cuffed and brought into a larger office with my parents already sitting there with a white-shirted uniformed police officer that I had not remembered seeing before. (The arresting officers, who were patrol officers, wore blue shirts. With the white shirt, I guessed then that this guy was a supervisor of some sort.) I was introduced to him by my parents. He was Lt. Jim Kehoe. I found out that he was a family member. He was my dad's niece's husband, but someone that I had not met or seen since perhaps earlier in my childhood. He was a veteran patrol lieutenant in the Philadelphia Police Department.

Apparently, after I called my mom, my dad then made a few phone calls before they left the house and somehow they got hold of my cousin-in-law by marriage. He just happened to be working that night, and not too far away. Talk about good timing. Well, good timing after some bad timing, I suppose. I found out later that upon his arrival the lieutenant had talked to the crazy running guy/off-duty police officer and the two other officers from the van. He also talked to my parents who confirmed that two nights ago I was with them, in the house, playing Scrabble until midnight with my mom, going to bed right afterwards.

It was quickly realized that there was no crime here, or at least no criminal here, meaning me. We were told that upon further investigation it wasn't clear that a crime had even occurred two nights before at the location where this all started, much less tonight. In view of this, Lt. Kehoe said I was free to go with nothing else to worry about. I would have no record for this incident because it was a case of mistaken identity and poor judgment (his words) on the part of at least one Philadelphia police officer.

In parting that night, Lt. Kehoe advised me that in the future I probably shouldn't worry about cats stuck on signs, in trees, or anywhere else. I agreed wholeheartedly with him. Like the walking on ice lesson learned a few years before, I would never again directly involve myself with a stranded cat. Or, if I was to, I would certainly handle it differently than Rob and I did that evening. Cats, I learned, can usually get out of any mess in which they find themselves very well on their own. Luckily for me that night, I did too.

This false arrest, and that's really what it was, although relatively minor compared to what many others may have experienced in their lives, and one adjudicated rather quickly to my great benefit, nonetheless left a permanent mark on me. I was unjustly accused of a crime, even if just for about 90 minutes total. I possibly could have been forced to pay a hefty price for it on multiple levels for a long time to come. After all these years, I would like to think that even without the intervention of Lt. Kehoe, my police officer family member, this matter would have somehow been resolved that night.

Or, would it have been? And if so, at what personal cost?

What if the crazy running guy/police officer's wife (maybe being crazy herself) somehow wrongly insisted that she saw me at her door two nights before? That could have changed everything. With any luck, if it did go that far, eventually through the legal system it would have been rectified. But, not before numerous court appearances, the hiring of lawyers, vast amounts of time wasted and money spent, etc., until I would have been acquitted of the charges. That is, *hopefully* acquitted of the charges.

Years later, as a law enforcement officer, based on most likely both a conscious and sub-conscious mindset as a result of this 1969 incident, as well as my own moral compass instilled in me by my family, it was engrained in me to never arrest anyone or charge anyone without the existence of valid and compelling evidence, aka probable cause. There would be no exceptions to this rule. Whether it was a traffic ticket, a minor criminal charge or a major federal violation, if I wasn't personally satisfied beyond a reasonable doubt and did not have probable cause that the person was culpable for a crime or series of crimes, I simply did not make the arrest. I was well aware that sometimes an otherwise "guilty" person was perhaps getting away with a crime. But, if the evidence wasn't there, then there wasn't meant to be an arrest, at least not at that time and place. More investigation and fact-gathering would be necessary. Then, perhaps the arrest could be lawfully undertaken and a conviction attained.

A good investigator knows this. A good police officer knows this. The crazy running guy/police officer was way out of line that evening, making rash decisions based on anger and emotions, based on alleged second-hand accounts from his wife, and as a result leaving his objectivity far behind. If he himself had called the police that night, waited for them to arrive, and then went down to calmly talk to us and the on-duty officers, it would have been determined in a non-biased and impartial manner that there was nothing to this situation. It was just two kids harmlessly (and yes, in retrospect, stupidly) checking on a cat that was seemingly in peril.

A few years later I became acquainted with some police officers who were familiar with other officers working in the 35th Police District. They were several years older than me and were friends of friends or brothers of friends. Bill McCarthy, Rob's older brother, was one of these officers. When I told them my almost-arrested-for-rape story, they claimed to have known this particular running guy/police officer and had worked directly with him. They told me he was a well-known "loose cannon" in the district and had made other questionable arrests and had numerous civilian complaints against him during his time on the force. Other than these anecdotes, I have no idea of what ever happened to him as I never personally crossed paths with him again.

In later years, this guy was one of the law enforcement officers I used in my own career as a role model. Make that a *reverse-role model*. In the case of this specific officer, it was to provide guidance on how NOT to do my job, how NOT to overreact in situations and potentially mark someone for life for a crime they didn't commit.

Just like Richard Kimball, aka The Fugitive.

Kimball, of course, was a fictional character. (Although, he's allegedly based on Dr. Sam Shepard who in the 1950s, in Ohio, was accused, arrested, convicted, sent to prison, and eventually exonerated through appeal, in the murder of his wife.) In February of 2009, I was introduced to Marty Tankleff. He is a real person, who was accused of two very serious crimes. I met him after I was invited to give a forensic linguistic lecture at John Jay College in New York City. Upon talking to him, I learned that he spent 17 years in prison in New York for the 1988 murder of his parents, a crime it was later determined to have been committed by others, not him. His arrest and conviction were based on a sloppy, unprofessional and ultimately biased investigation by Suffolk County, NY, authorities, to include police investigators as well as prosecutors and arguably even judges. He was the victim in a real life nightmare scenario of false arrest, conviction, and imprisonment.

Once we began talking, I realized that he was the same Marty Tankleff I read about in the local media coverage in New York City when I worked there as a young FBI agent in the late 1980s. It was a brief yet emotional discussion I had with him in the hallways of the college that afternoon. I told him I could not imagine being part of a law enforcement team (meaning investigators and prosecutors) that sent someone to prison for something he or she did not do. I was never on such a team and that is very reassuring to me.

Marty acknowledged that he is certainly aware that all law enforcement officials are not like the ones who falsely incriminated him for the murders of his parents. He was just unfortunate to have his parents' murder investigated and prosecuted by officials who fell outside of the norm in this regard.

Marty gave me a book that day, *A Criminal Injustice*, by Richard Firstman and Jay Salpeter, published in 2008. It tells his compelling story in very riveting and conclusive fashion. His perseverance and determination, and that of those around him, ultimately paid off for him when his freedom was finally attained in 2005.

I'm still in contact with Marty and he's now busy making up for lost time. He's enrolled in law school and his specialty upon graduation in 2014 will be representing clients who are also the victims of false confessions and wrongful convictions.

While I'm proud of and commend the work of the vast majority of law enforcement officers in the U.S., minor incidents like the one involving me, and especially major incidents like the one involving Marty Tankleff, must be avoided at all costs. The already built-in system of checks and balances within the U.S. criminal justice system, from the initial investigation to the appellate process, including defense attorneys and judges, serve to preclude such malfeasances of duty and responsibility. But, they can be circumvented at times, through a lack of quality training, by insufficient supervision, by unchecked political agenda, and out-of-control egos. Usually, it's a combination of several, if not all, of these factors.

The aforementioned checks and balances system must be maintained and adhered to religiously in every investigation and prosecution. The 2006 Duke lacrosse team incident is a clear example of a prosecutor abusing power entrusted to him by the citizens of his county. The investigators working for him weren't much better either. Luckily, these types of arrests and sometimes convictions are the exception to the rule. However, even one time wrong is clearly one too many.

Chapter Ten

My night-of-the-false-arrest was the summer of 1969. Obviously, I was "acquitted" of the charges brought against me that night and all ended well, actually in less than 2 hours. However, the outcome wasn't the same one year later, during the summer of 1970. I was arrested again, this time not as close to home and, I must admit, it wasn't a false arrest this time. There was no relative I could call (other than my parents, of course) and I spent a night in the lock-up until the matter was eventually adjudicated the next morning. Oh, and this particular incident didn't involve a cat on a ledge that I was attempting to help. Instead, it was a younger "friend" passed out under a seaside boardwalk who was in potential trouble. On that evening, yet another attempt at an altruistic act got me in trouble once again. But, this time I clearly contributed to it. Well, sort of....

By way of background, in the Philadelphia area, a generations-long tradition for many is going "down the shore," with one's family and friends. The "shore," in Philadelphia area parlance, generically refers to the southern New Jersey coast, all within a 90 to 150 minute drive from most anywhere in Southeastern Pennsylvania or New Jersey. The

Philly-area shore retreats generally lie on the Atlantic Ocean between Long Beach Island/Atlantic City to the north and Cape May to the south. There are at least 15 different towns along this approximately 50-mile stretch of beach, each with their own personality, look, and feel, most of these features evident during the summer season.

The shore towns are more than just beach and ocean, of course. They also offer such summertime amenities and activities as restaurants, bars, clubs, miniature golf courses, arcades, promenades, boardwalks, thrill rides, casinos (in Atlantic City starting in the late 1970s), and other fun type activities for all ages. The day, weekend, week, or seasonal trips to the shore between Memorial Day weekend in late May and Labor Day weekend in early September usually begin for Philadelphia area residents at a very young age as moms and dads bring their kids to enjoy playing in the sand and swimming in the ocean, just as their own parents did with them. Then, as the kids age, they come back as teenagers and college students looking to have other kinds of fun, usually without mom and dad nearby. For many, these trips to the seashore continue through the various stages of life, lasting through people bringing their own kids there, and later even their grandkids when many older folks would actually buy second homes and/or retire to their favorite seashore town.

In the 1960s, as well as before and since then, it was a rite-of-passage for Philadelphia-area teenagers at some point to go "down the shore" and stay somewhere on their own. The first time my parents allowed me to do this was in the summer of 1969, a few weeks before my cat-on-the-hot-tin-sign incident. With their approval and a little pre-planning, I went with Rob McCarthy and Tom Lubas to Wildwood, NJ.

Yes, it's the same town sung about in Bobby Rydal's 1963 pop song, *Wildwood Days*.

The three of us took a Greyhound bus from downtown Philadelphia to Wildwood. It was an uneventful weekend in terms of anything that occurred to us while there. We stayed at a boarding house type facility called the Pulaski Hotel, an older wooden building whose best days were clearly behind it, even back then. But, it was affordable, in the center of town, and catered to teenagers and younger adults, so it was the place to be for us. There, the three of us shared a room and we collectively shared a bathroom with multiple others on the same floor of the hotel. Our goal that weekend was to hang out on the beach, the boardwalk, and maybe even meet some girls. We did achieve all three goals, to some degree, anyway.

On the Sunday morning of that weekend, being the avid reader and news junkie into which I had slowly developed, I recall taking some time to read a *Sunday Bulletin* newspaper that someone left behind in the hotel lobby. While later sitting in one of the Adirondack chairs outside of the building in their small, shaded community garden, I became engrossed in reading an article out of Los Angeles, California, about a seemingly random pair of multiple killings of first some Hollywood types and the next night a grocery store magnate and his family members. Gruesome, violent deaths, "PIGS" scrawled on a wall with blood, celebrities and rich people, all seemingly meaningless...and it was still unfolding and unsolved. Who would do something like this? Were the killings even related?

It was eventually determined to be the Charlie Manson family murders. It was the weekend of August 8, 1969.

Even during this youthful get-away weekend for me, I had to be coaxed by my buddies to put down the newspaper and come join them for some teenage-related activities on the beach. I eventually finished the article and wound up meeting them there. After coming back home to Olney later that evening, I remember watching TV and then reading more that subsequent week about this tragic but fascinating case.

Flash ahead one year later, once again to the summer of 1970. The word got around that some friend of someone in my Olney neighborhood had access to a rental house on Roberts Ave. in Wildwood. A small group of local guys were invited, including me, and I wanted to go. So did other guys and those who could make the trip travelled there by various means. In my case, once my parents approved of this hastily planned trip they offered to drive me there, instead of me having to take the bus like I did the summer before. They also enjoyed the seashore; it had been awhile since they had been there, so a day trip there was to be a nice outing for them.

Coming with me was a friend from St. Helena and Cardinal Dougherty High School, named Paul Otto. Paul's nickname was "Mel," as that was bequeathed upon him sometime in grade school because his name was vaguely similar to the famous baseball player of yore, Mel Ott.

My parents dropped me and Paul/Mel off by noon that Wednesday afternoon at the Roberts Ave. house. Upon seeing the condition of the outside of the house, Wally and Alma decided, wisely, not to go inside of it. They had planned to grab lunch in town, walk the boardwalk a bit, and then drive home. I said goodbye and thanked them and Mel and I went inside. We quickly dropped off our bags, got into our swimsuits, and walked right to the beach as we knew our buddies would be there. We had a fun afternoon there with many of my Olney and CD friends. It was going to be a fun few days, with a house of our own, more or less, in Wildwood with no adults around. And with warm, sunny weather, what could possibly go wrong?

As it turned out, Mel and I were merely hours away from finding out what could and would go wrong.

When we collectively came back to the house later that afternoon, we saw that another one of our neighborhood guys showed up, an Olney and CD student two years younger than most of us. His name was Chas and he also learned of the available rental house and managed to get to Wildwood on his own.

Chas would be ultimately responsible for Mel's and my arrest that night. Looking back though, I should have known better. In acknowledging this, it clearly puts the blame squarely back on me. I can't blame Chas or Mel. In life, I found, it's rarely really ever someone else's fault when one does something wrong and/or gets caught for it. Others may contribute to a problematic scenario and play a role of some sort in what happened to go wrong. But, as older teens and adults, it ultimately falls on the person him or herself and the decision making process that they employ in their own questionable actions. That certainly applied in this situation of mine.

The beginning of the end for the three of us that day was when someone, somehow (not me) brought a case of 16-ounce Schlitz beer and a big, cheap bottle of wine, I believe Boone's Farm, back to the house later that afternoon. It was one of the older teenagers also staying at the house, I think, who made the illegal purchase. And, as the refrigerator was the one working appliance in the house, these items could even be kept cold, or at least moderately chilled.

Early that evening, I drank a 16-ounce can of beer. So did Mel and the others. No one was drunk, out of hand, loud, or doing anything stupid. We stayed inside, playing music on the radio, and generally enjoying ourselves, even if unlawfully as we were all under the age of 21. No one had a car there so driving under the influence was not an issue. We all knew better. Well, most of us.

Fifteen-year old Chas started drinking a bit before the rest of us. He also chose to drink a bit more than the rest of us, and it slowly began to show. Maybe he wanted to prove he could keep up with the older guys. He couldn't and he didn't, plus I don't believe anyone drank as much as him anyway that afternoon/evening. So, he was the "winner" of that contest.

Chas started slurring his words and saying and doing silly things in the house. Mel and I were clearly not intoxicated as we only had one beer each, and we drank our respective beers slowly. After all, we were only 17, and neither of us wanted to get in trouble for doing something we knew we shouldn't be doing. I can't speak for Mel, but I had "experimented" with drinking beer before this, on several occasions. No problems in doing so. I knew it was illegal, but I felt I was responsible in how I did it and wouldn't get in trouble because of it. Perhaps not this night though.

Mel and I decided after a while that we were hungry and wanted to go to the Wildwood boardwalk to get something to eat. We were fine and knew this wouldn't be a problem for us, with just one 16-ounce can of beer in us. Chas overheard we were leaving and said he wanted to come along as he was hungry too, not having eaten lunch that day. While clearly exhibiting the effects of at least two 16 oz. beers and a paper cup or two of wine (maybe more so because of no food in his belly), he nonetheless wasn't too wobbly or too out-of-sorts at this point. So, Mel and I reluctantly agreed to let him tag along with us. Looking back, if drinking in the first place was our number one mistake that late afternoon/early evening, allowing Chas to come along with us to the boardwalk was clearly mistake number two. The mistake count would continue upwards as others were to follow.

The three of us walked the several blocks eastbound on Roberts Ave. to the boardwalk. It was still daylight, perhaps around 8:00 or so. Chas was walking with us but was, at this point, not doing or feeling well. In fact, by the time we reached the boardwalk, he had deteriorated and could barely walk straight anymore. We had to practically carry him. He even vomited once on the way there in a local resident's flower garden. We laughingly called it "fertilizer" at the time. It was the last time we laughed that night.

Mel and I were getting increasingly concerned about, and quite frankly pissed-off at, Chas. How did we get stuck with this kid, now really drunk and showing it, and a whole five or so blocks from our house? As we approached the ocean, and the famous miles-long boardwalk that runs parallel to it, the two not-drunk persons among the three of us, that is, Mel and me, talked it over and came up with a plan. It was a sure-fire winner, or so we thought.

Mel and I decided to ever-so-cautiously walk Chas up and over the boardwalk. We avoided strolling multi-generational families, handholding couples, old folks on their nightly constitutions, and the seemingly ubiquitous tram cars blaring incessantly in a recorded monotone female voice, "Watch the tram car, please!" We were hoping the whole time that our young charge wouldn't up-chuck on any of them as we made the crossing. Fortunately, Chas managed to keep down whatever little food was left in his stomach for the zig-zag traverse across the wooden walkway.

We eventually got Chas down the steps on the ocean side of the boardwalk and onto the beach. We made an immediate U-turn at the bottom of the steps and walked/carried him underneath the boardwalk. There, on a plot of land all to himself, we gently placed him on the cool, white sand to allow him to sleep it off. It was dark, quiet, and safe there. It would be comfortable for him too, on his own sand-mattress and sand-pillow. It seemed like a good idea at the time, as we knew of other people who had "crashed" there before, although usually later at night and in better physical condition. So, why not now with him? We laid him down, and off we went to get some food.

"See ya, Chas," we each said to him as we walked away. He vaguely responded and then started snoring. The Sandman was clearly doing his job. Chas was now fine, we were hungry, so off we went for our pizza. All was good. Problem solved.

About three blocks away from Chas's makeshift bed, and near the pizza place where we wanted to eat, Mel and I saw what would change the course of our night and, for that matter, part of our young lives. That is, we saw a Jeep-type police cruiser, the kind designed for beach patrol, slowly driving alongside the boardwalk on the sand in the direction opposite of the way we were walking, toward where we left Chas. The officer in the passenger seat was using his searchlight to look under the walkway for whomever or whatever it was that shouldn't be there, such as lovers, druggies, bad guys, contraband, drunken 15-year-olds, etc.

Mel and I stopped and looked at each other. What do we do? Leave Chas to fend for himself? Why not? He caused his own problems by drinking too much earlier in the day. We didn't. We weren't like him. Plus, we were hungry, so let's just go and eat.

Or, do we go back and get the kid and walk him back to the house? He could just as easily sleep it off on one of the sandy beds in the place. He certainly wouldn't know the difference. Then, Mel and I would come back to the boardwalk and get our meal and enjoy the rest of the night.

Temporarily stopping our forward progress, we debated the issue at hand for the next minute or so.

We had to make a decision quickly though as the cops would be to his location in just a few minutes more and no doubt they would find him.

We slowly started leaning toward the option of going to help him. We felt sorry for young Chas and we knew he'd get in serious trouble in only a matter of minutes once the cops found him there. And, since we left him there, we figured it was our responsibility to remedy it. We trotted back on the boardwalk in the direction from where we just walked. Now a half block or so ahead of the slow but mission-oriented police Jeep, we went down the same steps as before to the beach, U-turned again under the boardwalk, and awoke, or at least tried to awaken, Chas from his stupor. This was mistake number three if you're keeping count.

We managed to get Chas up onto his feet, but as before, he could barely walk. He threw up one more time, fortunately missing Mel and me. We wiped his mouth with HIS shirt. No way we were going to use our own shirts for his mess. We then draped his arms over our shoulders and found a way to walk under the boardwalk this time and out the other side onto Roberts Ave. The police cruiser on beach patrol was just now driving behind us where Chas had been lying only seconds before. But, we were now out on the street side of the boardwalk we were out of range of their searchlight and we were pretty sure they didn't see us.

While walking a bee-line along Roberts Ave., en route back to our shack, we were supporting Chas's weight by his arms draped over our shoulders, with his feet barely doing their job on the ground between the two of us. We were moving though. We had already crossed Ocean Ave. and were now crossing Atlantic Ave. The house was only about three blocks away now. It was dusk, and our destination only a few hundred yards away. We were close, but not quite close enough.

When we were less than two blocks away from the house, having just crossed Pacific Ave., the last thing we wanted to see, a police cruiser, pulled up next to us on the southwest corner. It was not the same one we saw on the beach, but a regular marked patrol car. The lone late twenties-in-age officer walked up to us, did a quick up-close visual of the three of us, and quickly ascertaining that Chas was non-verbal, asked me, "What's his problem?"

I responded, nervously but respectfully, "Uh…he's sick."

The officer asked why he was sick. Mel said, also both nervously and respectfully, "We really don't know."

The officer asked if Chas could stand up on his own. Chas didn't respond. In an attempt to non-verbally answer the officer's question, we undraped his arms from around us and as Chas clearly couldn't stand up on his own, we lowered him gently to the ground. As soon as he hit the strip of grass we were standing on, he started snoring again. That pretty much answered the police officer's question.

The officer then looked at both of us who were still standing and asked us how old we were. Mel and I said 17.

"How about him?" pointing to the comfortably sleeping and once-again snoring Chas at our feet. We told him he was 15.

He asked if Chas had been drinking.

We said we didn't know.

He then asked if we had been drinking. We both initially said "No."

Mistake number four, lying to a police officer, especially when the evidence is indicative of something otherwise.

The policeman next asked to smell each of our breaths. We accommodated him by exhaling accordingly into his face.

The officer asked again, "Now tell me, and don't lie to me this time, I know he's been drinking (pointing to sleeping/snoring Chas). I want to know though, have you two been drinking?"

I hesitated at first but soon responded, "Well, I had one beer."

Mel said pretty much the same thing.

He said, "OK, I appreciate you being honest. That's important in today's world."

I responded, "Yes, Officer. We agree. Uh, can we go now?"

In a commanding retort, the officer barked, "No, you're now under arrest."

So here I was, the second time in a year, again in the summertime, being handcuffed and put in the back of a police vehicle. This time it's for underage drinking. Here, I was guilty. But geez, I was only helping a friend, a sort of friend, this younger kid. Was it so wrong what I did?

No, it wasn't, but as I had drank a beer and then later admitted it to the officer, and I was under 21, it was a crime, unlike what happened last summer with the cat escapade.

What will happen now?

I was soon to find out.

I was in the back of a regular police car this time, not a van, aka paddy wagon. And, at least I had Mel with me. For now. Another police car came along and the officer somehow managed to squeeze Chas's semi-limp body into the rear seat. I was wondering if Chas would puke in the back of the police car. I hoped not, for everyone's sake.

I never saw Chas again that night or the next day. He was on his own. Someone else would have to get him out of his mess this time. Well, once he regained consciousness.

Next thing Mel and I know, we're inside the Wildwood Police Department HQ being searched, giving information to the processing officer, and eventually being placed in a holding cell. Then, I was brought out shortly thereafter and told to call my parents. I was dreading this moment from the minute the officer stopped us on Roberts Ave.

The call lived up to all my expectations in terms of my parents' reactions. They were livid. Then, they talked to the processing officer. I heard him tell them to come in the morning for a hearing before the judge. I would be kept here overnight and once I appear before the magistrate the next morning, I'd be free to go. He said goodbye to my parents and handed me the phone. I told my mom I was sorry, really sorry. I told her I was just trying to help out a friend, but yes, I did have a beer that evening. She said we would talk more tomorrow. My dad got on the phone and after a few words he ended the call by stating, somewhat sarcastically, "Have a good night. And do some thinking about how you got there."

I did, all night long.

I had a cell entirely to myself that night. Lucky me. Mel and Chas were somewhere else in the building. So, I guess I was in a version of solitary confinement. It was for me that night anyway. There were bright lights on the whole time. I heard loud noises, doors slamming, and police radios crackling from outside the cell off and on during the entire night. My "cot" was a hard wooden bench, with no sheets, no blankets, and no pillows. There was a combination water fountain/sink/toilet in the one corner of the cell.

I hardly slept at all that night. An officer brought in some sort of toast and juice for breakfast around 8:00AM. Then, shortly thereafter, it was out to face the judge and my parents. Mel's mom was there too. She and my parents drove to Wildwood together early that morning after talking to each other the night before once the two of us independently called them. I spoke to my parents and a juvenile detective, and we agreed that I would plead guilty in front of the judge, I would get a $35.00 fine, plus costs, and if my parents paid it right then and there, it would be all over. No permanent record either. So, that's what we did. Mel did the same thing and we all drove back to Olney together on a very, very long and quiet ride.

We never saw Chas that day. We had no idea if anyone came for him or not. He wasn't in front of the judge with us that day. I didn't see him again for over a week or so. When I did next see him at the Lowell schoolyard I recall he had an attitude. He told me one of his older brothers came to get him the next day, paid the fine, etc.

Chas remembered nothing of what happened that evening. I then told him what occurred. He angrily questioned me as to why we did what we did with him that night. After listening to his rant for a minute or so, I eventually told him to "pound sand." The irony of that statement, however, was lost completely on him.

I told Chas that he would have been arrested either way that night, but the way it worked out, and the fact that Mel and I had TRIED to help him in his drunken state, got us arrested too. He didn't seem to understand. I never really talked to him much after that conversation, even with him being from the neighborhood and a CD student and someone I would see occasionally. He just wasn't worth it to me.

In retrospect, I broke the law that night and I got what I deserved. I was old enough and I knew the rules of what could and could not be done that night, even in Wildwood, NJ. It always bothered me though that Mel's and my attempt to help Chas is what really got us into trouble. If we ignored Chas's situation and the problem he clearly created for himself and just left him under the boardwalk, we never would have been arrested that night. If we never allowed him to come with us that night, I suppose that would have been even smarter. Mel and I were not intoxicated in any way then and there. But, we did drink one beer each, we told the officer the truth (eventually), and we paid the price. We paid the price for helping our friend and telling the truth. But, the law is the law.

Right?

About seven years after this underage drinking arrest, when a new police officer myself, I became friendly with a slightly older fellow rookie officer in my PD. He told me that during college he had been a part-time Wildwood officer the same summer that I was arrested. He remembered the policeman who arrested me. He was a year-round officer there and was known even among the other officers as being a "prick." We laughed and agreed that both of us, even as rookies, had to be "pricks" too at times while being law enforcement officers. Sometimes the situation simply dictated it. But not always.

In the course of my later duties as a police officer, I would come upon young people involved in underage drinking on numerous occasions. Depending on the situation, sometimes I would just have them pour out their alcoholic beverages and let them go on their way. Not if they were driving, of course, but if they were not drunk, could safely egress the location, and were respectful to me, I would let them go. Right or wrong, that's how I handled those similar type situations at times.

So, in summing up this most recent law enforcement encounter, at least four mistakes were made during that New Jersey summer evening in 1970 by Mel and me. I learned from them. No doubt, so did Mel.

By choice, my "Wildwood Days," and nights, were limited after that incident. It was onto other south Jersey seashore towns thereon for my summertime getaways. They tended to be not quite as "wild," as I was never arrested at the Jersey shore again. Chas didn't show up at those places either; probably because he wasn't told about them, at least by me or Mel.

Chapter Eleven

Other than these summertime out-of-school incidents, my high school years themselves were relatively event free. As I look back, they were good years; well, minus the two arrests.

I made the JV football team my sophomore year (that's why I quit my paper route), but broke my right thumb at practice about three weeks into the season. I was sidelined with my injury for about a month and I eventually decided to not go back on the team. My friend from St. Helena School, Mike Smith, a very good athlete who would eventually quarterback the team our senior year, suggested more than once that I should stay on the team. I appreciated his support but, for various reasons, mostly having to do with attaining a part-time job and getting a driver's license, two issues not unrelated to each other, I ended my high school athletic career with that thumb injury.

While remaining friends with Smitty throughout high school, and sharing a beach house with him and 10 other guys in Ocean City, New Jersey, during the summer of '71, it was during our respective freshman years at different but geographically adjacent colleges that I did my best to lend support to him. He was in a hospital bed at the time with severe cranial injuries, and they weren't football related.

More on Smitty's situation forthcoming.

Regarding Cardinal Dougherty High School football, the varsity team my sophomore year, in 1968, won the Philadelphia high school city championship. It's the only football championship my high school ever won. After my injury, the coach talked me into being one of the four managers of the football team that year. I recruited the other three guys, all from St. Helena's. One of the guys was Rob McCarthy, my cat-helping friend. While not a player on the team, it was a good experience nonetheless during that championship season, the only one ever for my school's football team. Maybe it had something to do with the excellent managers on the squad that year.

I always wondered if I hadn't been injured and kept playing, if I had listened to Smitty, where my future athletic career would have headed. In all likelihood, it probably wouldn't have gone too far, certainly not beyond high school. My skills were less in athletics and more in the social arena as I was learning about myself. I was elected to student council my senior year and proudly served in that position through graduation day.

I would be remiss here if I didn't discuss one of my more unusual friendships that was forged during my young teenage years. Looking back I wonder about it sometimes in terms of just what it represented and what it meant for the other person. For me and my friends it was pretty clear. But for him? I still am not sure.

The friendship was with a guy 14 years older than my Olney buddies and me. His name was Ed Fehrenbach. His nickname was Big Ed. He earned that name, well before we knew him, because he was about 6'3" and over 325 lbs. He worked his whole adult life in one of the local Philadelphia supermarket chains. When we first started hanging out, he was 29 and we were 15. Our mutual friendship went on for decades after it started at a nearby intersection almost every weekend in Olney in the late '60s.

My sister Alma actually knew Big Ed from when they attended St. Helena School together as they were in the same graduating class. Ed still lived in his parents' Olney rowhome when we met him. He had hit it off personally with his new paperboy, one of my neighborhood and St. Helena School friends, Tim Klarich. (Again, Tim is the younger brother of Steve Klarich, the boy who almost killed me, accidently, in the alley with a stickball bat during a game.) Despite the obvious age differences between my group of friends and Big Ed, the next thing we knew he started coming around and hanging out with us.

Ed owned a fancy, newer model, full-sized Chrysler automobile and it was great to have an adult driver with his own cool car to drive us places like school dances, sporting events, movies, and later, even bars. He claimed repeatedly he was a "regular guy" but that all his friends his age were now married, or were Catholic priests or Christian Brothers, and he was just looking for something to do and someone to do things with on certain nights of the week. My circle of buddies and I became those newly found friends of Ed's, despite being almost half-a-life apart in age, maturity, and world-ly experience.

Ed never had a girlfriend during those early years that we knew him, nor did he acknowledge any even short-term female relationships in his past. He had sex with women in the past, he confided to us, but he just never seemed to have had an actual dating life. Oh well, neither did any of us at the time. Not that unusual for young men our ages, but looking back, sort of odd for a guy his age. But, it didn't bother us at the time, so no big deal as far as we were concerned.

Big Ed made sure that when we first started going places together, he went around to all our homes and introduced himself to our parents. He didn't want to be a stranger to them while hanging around with us. It seemed to make sense to all of us, including our parents, who welcomed him into our respective lives. Because Ed appeared to be such a benign and innocent guy, a big and lovable teddy-bear some would call him, our parents, as well as my now-married sister Alma who knew him from years ago, didn't have any objections to this older guy/younger kids' relationship. At least we were all males, right? What could go wrong?

Whether on long drives into the far suburbs to go to movies or ice cream parlors or hamburger joints, athletic events, dances, running errands, or just sitting late at night at the intersection of 3rd and Nedro, we'd individually or collectively talk to Big Ed about lots of disparate subjects on these occasions. Obviously, some kid and school-related matters that concerned us teens were discussed, but also adult-related matters could be the topics on certain nights. It was actually cool having an adult male to talk to who was not one of our parents.

Despite how this relationship may appear at this time, I must say that I never experienced anything with Big Ed that was other than legit and on the up-and-up. Nor did any of my friends ever acknowledge any shenanigans or specific questionable behavior involving Ed. Well, besides drinking with him at times, but that was it.

In closing to this recounting of the Big Ed portion of my early life, despite this seemingly odd relationship, I want to re-emphasize here that I have no direct knowledge or proof of Ed ever doing anything untoward involving me, nor with my other friends. Ed was a decent man, a devout Mass-attending Catholic, and a good friend. He finally married a nice woman in the late 1980s when he was in his late 40s. He died unexpectedly in 1992, inside of a fitness center he was visiting because he was considering joining it in an attempt to finally lose some weight.

Interestingly, in the mid-1980s, as a police detective, I came across my town's "Big Ed." Well, sort of. He had many of the same characteristics and younger relationships in his own suburban town as Big Ed did in Olney. Except this guy went a bit too far with one of his much younger friends. Way too far. I had the proof, and I arrested him for it. It made headlines in the local newspaper the next day because he was also a township politician. And, his arrest almost cost me my job.

More on this guy, his crime, and the subsequent threats against me because of this arrest, in Book II.

Starting in the summer after my sophomore year in high school, and lasting through graduation day, I worked at a family-owned Olney drug store at the intersection of 5th St. and Tabor Ave. Big Ed Fehrenbach was related to one of the managers and he actually helped me get the job there. It wasn't a pharmacy, but simply sold over-the-counter products. I was a stock boy and sometimes a cashier when needed. It was mostly part-time, with a full-time week or so over the two summers I was employed there to conduct inventory. Dealing with the public and adult co-workers at my first real job was an interesting way to learn about life beyond that of my home and school.

One of the more interesting parts of my job I learned during the first or second week there. That was when individual men (and it was always men), would pull me aside while I was stocking the shelves with laxatives, hairspray, diapers, vitamins, or other sundry items, and while sort of suspiciously looking around would in whisper-fashion ask me for a certain item. Back in those days, these items were not displayed in the open as they are today in most drug stores and other retail establishments. Upon being asked, I would then go into the backroom and get the requested item for the customers. They would then take the product to the cashier, pay for it, and leave the store.

If not surmised already, the items I'm referring to are condoms.

I soon learned as a new and relatively innocent stock boy, there were different kinds of condoms. As time went on, I would ask the interested male customer if they wanted lubricated, non-lubricated, ribbed, non-ribbed, three, six, a dozen, more, a certain brand, etc. I never did ask what "size" they wanted, but a fellow full-time stock boy there would "just for fun" ask that of some men when they asked for the product. His name was Kerry.

Kerry also told me that sometimes, when things were quiet at the store, and he was bored, he would open the condom boxes, stick pins through the centers of the foil wrappers, and then put them back in the boxes. He would later brag that he was "indirectly" the father of dozens of kids in the Olney area. I wasn't sure whether to laugh at him or cringe at the time. I never actually saw him prick (pun intended) the condoms myself, but knowing him, he probably did so.

(Any person conceived in the lower Olney area during the late '60s or early '70s, when Kerry worked at this drug store, MAY have him to thank for their very existence. If, instead, it led to you paying child support for 18 or so years, or an unplanned pregnancy, you MAY have him to blame.)

Kerry was an interesting guy. He was about two years older than me and athletic in his own way. He had some notable talents besides his strange sense of humor, among them being his arm wrestling abilities. Despite his rather thin build, he would arm wrestle his co-workers, delivery men, and others who would challenge him. He would somehow always win, even over bigger, bulkier, and clearly stronger guys. He even made money at it when others would bet on the results. Most of these events of strength took place in the backroom of the Olney drug store on a cleared off desk.

Big Ed, being a supermarket employee, knew of a guy who worked in his store who was also supposedly a great arm wrestler. I forget how it all came together, but after a week or so of indirect negotiations and schedule comparisons between Big Ed, his co-worker and me, Kerry and the guy agreed to arm wrestle during their respective lunch breaks one day. Kerry didn't have a car at the time, so my friends and I picked him up and drove him to the supermarket for the showdown. We bet some money, probably $20 in total among us, and the other arm wrestler's friends and co-workers did the same. Winners would take all. This event was building in anticipation like the later Ali-Frazier boxing match. Well, at least in Olney among our small group of friends.

So, on that day, in the backroom of the produce department of the supermarket, with a circle of about 25 people around them, and with a pool of about $60 sitting on a produce scale as the winnings (not a small sum of money at the time), Kerry and the produce guy squared off with their elbows on a large metallic table surrounded by squash, cucumbers, and tomatoes. They struggled evenly for about 30 seconds, with each combatant seeming to have the advantage over the other at one point or another during this time. Downward Kerry's arm would go, but then it would come back up; same with the produce guy's arm, downward and then up.

However, it wasn't long until the produce guy had Kerry's arm down, all the way down. And, as his arm became one with the table, a loud snap-like sound was heard. Kerry lost the match. His first ever, he later said. The other guy had beaten him, fair and square. The money went to the victor and those who bet on him. Kerry and my crew said goodbye and left the store, somewhat dejectedly and minus the money we lost.

Although Kerry didn't say anything while still in the store, on the way out in the parking lot, he apologized for losing the match. We told him to forget about it and that maybe in a rematch with the guy we could recoup our money. He then told us that it may be awhile as after getting into the car with us he said his arm really hurt. As it turns out, after a later trip to the doctor's office, it was learned that the guy broke Kerry's arm during the match. He'd be in a sling for over a month afterwards.

The bosses at the drug store were not happy to hear about this. We both got in trouble for it and I wasn't even working that day. Kerry could still stock the shelves, but now at only half the speed as he was down to only one working arm. I'm not sure if he could still poke holes in the condoms with just one arm. I never asked him and really didn't want to know.

The supermarket guy who broke Kerry's arm actually played another role in my still developing young adulthood. Having stayed in loose contact with him through Big Ed after that match, he later sold me and my friends some items that would come back to haunt me a few years later. One was just a piece of paper. Another was a badge, of sorts. Both independently almost derailed my future career.

More on these items, their various iterations, and the subsequent problems they caused me, coming up.

Regarding my Cardinal Dougherty High School years and the institution itself, on a very somber note, I want to add that the school earned an ominous distinction during my time there. It is a very unpleasant one and to this day remains a stark reminder of the reality of our world back then. The distinction is that 27 CD graduates were killed in the Vietnam War.

CDHS is ironically tied with Father Judge High School, another Philadelphia Catholic institution and one-time sports rival, which lost the same exact number of graduates. These two schools individually lost more former students to that war than at any other Catholic high school in the U.S. They are in the top five of U.S. schools to lose graduates in Vietnam.

(Interestingly, and equally sad, three of those five schools, including my alma mater and Father Judge, were in Philadelphia. Thomas Edison High School, a public school in Philadelphia, had 54 graduates killed, the most of any one school in the nation.)

I remember very well, seemingly once a month or so, sitting in homeroom class when the principal, Father Howard, would announce over the school public address system that yet another former student from one of the mid-'60s graduating classes had been killed in combat. It was always a very sobering moment when these notifications were made. I knew of at least two of the dead, as they were older brothers of fellow students.

I don't remember overly fixating on this issue with my friends and classmates at the time. It was probably healthier for us that we didn't. But, on at least a few occasions, my classmates and I, and even some teachers and priests, discussed among ourselves that within a few years we may be the ones trudging through the rice paddies and killing fields in this faraway and very dangerous land. Fortunately, the war was scaling down around the time I graduated and no one from my graduating class died in Vietnam.

I returned to CD in the mid-1990s when, as an FBI agent, I was invited to speak to the students on their annual Career Day. While there I was shown the new Vietnam Memorial display on the second floor of the building. It was designed and dedicated only a few years before to complement the stone memorial on the front lawn of the school. These were in memory of the 27 graduates who had been killed during the war. It was a sobering reminder of those times for me as it brought back memories that I had somewhat suppressed.

While at CD that evening, I hoped the present day students appreciated what sacrifices some of their alumnae made for them. While touting various employment and career opportunities within the FBI that night, I made it a point to specifically remind them of this historical fact.

Lastly, Cardinal Dougherty High School no longer exists. It closed its doors in June of 2010 for the last time. The Archdiocese of Philadelphia decided this because of the changing demographics of the area and the subsequent lower enrollments there over the preceding decade. Though many CD graduates tried to keep it open through petitions, fund raising, etc., it was to no avail.

Both the exterior stone monument and the interior display dedicated to the CD graduates who died in the Vietnam War were moved to a Northeast Philadelphia Veteran of Foreign Wars post shortly after the school closed.

May their memories and their sacrifices live forever.

Cardinal Dougherty High School, 1956-2010.
Gone but not forgotten.

Chapter Twelve

I graduated from CDHS in 1971. My next stop was Penn State University (PSU), Berks Campus, in West Reading, PA. It was one of 14 PSU satellite campuses at the time. I wanted to stay local for my college career and live at home, but the nearby PSU satellite, the Ogontz (now Abington) Campus, in the northern suburbs of Philadelphia, was full. I didn't apply to the main PSU campus in faraway State College, so off to the West Reading campus I went. I spent the fall trimester of '71 and the subsequent winter trimester there, through March of '72. I came home to Philadelphia every weekend during that time and for the breaks.

The Berks locale was more of a commuter campus, with only a relatively small number of students living in apartments, or in converted attics, fixed-up basements, and the like. The rest of the students lived in the area full-time, with their parents, most having been born and raised there. I cohabited with three other male PSU students, each of us unknown to the other at first, in the converted attic of a large Victorian-style home in Wyomissing, a suburb of Reading. The home was within bike riding and even walking distance of the campus, which was actually a converted textile factory in West Reading. A family of four lived below us in the house and had earlier agreed to rent their finished attic to PSU students. The father/husband of the family was a high ranking administrator at a nearby hospital. His influence at his medical facility would come in handy for me only a few weeks after I arrived there.

Mike Smith, my previously referenced friend from Olney, St. Helena School and CDHS, who later became the quarterback on our football team, earned an athletic scholarship to another Pennsylvania college, not too far away from my school. In the early autumn of '71, while on campus one night, an elevator in his dorm building in which he was riding with a few others got stuck halfway between floors. They somehow had to jump from it down through the pried open doors to the floor below. The others made the jump okay, but Smitty misjudged his leap and fell backwards several floors down the elevator shaft. He sustained severe head injuries and was rushed in critical condition to a hospital in West Reading, not far from my campus and where I lived. A few days later, when word got to me of his accident, I visited him for the first time. He was in bad shape. What I could see of his head was shaved of hair, with a large wrap-around bandage covering the rest of it. Though groggy, he was nevertheless glad to see me.

Clearly, the Smitty in the hospital wasn't the same guy I knew from Olney and CDHS. His head and other injuries were very serious and his speech and reactions were definitely affected by it. I visited him several times over the few weeks he was there and kept him company when other family members and friends couldn't make it to visit him. I was even granted special permission to visit during off-hours because the administrator of the hospital was also my landlord.

Smitty was eventually transferred to a Philadelphia hospital closer to his Olney home and he recovered, at least to some degree. But, he never went back to college and never played football again. I stayed in touch with him during his recovery and for a while afterwards. He's getting by now, but not without some difficulty, as he suffered a stroke in 2013. No doubt his 1971 accident and its repercussions stayed with him for years to come.

What happened to Smitty that night on his college campus, and what I subsequently saw of him in the hospital over the next few weeks or so, perhaps marked the end of the innocence to life as I knew it. His accident slowly signified to me, and no doubt to him and those close to him, our respective entries into the real world. We were no longer invincible. Not even the high school football team star quarterback. We could get hurt; we could do things that could negatively affect us for life; we could even die. I naturally knew of older people getting hurt and/or dying both at home and in the war, and was familiar with stories of people I didn't know suffering such trauma, but never a friend as close as Smitty getting hurt such as this. It was a tough time for me and called for great personal introspection from all of us who knew him.

I'm not sure if one's life maturation process can truly be measured in specific stages or by specific incidents. What separates one level from another? Is it these types of incidents? I don't know. But if so, I believe it was around this time that I entered the next stage of my development. One's health and well-being cannot, and should not, be taken for granted. It can be taken away, or severely curtailed, at any time, and for seemingly the most innocuous of reasons.

I would experience this once again with another friend, just about a year later.

It was during my Friday afternoon and Monday morning rides back and forth to the Berks campus that I became friendly, or I should say friendlier, with John Welsh. John was attending classes there too and, like me, going back and forth to Philadelphia on weekends. He had his own car, and graciously offered to give me rides on occasion, including the weekend trips back and forth to home. He was an Olney guy and also attended St. Helena School and CDHS. We sort of knew of each other since seventh grade, when he first moved to our neighborhood and school, but through high school we never really had the occasion to "hang-out" with one another. We would, however, bond during our early college years and it would lead to a lifelong friendship.

John would ultimately have a pronounced influence in my life, during at least four different timeframes. The first was early on and a relatively innocent academic matter, yet nonetheless important to me; in less than a year, it was tragic with us experiencing a friend's serious and crippling accident, with John also being injured at the same time; another, before the decade ended, was very scary as it involved John sustaining a serious injury in a national headline producing event; and the last, some twenty years after that, involved one of John's immediate family members and it was, in fact, deadly.

The latter two events will be discussed in Book II and Book III, respectively.

John Welsh's initial influence in my life had to do with my potential future career direction. Or, more accurately, it was the lack thereof on my part at the time.

If I repeatedly dwelt on any one perplexing and confounding subject in my later youth, both internally and occasionally verbalized to others, it was, "What do I want to be when I grow up?"

I know many, if not all, young men and women go through this stage to some degree, and I'm sure I was not too much different from them in that regard. But, I just seemed to have no specific strengths or interests during this timeframe, other than playing schoolyard sports, reading, watching some TV, going to the movies, attending school, working various summer and part-time jobs, and generally having fun (all arguably being more "interests" than "strengths," of course). That wasn't necessarily a bad thing, but in my occasional contemplative moments, it could really bother me. What would I or could I be good at in the real world, which was slowly creeping up on me? Did I actually have to be good at something? Or, just do something, anything, to get by?

What did I want to do with my life? Was it about making lots of money or being happy? Were both possible? I honestly could not answer those questions back then. It was frustrating to me and others in my age bracket, no doubt.

I didn't even know what major to choose at Penn State. I was told by some adult at the time to put "Liberal Arts" on my college application form as it ostensibly covered courses from many different majors. Then, when one course or program subsequently interested me, I could choose that as my major. Since I didn't know what I wanted to do with my life that seemed to be the logical choice for now.

I recall taking one of those general career guidance tests right after I graduated high school. It was a necessary step to gain admittance to Penn State. One of its stated purposes was to assist first year college students in choosing a major. The other, obviously, was to help the student decide on a career track. When the results came back in the mail a few weeks later they indicated that based on my apparent interests and aptitudes I should strongly consider working as a...printer.

Me? A printer?

My opinion is that there's nothing wrong at all with the printing profession. I have no doubt it's an honorable and important job and I'm sure printers make a decent living at it and all that. One of this nation's founding fathers and a fellow Philadelphian, Ben Franklin, was a printer. Good for him. But, I didn't see myself as a future printer. It didn't seem to make sense to me. I must have some other calling. I must be able to do something else. But what?

As referenced earlier, I thoroughly enjoyed reading about criminal investigations and watching TV shows and movies regarding true crimes. The movie *In Cold Blood* (of which I also attended its opening night in Philadelphia) was one of my favorites of that genre from the late '60s, with *The*

French Connection and *Dirty Harry* coming a bit later in the early '70s. Each of these films is a classic in this genre. While sitting in the theaters, or reading the books, I would contemplate all sorts of issues and factors about how to solve the cases at hand and how or what I would do if somehow I was put in the shoes of one of the movies' or books' protagonists.

This interest included a fascination with the real-time, real-life case involving Charles Manson, in Los Angeles. I read everything I could on that investigation at the time, from that first getaway summer weekend in Wildwood as a young teen, to later reading the book *Helter Skelter*, co-authored by the prosecutor in that case, Vincent Bugliosi, along with Curt Gentry. But, despite this obvious interest, I never took it to the next conscious level in thinking that I would perhaps want to be a law enforcement officer/investigator someday. That just didn't seem to be what I thought I wanted to do for a career. The dots were just not connecting at that time. It was confusing to me.

Plus, this wasn't the best time in our country's history to consider donning a uniform of any kind. The late '60s and early '70s were a tough time for the police and military in the U.S. The Vietnam War, soldiers as alleged individual "baby killers" (an allegation later proven groundless), the Kent State University student shootings, numerous reports of police brutality at student campus protests (whether real or suggested by those with agendas), etc., were in the headlines almost every day. Would I really want to join a military branch or a police agency and take that kind of abuse before I even started my job? Of course, as I eventually did choose to work at two different law enforcement agencies in the future, these issues apparently did not ultimately make that much of a difference to me.

I knew, or at least hoped, that I was first going to get a college degree, but in what? Perhaps, looking back, it seems obvious, but it wasn't to me while living in the middle of it. That particular level of self-awareness was still undeveloped in me. Maybe by design....

I remember a conversation I had with my parents in my first few months of college when I was home for a weekend. My mom asked me, "So, Jimmy, have you picked another major yet?"

I said, "No, it's still liberal arts."

My dad, who was now fully retired from his Philadelphia Gas Works job, then asked, "Well, what do you want to do with yourself?"

I responded, "I'm not really sure."

He sat quiet for a moment or so and then eventually offered some very sage advice. He said, "Well, all I can tell you is this: Find something you like to do, get a degree in it, then get someone to pay you for it."

I know he didn't invent that axiom, but it was probably the first time I had ever heard it.

I remember saying back to him, "Hmmmmm... that seems like a good idea. All I have to do is figure out what it is I want to get paid for."

He then said, "You'll figure it out. Just follow your interests and don't let anyone talk you out of it. And, of course, keep doing well in school."

I ended the conversation with a simple, "Okay."

As it turned out, my decision making process had already started. One big decision was right around the corner or, to be geographically more accurate, somewhere on the Pennsylvania Turnpike between Philadelphia and Reading, just a few days later.

It was during a car ride back to Reading with John Welsh the following Monday morning when, after recounting what we separately did over the weekend, we started talking about school, courses, our respective majors, potential careers, academic advisors, parental talks, etc. I forget what John's original major may have been at the time, but he told me he was about to transfer into "Law Enforcement and Corrections" (LEC). I asked him to tell me more about it. He did. As I listened to him, while he drove us westbound on the turnpike, I was becoming truly interested in this as a potential major. He too was unsure what he wanted to do in the immediate future, but he was leaning toward becoming a Philadelphia police officer or firefighter. We both kidded that we certainly didn't need college degrees for those jobs, so why even bother. But, we both figured continuing with school for now would make sense either way.

I had been contemplating switching to Psychology as my major, after taking one whole course in this fascinating new subject to me. But, I was turned off by it as a major a short time later as someone had told me that one couldn't do anything job-wise with just an undergrad Psych degree. A doctorate was needed to get any sort of real employment in this field. I figured that at 19 years of age, in 1972, three and a half more years of formal schooling was about all I had left in me. So, I ruled psychology out as a potential new major.

With a little more research on my part, and thinking of what my dad told me just a few days before, I figured with LEC as my major I could learn how and why crimes were committed, how criminals think and act, and how crimes could be solved, and even make a decent salary, someday while doing it. I was already very interested in this field, given my penchant for reading all I could in this area in my youth, along with television shows and movies of the same genre. Oh yeah, and successfully launching my own investigation as a 6-year-old to recover my stolen bike. So, it was perfect! And all of this was in a four-year degree.

I proceeded early that same week to the academic office where students went to change majors. I read some of the brochures on this new major, and right then and there I did it. Before the end of my second trimester at PSU, shortly before transferring to the Ogontz campus, I was an LEC major.

John Welsh and I transferred to the Ogontz/Abington campus together, and I thanked him then and for years to come for telling me about the LEC program at PSU. While it was a relatively casual conversation between John and me on that ride on the turnpike, it led me into an academic program that would finally direct me toward an actual career goal. I never dared dream of where it would eventually take me, but it was clearly a start.

That was the next step, of course. A career. But, a career where? With whom? Doing what? Something within the world of criminal justice, of course, but exactly where I was to go was seemingly a long way ahead of me. For now, for me, just getting the B.S. degree was my goal. I'd worry about the rest later.

LEC at PSU was a brand new major. In fact, it was one of the first majors of its kind in the U.S. Many of the initial instructors in this new program, including several of mine, were retired New York City Police Department detectives and/or high ranking police officials. There was apparently some sort of real-world-to-academia pipeline between this fledgling new major at PSU and the NYPD back then. They were some very interesting faculty members and I learned lots from them. I preferred them to the professors who were strictly academics with minimal real-world experience. But, I did realize then, and certainly now, that instructors with both types of backgrounds, that is, real-world and theoretical, are the ideal in any university degree program.

Some of my friends, both at PSU and other colleges, were business majors, specifically accounting or finance. Others majored in social work or education. Some of these friends would joke with me, John Welsh, and a few others who slowly started switching to LEC. They would say, "So, you're going to get a four-year degree to become what...a cop?"

"No, of course not," we would respond, perhaps in unison, perhaps on our own, but internally realizing that, in fact, they may be right.

It should be noted that in the mid-1970s, virtually no local or state law enforcement agencies in the U.S. required any college education at all, much less a four-year degree. In fact, the police department in my home city of Philadelphia had no educational requirements at all. Not high school, a GED, or even a grade school diploma. My friends and fellow LEC students and I soon started to realize that choosing to become police officers was a potential reality, depending on the job market in the year or two when we would be graduating. Our real hope, we thought, lay with the state and federal governments, and law enforcement/investigative careers we could hopefully find within those branches. Most of those positions did, in fact, require a four-year college degree, but getting in the door right out of college was not going to be easy.

Despite my earlier misgivings, mostly based on negative media coverage, one potential career I still considered as an option was the U.S. military. The question back then for all similar aged males was whether it would be mandatory to join as there was still the draft or would we enlist voluntarily. I found out that it would most likely not be mandatory for me on February 2, 1972. That's when the draft lottery was held for males born in 1953.

On that cold wintery day, while I was still at the Berks campus of PSU, the well-publicized, several hour-long draft lottery was held in Washington, D.C. I remember many of the male students congregating in the school's community room that afternoon watching the single television set and learning our immediate fate as the corresponding numbers and dates were read off one-by-one. I was listening intently, as were the rest of the guys in the room as well as some of their girlfriends, in an attempt to learn of our pending immediate futures. When each number was called, starting at "1" with the corresponding date called next, there would be either dead silence or loud cursing. Once a guy's number/birthdate was called out, he would usually leave the room. The ones leaving the room early were generally not very happy, with the ones leaving later tending to be in a more jovial mood.

I left the room that day somewhat closer to the middle of the pack. I didn't curse either. My number was in the 90s. Not necessarily as high as I would have preferred, but safely in a numerical area in which I would not soon be forced to make a decision that would affect the next few years of my life. As the Vietnam War and the U.S. military's role in it had begun the process of de-escalation by 1972, the strong opinion was that no one with assigned numbers higher than 40 or so that year would be drafted. That turned out to be true.

So I, and anyone else born on my birth date in 1953, was saved from military conscription while still in college or doing whatever else it is he may be doing at the time. I'd come back to this topic of potential military service soon after graduation from PSU a few years later while on the hunt for a job and a career.

Chapter Thirteen

Before landing any job in my career field, which was still a few years away, I needed a few summer jobs. I had college bills to pay, after all. Thanks to my hospital administrator brother-in-law Jim, Alma's husband, the summer after high school I took a job at Nazareth Hospital in Northeast Philadelphia. I worked in the housekeeping department there. Not a thrilling or personally rewarding job, but it earned me some spending cash. My official title there was "Wall Washer." I expanded my skill set that summer to not only cleaning walls, but floors too sometimes. While I was grateful for the summer work, I was hoping to do something different the following summer.

During the winter months preceding the next summer, Bill, my sister Cass's husband, talked to me over a Christmas gathering in '71 and asked me if I was a good swimmer. I responded that I was a decent swimmer. He then asked me if I wanted a summer job as a lifeguard. He was the regional manager of a large, upscale residential apartment management company in the greater Philadelphia area. Many of the apartment buildings and complexes had outdoor pools. As per Pennsylvania law, these pools needed certified lifeguards to legally operate in the summertime. So, essentially he was guaranteeing me a job, and a pretty cool job at that. All I needed, he added, was to get my Red Cross Senior Lifesaving Certificate.

I told him, okay, I can do that. I can swim pretty well in a straight line, so how hard can that be?

I never really had an interest in being a life-guard before this conversation, so I really didn't know where to begin to find out the details of at-taining a lifesaving training certificate. I asked around to some friends and PSU schoolmates of mine if they knew anything about how or where to get it. It took a bit of personal research on my part, but I eventually learned that it was offered at most YMCAs, at various times of the year, and all I had to do was sign up, show up, and get the piece of paper after a month or two of weekly classes. I didn't think it would be that difficult as I was al-ways an above average swimmer. While my family never belonged to a country club, nor was I on any swim teams in my youth, I could do the basic swim strokes and tread water with no problem. I was good at holding my breath and swimming far dis-tances underwater too.

I figured getting this certificate should be quick and easy. After all, I've got the basic skills down. I'm in good overall shape. I can do this. And lastly, someone told me the course was taught by mostly 20-year-old suburban girls and the whole program itself was pretty much a walk, if not a swim, in the park. So, I signed up at the Abington, PA, branch of the YMCA (about 25 minutes from my Olney home and just minutes from my PSU Ogontz Campus) for the eight-week course.

I was ready to go. Just get this baby over with and it's off to poolside, great hours, rainy days off, girls, a nice suntan, all the while getting paid for it too.

I showed up at the Y the first scheduled night, swimsuit and towel in hand. It was sometime in early-April of 1972. I followed the signs to the up-stairs classroom for the Senior Lifesaving Course. I meandered in and plopped myself into one of the desks. There were around 25 people in the room. I didn't know any of them. They were boys and girls mostly two to three years younger than me, with only a few of them my age. I assumed at first that one of them was the instructor. I was waiting for him or her to suddenly begin the class.

After a few minutes, I learned that none of the boys and girls in the classroom with me was to be the course instructor. I couldn't have been that lucky. The actual instructor had just walked into the back door of the classroom. He was an older man, to us anyway, maybe in his early 30s. Not a tall guy, but he was pretty solidly built. It was a body frame that I would not normally associate with that of an everyday swimmer, but maybe a football fullback instead. He had short hair too, certainly for the early '70s. Actually, it was really short hair, almost military-like. Maybe he was a substitute instructor for the night. Maybe he was the father of the young female instructor who couldn't make the first class for some reason.

Again, no such luck.

This barrel-chested, military-haired guy slowly walked to the front of the room, glaring somewhat disgustingly at us as he walked forward. He slammed a clipboard onto the fixed-podium, and right out of the gate stated somewhat indignantly, "I'm not here to babysit any of you. I'm also not here to teach anyone how to swim. If you can't hack this class, if you can't pass the swim test down in the pool later tonight, you're out of here. Your certification by the Red Cross AND me is serious stuff. Get it?"

Get it? Get what?

What the hell? Who was this guy? I didn't sign up for this. What is he, some sort of drill instructor? I'm not here for military boot camp.

As it turns out, our instructor told us shortly thereafter that he was, in fact, a former military drill instructor and now a sergeant in one of the local police departments.

Hey, where's the nice, friendly, 20-year-old girl instructor from the suburbs who was supposed to be here?

The first hour that night was spent going over various classroom materials, future assignments (yes, we were to have actual homework in this course), class protocols (we were not to be even one minute late for class, not miss any class), etc. He then told us that he was going to work us hard over the next eight weeks and some of us would not make it. In fact, he told us to look to our left, and then to our right, and that one of those people would most likely not be here at the end of the course, or even the end of this first night.

Geez…was I to be one of them? I didn't know. I really didn't want to even look at the students next to me as I knew they'd be looking at me too.

At the end of the classroom session, when we were instructed to meet down at the pool, I think five of the other students simply stated to us that they were quitting. They said they'd come back in the fall when instructor so-in-so was in place. Should I follow them? Was this course really worth it? But, going in the fall wouldn't do me any good. My job opportunity was for this summer.

So, I decided to stay, at least for now. We remaining guys and gals in the class went to our respective locker rooms, got into our swimsuits, got to the pool area (those of us who hadn't quit), and the instructor started barking at us. He didn't need a megaphone or a microphone, as his natural voice projected and echoed plenty well in the long and narrow natatorium.

Into the water half of us went. Luckily, having initially stayed in the background, I was in the still-out-of-the-pool half, as he started giving those in the pool orders that I didn't really understand.

With each lap, he'd yell, "Give me a lap of front crawl; now breaststroke; give me a full lap of backstroke; give me a full lap of butterfly; now, do inverted butterfly."

I wasn't even sure what some of these strokes were. I was just a regular swimmer, which I learned that night is officially called "front crawl," and I'm not even that good at it, at least in terms of my form, style, and overall speed while doing it.

I watched the other swimmers. I tried to memorize their motions. Not easy, standing nervously at poolside. Not an ideal way to learn swim strokes, I learned.

It slowly, but very deliberately, started happening. While pointing at individual swimmers, the instructor bellowed to them, "You, go home!" "You, you're outta here!" "Not good enough, see ya!"

Yes, these kids were being thrown out of the class. They looked to me like they were actually decent swimmers. I wasn't even in the water yet, but I felt my minutes here were numbered.

Do I even jump in when it's my turn? I don't think I'm going to be a lifeguard this summer. Maybe back at the hospital, cleaning walls again. Or, maybe the "Ack-a-me" supermarket will be hiring experienced stock boys.

The still-remaining swimmers from the first platoon were told to exit the pool, all puffing hard and out of breath. Now it was my group's turn to go in the water. We each took a lane. Then, the instructor started barking his commands. I did my best to mimic those who went before me and those alongside of me. I could make it back and forth from one end to the other okay, but I know I was not earning any points on style. I was probably losing points, as a matter of fact. My front crawl and breaststroke were relatively good, and I upped my speed in the water by pushing really hard off the pool walls. I was hoping this attempt at speed would compensate for my lack of actually knowing the majority of the strokes I was being asked to perform. Maybe if I simply went fast enough, he wouldn't be able to really see my individual strokes.

Unlikely....

Then, his voice bellowed once again, this time to my group. This was it, I figured. "You're out;" "See ya;" he was heard loudly saying.

I assumed he was talking to me, but instead it was to two other swimmers. So far, nothing was said to me.

Finally, at the completion of the last lap, as I'm holding onto the side of the pool catching my breath, the instructor walked over to me. He bent down. He said, "What's your name?"

I told him. He responded, "You're close, kid. I'm gonna leave you in the class for now, but I'll be watching you."

With that, I wasn't sure if I was to be proud or disappointed in myself. I made it, but just barely that first night. I suppose I did better than the one-quarter of the class that had showed up that night but who either quit outright or didn't finish the "tryout." But, what happens over the course of the next seven weeks is far from determined. This is not a done deal. Not even close.

Would this even be worth it for me? Did I really want to be pushed this hard for a lifesaving certificate?

For what? For who?

I must confess here that, at times in my early life, I had not always successfully followed through with, shall we say, various youthful endeavors or challenges. In other words, sometimes, I could be a quitter. I quit the Cub Scouts after one meeting; I quit drum lessons after one quick lesson with my potential instructor; and, even though I had broken my thumb early in the football season my sophomore year in high school, and was forced to miss a few weeks of practice and games, I did make the team and I could have gone back to it. But, I didn't.

For reasons not sure to me after all these years, I didn't follow through on some of these endeavors. Why? Because they challenged me in ways that made me, well, uncomfortable and pushed me in ways in which I wasn't prepared to be pushed...at least not yet. Now, it was a senior lifesaving course. Do I quit again? I made it through the first night, but so what. Would I get "cut" the second night, or later in the program? These questions would eventually be answered for me, in a very surprising and life-altering way.

I thought a lot about that first night of senior lifesaving over the next six days. I seriously considered not showing up for the next class. Two hours before it was to start, I still wasn't sure if I was going back. Hey, I could find a job somewhere else that summer. I didn't have to be a lifeguard, right? I could get dismissed on some other night too, couldn't I? He was a tough guy. Did I really need a guy like him barking orders at me just to be a lifeguard?

To this day, I'm not sure what mental processes of mine kicked in toward the approach of that second class, but whatever they were, they told me to go. Maybe it was that ongoing and still developing phenomenon known as maturity. Maybe it was something else like thinking of what a potentially cool job this could lead to. I don't know, but for whatever reason, just an hour before it started, I decided to go to the second class. I had already done the reading and written assignment earlier that day, just in case.

I went back for the remainder of the course too. I never missed a class nor was I ever late. I got better with each subsequent night of training and my confidence slowly grew. The instructor lightened up a bit too. Not much, but he came across as slightly more of a human being than on that very first night.

As it turns out, I eventually completed the course. I not just completed it, but I actually aced it. The instructor graded us on homework assignments, written tests, the all-important actual in-pool lifesaving techniques, general attitude and aptitude, and other matters. On the last night at the end of the course, after performing all the required tasks in the pool, he announced to my fellow students that Jim Fitzgerald, someone he admittedly wasn't even sure he was going to allow to continue after the first night, graduated number one in this Senior Lifesaving class. My classmates applauded me and some even patted me on the back. All this after I had considered quitting the course after the first session. Needless to say, I'm glad I didn't.

At almost 19 years of age, in the spring of 1972, believe it or not, this accomplishment became a life-changing event for me. I know, I know, it was only a YMCA senior lifesaving certificate course, not a U.S. Navy Seal, Olympics, or an NFL team tryout or even basic training in the military. I'm not pretending it came even close to those levels of personal and physical challenge. However, it was the first time I was pushed into doing something relatively difficult, relatively challenging and something that I could have unceremoniously and easily quit if I had wanted.

But, I didn't.

Through the rest of the 1970s and into the mid-1980s, if asked, I would tell this little success story; that of the young man (me) who for one of the first times in his life, didn't quit under pressure. And, I'd tell of that former drill sergeant and present-day cop/senior lifesaving instructor who also didn't quit on me. He, and this eight-week course, ultimately made me a better person.

This was, no doubt, yet another defining moment of my young life. Perhaps it was me further transitioning from boyhood to manhood with much of it thanks to that hard-nosed lifesaving instructor who gave a kid who was struggling, but really trying that first night, one more chance to make it. I did make it, all the way to "number one" in his class. I thanked him profusely that last night and meant every word of it.

From a coping perspective, when life and its related issues would get difficult over the next decade-plus, and I may have started considering an easy way out, that is, quitting some task at hand, or retreating to an otherwise safe redoubt, I would think of the instructor, how he pushed me to be better, stronger, and that he somehow saw in me that perhaps I could accomplish my goal. He was right, and now I knew I could achieve the difficult tasks in life if I really wanted to do so and not quit them prematurely. I thought of him often over those years, always in a positive light, when tasked with the very challenging issues that would present themselves to me. He was a hero to me, in his and my own special way.

Until, that is, in the mid-1980s, when my opinion of this guy changed drastically. I ran into that same cop/senior lifesaving instructor again, strictly by chance. I didn't even know it was him at first as his hair turned white and he had put on some weight. He barely remembered me at first, too. But, over a brief time while taking another course, this one a Villanova University Graduate School course, he would again act in such a way as to alter my life.

I really resented this guy for a long while after that mid-1980s encounter. What a turnaround this created for me mentally, from what I DID think of him to what I NOW thought of him.

More on this next meeting, and that second life-changing experience involving him, in Book II.

With my Senior Lifesaving Certificate in hand, the summer of '72 was a blast for me. I started my lifeguard career in May of that year at an apartment complex in the East Falls section of Philadelphia. It was at a place called the Gypsy Lane Apartments. It was a garden complex layout, sprawled out over at least ten wooded acres. Like all the apartment complexes in my brother-in-law's management company, it was an upscale one. It had a 25-yard pool and a baby pool, both of which by Pennsylvania law needed a certified lifeguard when open to the public. It was mostly young couples, with young kids, who lived there and used the pool. This place came to be my first assignment of that summer season.

During my first few days there, leading up to Memorial Day Weekend of '72, I initially met that other Jim O'Brien in my young life. He was then one of the very popular "Boss Jocks" on the local radio station, WFIL, "...56 on the AM radio dial." He and several others, including George Michaels, who later became a very popular sportscaster in the Washington, D.C. television market, were big-time disc jockeys in the Philadelphia AM radio scene. Jim, like the other DJs, was one of those fast talking record spinners who introduced and ended each song with a voiceover that was electronically modulated to some degree to make it sound as if he was broadcasting from an echo chamber. It didn't matter how the technology made him sound. He was cool, the station was popular with us young adults, and the music was great.

The early 1970s was clearly a crossover period in music radio in the U.S. The popular top 40 (in this station's case, top 56) genre and the burgeoning FM progressive radio stations were slowly becoming at odds with each other. The former genre would slowly die out, and the latter would become a mainstay in music radio broadcasting for decades to come. But, during this particular time frame, WFIL in Philadelphia was about as "boss" or cool as it could get in radio music circles.

O'Brien lived in this apartment complex and was easily recognizable because he sometimes drove a customized bright red sports car with the station's call letters emblazoned on it. I suppose it was his "company car," a perk for doing a good job and getting high ratings in the Philly radio market. His apartment wasn't too far from where I would park my car (actually, my parents' un-customized blue 1966 Ford Fairlane), to go to perform my lifeguard duties at the outdoor pool.

Several times, just coincidently, as our respective coming-and-going schedules coincided, Jim and I would cross paths. He had dark hair and chiseled good looks, probably in his late 20s then, and as his picture had been prominently displayed in TV and newspaper advertising and on some highway billboards and sides of buses too, there was no mistaking it was him. The nearby bright red racing-style car that he drove, with "WFIL" painted on the side of it, was a big clue too.

After once passing each other without saying anything, I finally mustered up the courage to say a friendly "Hi, Jim" to him as we approached each other in the parking lot the next time. He was polite, would nod his head and give me a nice reply. Usually, it was simply, "Hey, kid, how's it going?"

Somehow eventually figuring out that I was the lifeguard there (although I never actually saw him at the pool itself), he asked me at a later by-chance meeting, "How's the water?"

I said, "Fine. You oughta stop by sometime?"

He replied, "Maybe, one of these days, if they ever give me a day off."

Not knowing exactly how to respond to that, I simply said, "Okay. That would be cool."

These were I believe my last words with him. I probably only saw him about four times that late spring, each time just walking to or from the pool, in and around the adjacent parking lot. That was the extent of my in-person contact with this ultra-cool and growing-in-popularity Philly Boss Jock.

Jim O'Brien would eventually move from the AM radio to being a fixture on the local ABC-TV affiliate, Channel 6 WPVI, evening news program. He became a very popular weatherman and a news anchor later in the 1970s and 1980s on "Action News" in the greater Philadelphia metropolitan area. It was also learned years later that his then young daughter, still living in his home state of

Texas, would become an actress and a popular member of a very successful 1990s TV show.

But, it was in Jim O'Brien's TV role early one summer evening in 1980 when I would hear from him, and unbelievably from no one else before him, very disturbing and tragic news that would affect me and many others in a very profound and personal way. My coincidental TV-watching experience with him that early evening, about eight years removed from my casual and friendly interactions with him near the Gypsy Lane Apartments pool, then as a young lifeguard to a young radio DJ, contrasted greatly in nature, meaning, and importance. The latter event shook me to my very core and made me question what I was doing in life, and why.

Ironically, and again tragic, several years after that fateful and very personal news announcement, Jim O'Brien himself would be the focus of the local news.

This sad part of my life, and later what happened to O'Brien, will be further addressed in Book II.

Back to my first lifeguarding assignment, after about three weeks at the Gypsy Lane Apartments pool, finishing my freshman year college courses and handling my pool duties at the same time, the manager told me there was a possible transfer in the wind. The company needed me at the Plaza Apartments in downtown Philadelphia. They sort of asked me, but I knew that they were sort of telling me that I was going there, with no real choice. I didn't do anything wrong at this initial assignment, and it was actually going to be a promotion as I was to make more money at the downtown location. I think I was to make a whole $2.50 per hour there, instead of the $2.25 I was making at the Gypsy Lane pool. It was clearly an offer I couldn't refuse.

So, I silently said goodbye to the Boss Jock, his fancy car, the big outdoor pool with the young moms and their kids, and it was on to the cosmopolitan and very swanky Plaza Apartments I went.

The Plaza is a distinctive round building at the intersection of 18th St. and JFK Boulevard in Philadelphia. It is a 20 or so floor building, yet with a really small outdoor pool on the second floor terrace. When I saw it for the first time, I wondered why I had to train so hard in senior lifesaving for this barely 25 feet in diameter pool, which was no deeper than four feet in any part of it. But, I suppose it now would be just that much easier to rescue someone if I had to. Maybe it wasn't a bad place to relocate after all in that regard. It was a whole .25 cents an hour more, too. But, after getting several parking tickets that summer, then having to pay for parking itself there in the underground garage, even at a discounted rate, it was probably a break-even scenario for me, income-wise, moving from the Gypsy Lane pool to this one.

My new boss, the building manager, told me my first day there that, unlike my previous pool, use of this one was by separate paid membership only. In other words, people needed a pre-paid seasonal pass to get onto the terrace and sun by the pool or go into the pool itself. He warned me that even though many of the residents were very wealthy, they would still try to use the pool for free without paying the seasonal membership fee or attaining a daily use pass. As lifeguard, the manager told me that besides being on the lookout for drowning persons and generally maintaining the pool area, I was also the one who had to police the pool area and ask those who showed up for their pool ID. That is, if they didn't at first volunteer it to me or have it prominently displayed.

The apartment building, I was to learn, had some interesting and well-connected people living in it. One of the first of these persons I met there early that summer was a guy that I politely but firmly challenged when he came to the pool early one Saturday afternoon. It was a warm day in mid-June and the pool was getting crowded that day. He sat down in one of the few available chaise lounge chairs at the rear of the pool deck. He didn't have his pool membership card displayed and I didn't recognize him from having been there previously. Remembering my boss's admonition, I walked over to him as he was just applying his sunscreen and nicely asked this guy for his membership card.

The man responded courteously, but in somewhat bothered fashion, that his card was "up in his apartment."

I asked him again, sort of apologetically but still as firm as I could muster, to see his pass. With that, he said, respectfully but in a bit more agitated mood, "Do I really have to go up there and get it? I'm only going to be here for an hour or so. I'm telling you, I do have a current pass."

Again, thinking of my boss's recent strongly worded suggestion, I responded, "Uh, yes sir, if you don't mind."

The man immediately got up, put his white robe back on, and walked out of the pool area. As he left, I thought to myself that in a strange way, he looked like Clark Kent, Superman's alter ego, to include his somewhat bookish-style eyeglasses. He was probably in his early 40s, built really well, and obviously took good physical care of himself. I was hoping he wasn't too mad at me. But, hey, I did have my orders.

The gentleman came back to the pool area a few minutes later. He then walked all the way up to my lifeguard chair at poolside and showed me his card. I made sure, as I had been advised by the manager, to confirm that it was the current year's card (as opposed to last year's card), and upon taking it from him and examining it for a few seconds, I determined that it was legit. I also took note of the name on it.

I then said, "Thank you Mr. Kelly and have a nice day at the pool."

He responded politely, if not bemusedly, while walking away, "Yes, yes, you're welcome."

I knew I recognized his name, and maybe even his face, but as I was then interrupted by some playful juvenile activity in the pool, I didn't think much of it afterwards. Eventually, a woman who had been at the pool for a while that day (and who had, in fact, showed me her card upon entering the pool area when it first opened), walked up to me and formally introduced herself. After some small talk, she asked me if I knew who it was that I challenged earlier and made walk back up to his penthouse suite for his pass. I responded that I knew his name was Kelly, but that I really didn't know him beyond that.

Before responding any further I instead asked her, "Wait, there's a penthouse suite in this building and that guy lives in it?"

She replied in the affirmative. She then proceeded to tell me that the man was John B. Kelly, Jr., former Olympic gold medal winner in rowing, elected Philadelphia Councilman-at-Large, and last but not least, the brother of Grace Kelly, the former movie actress and then Princess of Monaco.

I replied to her, "Oh, THAT Mr. Kelly...."

The following Monday morning the apartment manager summoned me to his office. He told me he heard through his "people" that I had asked Jack Kelly for his pool pass. I thought I was in trouble. Maybe there were certain people that I should NOT be asking for their pool passes. What's going to happen now? Is a reprimand in order here? Something worse?

As it turned out, the manager was fine with it, laughed a bit, and told me not to be afraid to challenge anyone, even those living in the penthouse, when they first arrive at the pool. He even told me that on Sunday his (the manager's) adult son and his son's girlfriend came unannounced to the pool. They didn't even live there. I fortunately challenged them too and had them pay a guest fee after they told me who they were. My boss had no problem with that either. He told me I was doing a good job. That was nice to hear, especially after questioning the poolside legitimacy of a scion of one of Philadelphia's most famous and wealthy families.

There were some other well-known local Philadelphia celebrities there too. One of the coaches of the 76ers basketball team lived there. Another was

Phil Jasner, a popular local newspaper sports columnist whom I read all the time. And, Bett, the woman who told me about Jack Kelly, later told me that she was the ex-girlfriend of the brother of local singer and The Twist dance inventor, Chubby Checker. Cool! I was impressed with her too, more at first for who she used to date than who she was. I did get to know her a bit better before that summer ended. I learned later that she was a school teacher. She was a nice person and no doubt a good teacher too.

No one drowned on me that summer. Not even close. That's not just a good thing, that's a great thing if you're a lifeguard. My Red Cross certification apparently paid off, perhaps in some proactive way. The pool closed down that Labor Day weekend and it was back to Penn State for me.

The following winter my brother-in-law asked if I'd be interested in going out to the suburbs and actually becoming the pool captain at a much larger pool in a much larger garden complex, with several lifeguards working for me. I said sure, why not? Another promotion as it involved a bit more money and, I was assured, free parking. The complex actually had an executive golf course attached to it, tennis courts, and the whole outdoor facility was run by a tennis-pro of some sort. He was to be my boss.

I started at this large apartment complex in late April of '73, helping to get the pool and surrounding grounds set up for the Memorial Day weekend opening. Prior to that, I encouraged my good friend, Bill Sena, to get his Lifesaving Certificate. He did, but from a very easy going, barely-twenty year old female instructor; not the drill sergeant-cum-poolside taskmaster of my experience. I had told him in advance of the drill sergeant. He opted to find another YMCA to get his certificate. He still earned his legitimately and worked hard to get it, but we agreed with much less angst than it took to earn mine the year before.

As per the tennis-pro/boss, our first tasks at our new job that spring were anything but lifeguard related. Bill and I were ordered to dig fence posts, then erect the wooden fences, pull weeds, clean bathrooms, paint walls, move pool equipment, chairs, tables, etc. Okay, whatever was asked of us. This was to be our pool area too, so let's get it clean and set up right.

In the middle of those jobs, we were assigned a most ludicrous and time *in-effective* task. That was to attempt to match up about 150 unmarked keys in a shoebox to about 100 lockers in the club house. Bill and I, and eventually another lifeguard I was authorized to interview and hire, spent three solid days simply and repeatedly sticking random small keys into random locks to see if they would open the lockers. The tennis-pro would stop by every few hours to ask how many key-to-locker connections we made. Eventually, about ten keys fit into their corresponding lockers. The rest of the lockers had to be rekeyed by a local locksmith.

It cost less than $200 dollars to key the other 90 lockers. To this day, I feel that was one of the stupidest jobs anyone ever assigned me, and two other employees at the same time, in any time in my life. However, even though these were not very life-guard-like jobs, we didn't complain. We were getting paid for it, after all.

As time went on that spring, it appeared that the tennis-pro and I weren't hitting it off very well. I had never dug fence posts before, and when I didn't dig deep enough in the first few holes, he got mad at Bill and me, grabbed the posthole digger, and attempted to show us how to do it. He didn't do it very well either, but Bill and I eventually did manage to get it right. On another occasion, the women's bathroom wasn't as clean as he would have liked (after numerous women used it over a certain weekend) and he chastised us for that too. For this and the fact that only ten locker keys could be matched up with their respective keyholes, he wasn't very happy with me and my lifeguard team at first.

With these problems, what kind of pool captain would I be this summer? This, the tennis-pro would ask me in his office more than once that spring, almost as if it was a set-up question of some sort for a yet unknown agenda of his. I told him when the pool officially opened on Memorial Day weekend and there were swimmers in the water, and the pool area itself would be clean and safe and properly staffed, he'd know what kind of pool I run and what kind of pool captain I would be. He didn't like that curt yet honest response from me. I didn't see anything wrong with it.

For the record, I didn't mind doing the work of the groundskeepers, maintenance men, and janitors before the season started. But, once the pool was open starting Memorial Day weekend, and when my semi-pro boss or whatever he was would ask me to run various errands for him around the complex, the restaurant, and the general area while people, including little kids, were in the pool, I would tell him I would, but not right then. This was for safety reasons, even with another lifeguard on duty at the deep end of the pool. He didn't like that response from me either.

My lifeguard instructor the year before had taught us over and over again, more than any other related issue, that when little kids were in the water, even in the shallow parts, 100% focus had to be given them. There were no exceptions to that rule, he repeatedly stressed during that course, as young kids could go under the water and drown in seconds. I didn't lose anyone the summer before, and I wasn't about to lose anyone this summer, especially a little kid. My tennis-pro/boss didn't seem to understand this notion. If a toilet had overflowed in the men's room, he wanted me handling it. He actually told me once at poolside, "The kids in the water will be fine, they have parents watching them."

Several weeks into the actual summer season, I stopped by after pool hours one Saturday evening with some friends. It was around 10:00PM and I was there to check on the water level to make sure the pool wasn't overflowing. I had routinely turned on the water to the pool before I left that day as the level had gone down. I happened to be driving by that evening and decided to make sure the water flow wasn't too strong or too weak. While there, I had some words with the clubhouse chef, a guy who was very friendly with the tennis-pro, when he challenged me for being by the pool when it was closed. He said he was told by our boss that he (the chef) could check the pool's water level. I advised him I didn't know of that arrangement and there ensued a mild disagreement as to who was in charge of the pool and who was in charge of the grill. I eventually left, but not before I decided for myself that the pool water level was fine.

The next day, Sunday, the tennis-pro was off or at least didn't come to the swimming pool area. On the following Monday morning, he called me into his office. He immediately referred to my stopping by the pool that Saturday night and allegedly arguing with the chef. I thought he may have appreciated me checking on the pool while technically "off-duty," but that wasn't the case as I was soon to learn. I also attempted to explain that the chef had been a bit aggressive and argumentative with me that night and that I had not appreciated it.

Apparently not hearing a word I said, the tennis-pro, in what sounded like a pre-prepared speech, then told me he didn't think I was the right "fit" to be pool captain at this facility. Without skipping a beat, he also told me he already called my brother-in-law and told him the situation. Well, the situation as he saw it anyway. Then, he told me it wasn't that bad though. I wasn't going to be fired. I could stay on as a regular lifeguard, but I was no longer to be the pool captain.

Now it all made sense. It seems, coincidently, at the end of the previous week, the tennis-pro, unbeknownst to me, had himself hired a comely young female that I had never met or even seen before as one of our new lifeguards. I thought we had our lifeguard staff complement filled at six of us, but I found out evidently we didn't when she showed up that day. He decided we needed one more, without even consulting me, his pool captain, about it.

The new lifeguard had told me that previous Friday that she had a Senior Lifesaving certificate but when I asked for the requisite card, as I did with every other lifeguard I had hired, she said she didn't have it with her. She said she would try to remember to bring it in the following week. I never did see it.

The boss then told me during my "demotion" conversation with him that Monday morning that she was now going to be the new pool captain, even though she just started three days ago and had minimal experience before being hired. It was pretty clear to me that as far as the tennis-pro went, this new pool captain's talents lied less with her breast-stroke than with her...well, other attributes.

The boss actually said to me that morning, "I think of everyone else here she is *breast*, I mean BEST, for the pool captain job."

I learned in my psychology course that year at PSU that what I heard him say is known as a Freudian Slip.

Obviously, she got the *breast*, I mean BEST, of me that summer.

Back to our brief conversation, I politely thanked the tennis-pro for my time there, but told him I was not interested in being demoted to a regular lifeguard. So, I quit on the spot. He said okay, but then asked me, as I was walking out of his office, to show the new pool captain how to backwash the filtration system and how to regulate the chlorinator.

Up until then, I was the only one there who knew how to do these every-other-day required tasks as I had learned them the year before at my two other pools. It wasn't a difficult task, but a bit tricky with the various valves and levers and chemical mixes that had to be coordinated in specific ways. I simply had not yet found the time to train the others. I would have eventually, but since I was demoted that day….

So, I took the new pool captain to the pump room and showed her everything I knew. Except, it MAY have been in the reverse order of how the tasks should have been undertaken.

I learned from Bill that in the next few days they had to call in a pool service for several hundred dollars to instruct her and the others how to properly undertake these every-other-day protocols.

What I did or didn't do in my final few minutes at the pool was probably less than professional on my part, I do admit, but I was upset, not thinking, and that's just how it happened. I'm sure the new pool captain learned the process eventually.

Also according to Bill, who worked there the rest of the summer, the pool captain and the tennis-pro would meet surreptitiously in that same pump room about once a week. No doubt, to make sure the requisite plumbing systems were backwashed and cleaned out as needed.

While this was a difficult moment in my young life, which also upset my parents as I was now out of work for a while that summer, as it turns out this was the only job I ever held in which I faced a demotion, or worse. I was never fired or demoted again at any job. Better it happened at that job, I later reckoned, than in one of the more critical positions I held as I moved on in my chosen profession. A life lesson there to be sure, learned by me while wearing swim trunks and sunblock.

My quitting this lifeguard job, more out of pride than anything else, marked the end of my relatively brief lifeguarding career. It only lasted one full summer and about one-third of another. After a few weeks off, it was to nearby Fleer's (the bubble gum factory), and Sears (the retailer, in their warehouse), for my next jobs over this and the part of the following summer. Not as glamorous as being a lifeguard, but they paid the bills. Most importantly, to this day, I can still say I never lost a swimmer; a pool captain title yes, but never a swimmer.

Lastly, on the topic of lifeguarding, as it happens, the following summer I did, in fact, rescue a young woman from some rough surf off the beach of Ocean City, New Jersey. On that late afternoon, I recall walking along the beach with a friend in an area that was not presently under lifeguard supervision. (I believe it rained most of that day, and the lifeguards didn't have to report to their posts.) I first heard and then saw, a young woman, perhaps in her late teens, beyond the breakers and calling for help. She was in the water with a friend, who wasn't out as far and was not in distress. The woman wasn't overtly panicking, but she definitely was yelling for assistance of some sort as no one else was attempting to help her. She apparently had no flotation devices anywhere near her.

I went running toward her and then swam out to her location, talking to her on the way, and did my best to calm her down. As the water was over her head, she had been bouncing up and down from the bottom to take in breaths of air. But, she couldn't swim or bounce back to shallower water on her own because of the strong current. I got to her pretty quickly and right away put her into the standard arm-across-the-chest-her-back-to-my-side carry position as I was taught and swam on an angle, sort of with the current, to shallower water with her.

When we reached around chest high water, I slowly released her and made sure she could stand on her own. She could, although just barely at first. Without even looking back at me, she immediately waded over to her friend and once on the sand they walked away, giggling while doing so. She never said thanks, or that she appreciated my effort, or that I'm a nice guy, or can she buy me a hotdog on the boardwalk, or anything similar. Honestly, it really didn't matter that much to me, but I thought she would at least acknowledge to me to some degree that maybe, just maybe, I got her out of a potentially dangerous situation. But, alas, she didn't.

Oh well, I was just doing my job. Wait! Actually, it was NOT my job that day. I was a "retired" lifeguard at that point, although my three-year Red Cross certificate would still be valid for another year. I was just taking a stroll on the beach that day and helped this damsel in distress whilst in over her head, literally. Hopefully, she learned someday to thank people who may have potentially saved her life, got her out of harm's way, or helped her out in ANY way, for that matter.

Geez, what is it about me helping out animals and/or people on or near the beach? Never even a thank you from them.

At least I wasn't arrested this last time.

Chapter Fourteen

With summer over, it was back to school for me. It was the beginning of my sophomore year at Penn State's Ogontz campus that I met a fellow sophomore who later would become semi-infamous in the Philadelphia area. His name was Dave Downey. Years later, while reading of his deadly exploits, I would put my then-profiling skills to work in an erstwhile attempt to determine if there was anything I may have noticed about him, retrospectively, in the relatively short time we hung out together as young college students. If only, I thought later in life, if only....

I met Dave through mutual friends at the Penn State Ogontz campus. Like all college students, I was sharing classes and the accompanying academic settings with a growing number of new friends. We hung out during lunch, between classes in the large community room, after school, in the parking lot, and as we became friendlier, more and more on Friday and Saturday nights.

During this time we were experiencing the party scenes at various locales, mostly at other nearby colleges, and on Boathouse Row, along the Schuylkill River in Philadelphia. These were several old, well, boathouses, where local colleges maintained their equipment and their teams were headquartered. The large buildings also had second floors above where the boats were stored in which lots of college parties took place, usually sponsored by various fraternities, athletic clubs, etc. These were usually called "Beef and Beers," and the admission price back then was $5.00 for all the roast beef sandwiches (of varying quality) one could eat and all the beer (also of varying quality) one could drink. These weren't Penn State parties as Ogontz was a commuter campus with no dorms or any real local party scene. But, as I had friends at other Philadelphia area colleges, we always had something going on somewhere on their campuses or on Boathouse Row, quasi-school related, on the weekends.

Dave Downey became part of this newly formed hybrid crowd. It was an interesting mix of my core Olney and Cardinal Dougherty High School friends and then each of us now meeting new friends at our respective colleges. These other schools included St. Joseph's College where Bill Sena and Tim Klarich attended and Philadelphia College of Textiles and Science where Tom Lubas attended. We would integrate these campuses into our weekend social scene, wherever and whatever that may have entailed. I had numerous new college friends, male and female, all relatively (well, mostly) stable and balanced and virtually all of them getting along with my Olney and high school friends, and in turn their new friends from their respective schools.

I wasn't completely sure about Dave Downey back then as he was a strange guy in some ways. But, we all sort of put up with him. He could be funny at times, cool at times, but again, with some odd ways in what he said and did. Years later, that oddness was certainly confirmed, in glaring and very disturbing newspaper headlines.

Unlike us Olney guys who grew up in rowhomes, Dave grew up in a large single home in the suburbs, specifically Montgomery County, PA. His dad was a successful businessman and his older brother was an equally successful attorney. Out of his presence, we would kiddingly refer to him as one of the "rich kids." He was a very good golfer and was even on the PSU Ogontz golf team. He wasn't a bad looking guy and had a very cute girl-friend, soon to be his fiancé, then wife.

Dave came to my 3rd Street house on a few oc-casions where we would watch sports on the black and white TV in my parents' living room. (Yes, at this stage, I was allowed to bring friends in the house, and not restrict them to just the front porch.) I don't think I was ever invited inside Dave's sub-urban home, although I drove there to pick him up or drop him off on occasion.

As New Jersey had lowered the drinking age to 18 sometime in the early 1970s (but Pennsylvania did not), when the weekend college party scene wasn't happening we would sometimes drive across the Tacony-Palmyra Bridge to socialize at the NJ bars and clubs. Dave would invariably come with us on some of those nights. Suffice it to say, he didn't handle alcoholic beverages very well. On more than one occasion, he would do and say em-barrassing things to us and to others, sometimes causing problems for all of us. He was one of those guys who would get in a heated argument with someone or some group and then miraculously be nowhere around once the fists started flying.

After one such night visiting some NJ bar, fortunately with no such fights breaking out, before leaving for home and still in the parking lot with me in the back seat of Dave's car with my girlfriend Eileen, and him in the front seat with his recently announced fiancé, he surprised me by asking me in a somewhat drunken state a question.

He mumbled in barely recognizable interrogatory form, "Fitz, would you be in my wedding? You know, one of my groomsmen?"

Upon hearing the question and before I could answer, his fiancé immediately turned her head to her left and glared at him. It was pretty clear that her look was a distinct non-verbal reaction to him indicating that perhaps she would have liked to have been a part of this request of me. She evidently wasn't. It's not that I think she had a specific problem with me, or didn't like me; it's just that she probably would have preferred to have been asked first about the possibility of my joining their wedding party, being in their photos for life, etc.

In the meantime, from the backseat I responded matter-of-factly, "Sure, why not? What's the date again?"

Then, off we drove, back to PA. Actually, Dave's fiancé got behind the wheel and drove us home. She was in much better driving shape than Dave. And, she didn't say a word the whole way home. Her non-verbals were speaking volumes.

Interestingly, the subject of Dave's wedding never came up again. I was not a member of his wedding party for this marriage or any subsequent marriages of his. As it turned out, I wasn't even invited to his wedding the following year. Strange, I know, but it gets stranger.

It was at a New Year's Eve party as 1972 was turning to 1973 that Dave really pushed his luck with some people in this ever-growing mixed crowd of mine. I sort of reluctantly invited him to a party that night thrown by some friends in East Oak Lane, a Philadelphia neighborhood directly adjacent to Olney. Later that night, I saved his butt from a severe beating. Years later I realized that my interference may have been a mistake.

Somewhere approaching midnight that New Year's Eve, among the mixed group of people at this party, Dave was doing his well-worn "frog impersonation" on the floor. His act involved him crawling along the floor making sounds like a croaking frog. It was probably funny maybe for 10 seconds the first time he did it. Actually, in retrospect it was never funny, not even the first time. But, it got even less funny, if that's possible, every single time afterwards that he chose to do it. That night, he probably did it for upwards of ten minutes in front of many people he didn't know. Yes, consumption of alcohol was involved, more on his part than most others that night.

There was one guy at the party who was not one of our college friends. His name was John Pat Loughran. After graduating in my class from CDHS, he worked at a manufacturing company somewhere in Philadelphia. He was a guy I sort of knew from high school. He was a nice guy, a funny guy, and I always got along well with him. Oh, and he liked to drink and when the situation presented itself, he liked to fight. He could handle himself very well in both categories, especially fisticuffs-wise. It was clearly in John Pat's DNA. His uncle was 1920s Light Heavyweight Champion, Tommy Loughran. One just had to be careful not to cross him at certain points of certain evenings. John Pat and I never had a problem in that regard though.

I once saw John Pat in a rematch with a bouncer who, on the previous Memorial Day weekend one summer, had sucker-punched him and physically got the better of him at a New Jersey seashore bar. John Pat went back three months later, on the Sunday night of Labor Day weekend, waited for the bar to close, went up to the bouncer and said, "Remember me?"

The bouncer said he did and agreed to fight John Pat in the parking lot, one-on-one in this rematch. Needless to say, the bouncer, without the benefit of a surprise punch, and now in a "fair" fight this time, lost badly in this sequel bout with John Pat.

Back at the New Year's Eve party, John Pat, along with the rest of us, was watching Dave do his stupid frog act. He had never met Dave before, but I could tell he clearly didn't like him, even before Dave's reptilian beer-crawl. I should add here that Dave could also be a wise guy and his attempts at humor and insults could push the limits, especially of those who did not know him or his personality very well. I believe he tossed a few playful insults in the direction of John Pat that night, which only served to foment a slowly building anger. I could clearly see, knowing John Pat, how he badly wanted to kick Dave's ass. His ongoing consumption of alcohol and Dave's ongoing bizarre behavior both continued to fuel that interest.

John Pat looked at me a few times and simply said, "Fitz, I just gotta kick this guy's ass. He's such a f***in' asshole. Who invited him here, anyway?"

I dodged the last question, but I wholeheartedly agreed with John Pat in his former two statements, and I told him so. Nonetheless, I proceeded to talk him out of what would have clearly been a very one-sided beating. It took a while, and not without some attempted use of beer-laced logic and rationale, but John Pat eventually changed his mind. Perhaps it was less me convincing him to abstain from initiating a Dave Downey bloodbath than his newly formed attention to a young woman at the party with whom he was hoping to plant a stroke-of-midnight kiss. I gently directed him to that alternative by calling her over and introducing John Pat to her. Dave's beating was thusly averted.

I managed to get Dave off the floor and into his car (again, with his fiancé driving him home) shortly thereafter. He never knew how close he came to getting his clock severely cleaned that night, perhaps well into another time zone.

But, was it a good decision on my part to intervene and alter Dave's destiny that night? Starting in 2005, I asked myself that question repeatedly.

Later that summer of '73, after my shortened lifeguard season and a few odd jobs, I went with Rich Davoli, a good friend of mine since first grade at St. Helena School, all through CDHS, and now PSU, to a fellow Ogontz campus student's house in the Philadelphia suburbs. It was a mini-going away party for the three of us who were leaving to go to PSU's Main Campus at State College to do our last two years there. We stayed overnight at the friend's house listening to music, having a few beers, etc. Dave Downey was there too. The party was his idea as he was not heading to State College that fall. And, much like Dave, he planned for the party to be at someone else's house, and with him contributing little to it.

Later that night, maybe around 3:00AM, Dave suddenly said goodbye and left, we thought to go home. The rest of us then proceeded to go to sleep on a pair of couches and a recliner in our friend's rec room. It was time to settle in for a peaceful, late night respite.

But, Dave's night wasn't yet over. He came back around 4:00AM, woke us up, and asked me and Rich to go for a ride with him. We initially said "No," it was too late, we were tired, etc., but he kept bugging us to go. He said he wanted to play a really cool practical joke on someone and he wanted our help. Rich and I looked at each other from our respective sleeping posts and reluctantly gave in to Dave's request. He then drove us a relatively short distance in his car to a supposed high school buddy's house who he "knew" was home but his parents weren't, and he wanted to play this trick on him. We weren't sure exactly what he wanted to do, but we went along with his idea anyway.

When we got to Dave's alleged friend's house, a large single home in one of the adjacent neighborhoods to where we were staying, he wanted to go inside and awaken him with a cold bucket of water, or something like that, as this guy supposedly did the same thing to him once before. The back sliding glass doors there were usually unlocked, Dave told us, and he was proven right that night. I questioned aloud the rationale of the three of us doing this, but nonetheless, and stupidly, we went along with Dave.

Next thing we know we were inside this guy's darkened house. Upon going upstairs to his bedroom, Dave leading the way, it was determined shortly afterwards that he was not there. In fact, no one was in the house. It was at that time that I realized we were...gulp...committing a burglary, as in a felony offense.

In no small way did I like what was happening here, and as the sun was not far from rising, I suggested that we get out of the place. Dave insisted on going to his buddy's bedroom and taking some record albums, "just for fun," as the guy had not returned some to him that he borrowed, or some such story like that. Rich and I told Dave to do what he wanted to do and we'd meet him out in the car. We then insisted on leaving now before one of the neighbors saw us three guys and called the police. He had a handful of something when the three of us exited the house and we walked to the car. Then, we drove off and went back to the now darkened party house. Dave then went home.

Nothing further ever happened regarding this "burglary." I'm not sure if Dave ever re-contacted his buddy or not about this clandestine entry or returned what he took "...just for fun." I was an inadvertent burglar that night and in months and years to come I often thought that if the police had arrived that morning and arrested us I doubt if Dave's story to them would have sufficed. I don't know if his alleged buddy OR his parents would have "vouched" for Dave or the two of us (whom they had never even met before) if ever confronted regarding this burglary.

Rich and I clearly made a bad decision that night. We should not have gone with Dave to play the "practical joke" on his real or imagined old high school chum. I'm not even sure after all of these years if he really did know the guy who lived in that house. The few times I saw Dave afterwards, when asked about that night, he would only half-jokingly reply, "Hmmmmm....I THOUGHT that was my buddy's house, now I'm not so sure...." He'd then laugh out loud. Geez, where was John Pat when I needed him? Not that I couldn't have handled the task myself, but watching John Pat do it would have made it much more enjoyable.

I was sure then that I didn't want to hang out with Dave anymore. Luckily, he was not going with us to State College.

I lost track of Dave Downey over the next year and the subsequent three decades. He decided, like some other of the PSU/Ogontz sophomores, that he did not want to go to the main campus of Penn State for his last two years. He instead transferred to Temple University in Philadelphia. I doubt if I saw him more than two times again after 1974.

Beginning in 2005, however, I learned more about Dave Downey's life than I ever knew about him even back in the early '70s. It was way more than I would have ever cared to learn about him. Most other people, too, as he apparently developed into a truly creepy adult. As it turns out, he was the "Montco (for Montgomery County, PA) Business-man" that the newspaper headlines and local TV news anchors referenced after his complicity in the death of a 17-year-old woman.

It seems that after two failed marriages, and bouncing around a few technology consulting jobs in the area (albeit with some level of financial success), Dave was single again and liked to frequent strip bars and engage various "escorts" on given occasions. He apparently had a propensity to lie about his background to the people he would run into at these various venues. He had a U.S. Navy Seal tattoo on his leg and would advise some that he was retired from that specialized unit. He told others he was a CIA operative, and still in "operating" mode. Women and men seemingly believed him, or at least some of them. He apparently could be a convincing liar.

On July 30, 2005, according to media and police sources, he contacted one of his former escorts and requested yet another "girl," and also some cocaine. As a result, 17 year-old Ashley Burg was dropped off at his Montco residence along with two "8-balls" of cocaine. Exactly what happened that night is now known only to Dave, but somehow drugs were ingested and the young woman passed out on his living room couch. She then essentially stopped breathing. She later died on his couch, according to the subsequent autopsy.

However, instead of calling the police, Dave waited until the next day to re-contact the escort service complaining about the lack of "service" from young Ashley. Two of their representatives came back to his place the following night. There they apparently argued with Dave, but after he agreed to pay them an additional $2600, they eventually agreed to take the young woman's body and dump it somewhere. Ashley wound up in an empty lot in Northeast Philadelphia.

Ms. Burg's body was found within minutes after it was placed in the lot on the morning of August 1. She was identified shortly thereafter. The subsequent investigation led to Dave, and he was arrested by Montgomery County detectives, as that is where her death occurred and they had jurisdiction of the crime. The police allege that he provided the drugs to the young escort, which directly contributed to her death. Then, he conspired to dispose of her body.

Despite these charges, Dave's bail was set at $250,000, and he managed to post ten percent of it and was released from lock-up. Within days, he was spotted at some of the same strip clubs. While there, he actually contracted with yet another escort, this time asking her if she could get "stuff" (drugs) with which to "party." This information eventually got back to the judge who originally issued his bail and it was subsequently revoked. He was then held in detention awaiting his trial. All of this was covered extensively in the Philadelphia area media.

Dave's trial a year or so later was a relatively brief one and reportedly very one-sided. He attempted to have character witnesses testify on his behalf, but none ultimately agreed to do so. They'd have to tell the truth about his character and that wouldn't work well for Dave in front of a jury. In fact, people came forward from various personal and professional aspects of his life to say how much he was a bully and a jerk to them and others.

With the jury returning a guilty verdict on the charge of delivery of a drug that caused death,

Dave was sentenced to 8 to 17 years in state prison. As of this writing, he's still incarcerated somewhere in the Pennsylvania penal system.

Of course, I realize that even if I had let John Pat kick the crap out of Dave on that long-ago New Year's Eve (or even if I undertook the pleasure at some later date), it would not necessarily have made a difference in his life, certainly not as it relates to the death of Ashley Burg. But, part of me, just a small part of me, after the tricked-into burglary, and especially after the death of young Ashley in Dave's company years later, had me wishing I had done nothing to interfere with a beating that he arguably had coming to him. If not for what he was doing that New Year's Eve, then for what he would do to that young woman three decades later.

I know, life shouldn't and doesn't necessarily work that way. But sometimes, just sometimes, people deserve life lessons, even if in unorthodox ways and years before it may be so earned, as in this case. Believing in cause and effect, I'm convinced it's not necessarily disconnected in situations such as this.

I deprived Dave of that beating by John Pat that evening as the clock approached midnight. I'll never know if it would have made a difference to him, or for Ashley Burg many years later, as midnight approached in her young life. I can only imagine....

In the fall of '74, John Pat would figure into another almost-fight in which I played a role in preventing. This time, it was at the PSU main campus. It was almost a career-ender for me, before my career even started, and with Dave Downey nowhere to be found.

More on this crazy scenario forthcoming....

Chapter Fifteen

On Easter Sunday of 1973, John Welsh was in a very bad car accident in New Jersey. He and several other friends were driving back around 5:00AM from a popular bar in the shore town of Margate, NJ, which is near Atlantic City. Denny Friel, another Olney guy who lived not far from me, was driving his large station wagon and John and Joe Widmeier were asleep in the back of the vehicle. The rear two seats of the station wagon were in the down position. On the way home that morning, Denny also fell asleep, crossed over several lanes of traffic, and slammed into another car. Everyone sustained injuries, but Joe was hurt the worst. John, fortunately, only suffered relatively minor injuries, Denny too.

Many of our circle of friends, including me, didn't learn of the accident until the following Monday. I finally saw John back at the Ogontz campus on Tuesday or Wednesday of that week. He was banged up, but able to attend classes. The news for Joe wasn't good though. As it turns out, he would never walk again. He was paralyzed from the waist down as a result of this car crash.

I wasn't best of friends with Joe Widmeier before the accident. I knew him from St. Helena

School and the general Olney area, but as he didn't attend Cardinal Dougherty High School, I simply wasn't that close to him back then. As John Welsh was getting friendlier with him, and as I was getting friendlier with John, I did socialize with Joe a few times in early '73.

After several months recovering from his treatable injuries in an area hospital, Joe would eventually be sent to Johnstown, Pennsylvania, to a special rehabilitation unit for paraplegics. Among other things over the next half-year there, he learned to drive a car using hand controls. He acquired his own car and would come to visit us on weekends at the main campus of Penn State, in State College, which was only 90 minutes or so away from Johnstown. John Welsh was there too that year, our junior year, and Joe added quite an interesting dynamic to those of us from Olney and CD now attending school in the foothills of central Pennsylvania.

Pushing Joe around in his wheelchair attained him, and sometimes us, many benefits on or near campus, including free meals in the dining halls (for Joe and other visiting friends, the rest of us already had our meal passes), drinks in bars, etc. To Joe's credit, he rarely if ever complained out loud to any of his friends about his condition. I've always said that I wasn't sure if I would have handled the functional loss of my legs with the same aplomb as did Joe. But, he was a fun guy who did not want to miss out on any activities wherever he may be, stuck in a wheelchair or not. At Penn State, that would include football games, frat parties, the bar scenes, etc.

Joe soon learned it was much more beneficial for him to tell young women he would casually meet that he was a military vet and had been critically injured in the jungles of Vietnam. As the war had effectively ended the year or so before, his story was perfect. Even some actual Vietnam vets we got to know on campus told him to "go for it." If it helped him with the ladies, they said, why not?

While I would never have used the wounded vet storyline myself, nor recommend it to others, I figured a guy in a wheelchair, recently paralyzed, can tell any story he likes in this regard if it makes him feel even temporarily better about his difficult situation. He didn't use this story all the time, but when he did it seemed to work for him, socially-speaking, that is. He would get invited back to more women's dorms and apartments than most of us, his otherwise able-bodied friends. The stories he would tell us the next day, after the young women would somehow roll him back to our dorms, were always good ones.

Talk about a "walk of shame," make that a "roll of shame." It didn't bother Joe though, or apparently the women who walked/rolled him back to us.

Whether all the stories were true or not, it didn't matter. Joe, while not being a college student at PSU, was having as much if not more fun than many of the students there, certainly among our crowd, and with no exams to take or papers to write either.

Knowing Joe, a guy who was healthy and with use of all his limbs just a relatively short while ago, to then suddenly lose use of half those limbs to a car accident, made it very difficult for me to deal with when it happened. It was scary too that John Welsh, with whom I was much closer at the time, could have been just as easily paralyzed or killed. Much like with Smitty who fell down the elevator shaft a year-and-a-half before, these were guys I knew, in my loose crowd of friends, from my old neighborhood, who were learning the very hard way the reality of life.

We were slowly deducing, explicitly and implicitly, that we were mortal and bad things could happen to those who took unnecessary risks, or to those who fell asleep in the back seats of someone's moving station wagon. Guys in their teens and early twenties have to learn this sometimes the hard way, and sometimes after it's way too late.

Besides experiencing all I could on campus from a social perspective, to include the positive and the negative, I was, by the way, also attending my LEC and other classes at PSU. A fellow student in at least two of my LEC classes was John Cappeletti. He was on the PSU football team and he won the Heisman Trophy in 1973. On the day it was announced, there was an impromptu parade around and through campus with John sitting up on the back seat of a convertible. I didn't know him all that well, but we would chat before and after classes on occasion. He was a friendly and humble guy and a great PSU football player and role model for others.

The LEC program itself was valuable because, besides the interesting academic courses offered, it was also mandatory that students undertake at least two internships, or practicums as they were called back then. We could choose them from a wide selection of local, state, and federal agencies. My first one was the summer of '74 with the Pennsylvania Board of Probation and Parole. It was at one of their satellite offices located in the Kensington neighborhood of Philadelphia. It would eventually become a very meaningful experience for me, in more than one way.

While doing my practicum at the Probation and Parole office, I got to interview real "criminals," well, criminals on parole (supervision after their release from prison), and probation (supervision in lieu of them going to prison). Some I interviewed in the office, some when I would travel to their homes. While I was teamed up with a seasoned probation officer initially, I did eventually undertake some of these routine status-check interviews on my own. These were not necessarily hardened parolees or probationers, as most had been previously convicted of non-violent type crimes. All of these guys were well on their way to "rehabilitation," long-time parolees or probationers, and did not cause any problems for me. Either way, it was really cool at the time to have an actual caseload of eight "clients." I completed a brief "contact report" after each meeting, and these reports became part of their official files. These were the first group of people in my life to refer to me as "Mr. Fitzgerald." I guess I was becoming a real adult. Well, at least during these eight weeks, anyway. But, there would be relapses coming up; two big ones, to be sure.

This proved to be a very interesting and enlightening summer for me, working for the first time in an office environment, being dressed up in a jacket and tie for a job (albeit, a non-paying job) every day, handling phone calls having to do with official criminal justice business, hanging out with real members of the criminal justice system, attending parole revocation hearings, etc. The staff, comprised of a few retired Philadelphia police officers, other career probation officers and two secretaries were very nice and treated me very professionally, even though I was just a third-year college student. One night, I even brought one of the agents back to my parents' home for dinner as I was giving him a ride to his house that evening. My parents liked this guy and so did I. He became one of my early professional mentors.

On my last day at my office internship, the boss sent me with another agent to Philadelphia City Hall to pick up some routine paperwork. When I got back in the afternoon, the office personnel had arranged a surprise going-away party for me. It was great. My first surprise party since I was a little kid. The boss called me into his office that day and said he liked how I handled myself over the summer internship and he'd be glad to help facilitate my way to becoming a state probation officer someday. I was to let him know when I was about to graduate (in less than a year from that point) and he would see what he could do with references, phone calls, etc., to help me get on board with the State.

Apparently, I impressed these people, these real working professionals. They liked me and told me they thought I would make a great probation officer one day. That was such a good feeling. It was an accomplishment, in its own little way, actually make that in a big way, and one of which I was very proud. I spent time in a real criminal justice-oriented office and I impressed the people who worked there; people employed in the field for decades in the case of some of them. I was on my way in my newly chosen profession.

Or so I thought.

But, I blew it. I did something really stupid one night, less than two months later, while back at the PSU main campus. It had a tangential connection with my just completed internship. That problem was then compounded at virtually the same time by yet another potentially serious problem having to do with that piece of paper and badge I attained from the guy who broke Kerry's arm awhile back during the supermarket arm wrestling match.

There were two perfect or perhaps very much imperfect storms coming at me at the same time, with me alone as the rainmaker.

I clearly had not matured yet, no matter what the folks in the probation and parole office thought of me.

Damn...!

It's possible though, what happened over the next few months, forced maturation on me for good, even if a bit late in its arrival. And it was like a sledge hammer to the head; actually, make that two of them.

I went back to PSU in September of '74 for my final trimester at the main campus. I had two more trimesters of undergrad schooling to go, but this was to be my last college term away from home. While I lived in an apartment building my junior year at PSU with three other guys, Rich Davoli being one of them, it didn't work out so well in the long run. So, for my one term left at the main campus my senior year, about seven of my other CDHS and Ogontz friends (none that I lived with the previous year), and me, all decided to stay in the Nittany Dorms, aka the Barracks, aka the Chicken Coops, in the northeast quadrant of the campus.

These dorms were around 20 older style single story dorm buildings, built during World War II, that while not as fancy as some of the other dorms on campus, they had one distinct advantage over the other dorms. They were all single rooms, and at no extra cost. So, the eight of us were spread out over several of these buildings. We kiddingly referred to ourselves as "The Nittany 8." Jim Coyle (the future best man at my wedding), Ray Geary (with whom I would attain my first official law enforcement job), Larry Morrissey (a future Bureau of Alcohol, Tobacco, and Firearms agent), John Welsh, and weekender Joe Widmeier, an honorary member, were among the eight.

As one of the Nittany 8ers that trimester, John Welsh somehow managed to have a dorm room with bunk beds. When Joe Widmeier would come for a visit from Johnstown, John would sleep in the top bunk and Joe in the bottom. It was a great set-up. While we were all good friends, after some of us had roommate problems during our respective junior years at PSU, we found it better to live in our own individual rooms, even if it was with a large shared bathroom down the hall and very close to the chicken coops on campus. And yes, we heard the chickens every morning at sunrise. It didn't mean we necessarily got out of our respective dorm room beds then, but we certainly did hear them.

Interestingly, since my early college days, along with my fascination in ongoing crime related stories, I had also been following in the media the burgeoning radical movements that had developed across the U.S. These were mostly left-wing groups originating at some of the more prestigious universities throughout the country. The protesting of the Vietnam War was the genesis for many of these groups, but they evolved to general anti-government ideologies once the war ended. Some of these protests, all non-violent, took place on the PSU main campus, but our school was by no means a hotbed of this sort of activity.

My interest in this aspect of our culture was piqued with the kidnapping of newspaper heiress Patty Hearst in 1974 from the apartment she shared with her boyfriend in California. The Symbionese Liberation Army (SLA) claimed responsibility for it and before long it was determined that at least some of the members of this violent and radical group were former college students and left-wing activists. The non-student members of these groups tended to be hardened criminals and ex-cons. These people, at least the student members, were around my age and in many ways not too dissimilar from me in terms of our general backgrounds.

As I read and assimilated more information, specifically about the Patty Hearst kidnapping, more questions followed. How could a group such as this successfully kidnap someone like Hearst? And, how could they not only control her while holding her as their hostage, but also get her to seemingly join their radical, anti-government movement?

It was only weeks after her abduction that Hearst was committing bank robberies and other violent crimes with her kidnappers, even shooting at people during the commission of these acts. The answers to these questions for me, and no doubt for many other interested parties, wouldn't be known for a few more years.

Patty Hearst was the most wanted person in the U.S. in the mid-'70s, with her picture posted almost everywhere, including on the FBI's Ten Most Wanted List, and with frequent media coverage of her and what she and her group may be doing at a given time. I used to occasionally fantasize about being the one who somehow spotted her in a public place, which would then lead to her capture and arrest.

I was at PSU in State College for some of Hearst's time as a fugitive, and while there and when sometimes driving back and forth to Philadelphia, I would half-kiddingly tell my fellow Nittany 8ers, and whomever else would listen, that I was earnestly looking for her on campus and in passing cars and roadside rest stops in my quest to hopefully find her. After all, her and her generally college-aged associates hiding out in a large campus environment was not that much of a stretch. I figured if I somehow found her, firstly, I'd get the very healthy monetary reward. Secondly, the FBI would be very appreciative of it. And thirdly, it would be great on my resume to then get a job somewhere in the law enforcement community.

During those days of my Patty Hearst lookout, I would envision the latter scenario in future job-related interview sessions.

"So, Mr. Fitzgerald, why should we hire you as an officer/investigator at our agency?"

I'd of course reply, "Well, let's see...I have an LEC degree from PSU, I'm in overall good shape,

I'm bright, well-read, dedicated, hard-working, and oh yeah, I helped the FBI arrest Patty Hearst. Does that help?"

My PSU buddies used to kid me over this semi-serious "fugitive hunt" of mine. They would say to me, "What would Patty Hearst be doing in Central Pennsylvania? She's from California."

I'd respond, semi-seriously, "Exactly! No one is looking for her here. What better place to hide out."

Despite their reservations, and sometimes mine too, quite frankly, I nonetheless did keep my eyes open for her. I never saw her though, although a few look-a-likes crossed my path. I even bought a beer for a Patty Hearst-esque looking woman at the My-O-My bar in State College one night, using her facial and general overall similarities to the wanted fugitive as my introductory line. That was, of course, once I clearly determined it wasn't her, or at least I was pretty sure it wasn't her. Later that evening, the woman commented that it was a very different sort of pick-up line I used on her. I told her it wasn't really a pick-up line, but that I was on an actual quest to find the wanted heiress *cum* bank robber. She didn't seem to understand my meaning and left after finishing the three beers I bought her.

By the way, I did confirm she was NOT Patty Hearst. At least I'm pretty sure it wasn't her. It would have been truly devastating if, let's say, we had kept talking at the bar that night and then afterwards if I had taken her back to my dorm room, and let's say she somehow stayed over and, well, you know, and then after she left I found out it was actually Hearst. That scenario would NOT have played out very well at any future job interviews. I think I'd have to keep that little barroom and dorm room incident to myself, if it ever did happen. I'd rationalize it somehow in that I don't "kiss and tell."

And, for the record, that scenario did NOT happen.

When Hearst was eventually arrested in San Francisco in September of '75, it was revealed that while on the lam she had, in fact, driven to and spent some time in the Pennsylvania Poconos, a region about 100 miles from PSU. She and her cohorts undoubtedly passed within 20 miles of the PSU campus while en route there and back.

When this information became public, I had to contact my various PSU friends with whom I shared this quest. I said a simple "See, I was right!" They reluctantly agreed.

Back to my everyday life on campus that term, on random days during the middle of the week during the fall football season of '74, I would observe then-head coach Joe Paterno walking through our part of the campus, cutting right between some of our Nittany dorm buildings. It was never clear to me from where he was coming or to where he was going. He was always alone, carrying a large manila-style envelope of some sort, and tended to be walking in the direction of the nearby football stadium when I would see him.

On occasion, my friends and I would toss a football around in an open area in the center of our dorm buildings. One of these times, Coach Paterno just happened to be walking by when we were out there with football in hand. I had one of my friends throw me a long pass as I did a buttonhook pattern pretty close to where Joe was walking. Not right in front of him to make it too obvious, but near enough. I caught the football and slowly looked up at him as I ran back toward my friend. From a slight distance when our eyes met and without slowing his pace at all he calmly said to me, "Nice catch, kid."

I replied, somewhat ecstatically, "Thanks, Coach," and ran back toward my buddies. They didn't hear what he said to me and didn't believe me when I told them what he said. It was our little secret, I guess.

Coach Paterno never reached out to me after my version of "the catch." He never sent his recruiters around my dorms attempting to find out who that guy was who made such a great reception right in front of him that day. No doubt, his complement of wide receivers on the team for that year was complete with guys all much faster and bigger than me. But, it was nonetheless a small honor to have him comment aloud on my catch, lo those many years ago.

While I certainly saw Coach Paterno on the sidelines at football games at Beaver Stadium over the years, and for decades watching my college team play on TV, this was my one and only close-up and personal experience with him.

I admired Joe Pa and continue to respect him greatly, even after the child abuse scandal unfolded at Penn State in 2012.

I was now in my senior year at PSU. I knew I needed a break from academic life before long and graduate school was simply not in the plans for me at this time. After now being in my 16th straight year of formal education, I wanted to get into the real world, have a real job, and earn some real money. Doing what, exactly, with my degree in LEC, I did not yet know.

This was to be my last trimester at the main campus of PSU. The upcoming winter term would be another practicum, and for the final spring trimester I somehow managed to work it out where I could live at home and finish up my degree back at the Ogontz campus. I had my senior year planned out, I knew what lied ahead, at least for the rest of my academic year, and was all ready to graduate in June.

My academic standing at PSU was fine. Not necessarily stellar, but I knew I would be graduating soon, certainly with a good GPA in my major of LEC. But, there were two other issues I had to address. They were separate, but somewhat comingled, and they would potentially get in the way of my further entry into adult life, my post-graduation, and oh yes, possibly curtail my entire future career. Two bad and stupid decisions were made on my part; one done in almost an instant, and the other over the course of a year or so.

Would I ever learn?

Chapter Sixteen

It all started this way....

While working at the aforementioned previous summer's practicum at the Pennsylvania State Bureau of Probation and Parole, at their Kensington (Philadelphia) neighborhood office, I was allowed to use generic business cards to identify myself to my eight parolee and probationer clients. These cards had the official seal, agency name, phone number and address on them, but the name and title area in its center was left blank. I had received authorization to type my name on them, thus making them official business cards and thus identifying myself as a representative of the agency. I provided the cards to the eight or so clients that I was handling that summer and instructed them to contact me if they had any problems. This was long before the advent of email and cell phones, so only the office landline number was included on the card. If they needed me after my summer practicum ended, they would simply deal with a full-time probation officer then.

The cards worked fine and there was no problem with them during my practicum. I had inadvertently made an extra one earlier that summer and decided to keep it with me in my wallet as a keepsake of my work in the office. No one in the office asked me for the extra one back, so I figured it was no big deal. Well, the extra business card shouldn't have been a big deal, but I made it into one while back on the PSU campus in October of '74.

Joe Widmeier was visiting for a weekend, along with John Pat Loughran (the guy whom I should have let beat up future convicted murderer Dave Downey), and another Olney and CDHS guy named Ned Graham, who was a year younger than me and enrolled at the PSU Ogontz campus. Visitors such as this weren't uncommon as friends from other Philly schools would travel to PSU on a semi-regular basis and crash in our various Nittany barracks dorms. This weekend was destined to be different though.

On the Saturday night of that weekend, after an exciting afternoon football game at Beaver Stadium (it was either against Wake Forrest or Syracuse), and after dinner at the dorms, my buddies and I with nothing else specific to do walked (and rolled Joe) through the campus and its immediate environs. This was not uncommon as there was always something happening somewhere on or near campus on football weekends, either inside or outside. So, we roamed around that night looking for something to do.

After bar hopping a bit, we eventually found ourselves along fraternity row on the south side of campus. We heard from a distance what sounded like an interesting social event and decided to follow the noise and check it out. We turned a corner, saw a bunch of guys and gals throwing around Frisbees and footballs on the front lawn of a large frat house, with loud, live band music emanating from their basement, and realized this was the party we had been hearing from a distance. It was the Pi-something-something fraternity house.

Upon getting closer and seeing the Greek name on the side of the frat house it hit me. This was the place where, just a few weeks before, two other Nittany barracks dorm mates of mine were assaulted. They were not officially Nittany 8ers (as they weren't from Philadelphia or the Ogontz Campus), but they were friends of ours nevertheless. On that night they had been walking by the frat and, after some comments from several guys on the porch, a fight ensued on the front lawn. They were beaten-up pretty badly. I knew they were not the type of guys to start a fight, especially when outnumbered and on the home turf of these particular frat boys.

These friends told us that one of the frat guys there even pulled a baseball bat and swung it a few times at them, but fortunately didn't hit either of them directly with it. They described the bat-wielder as a short guy wearing a Pittsburgh Steelers jersey with #12 on it. For some reason, I remembered this guy and their description of him. Despite the near misses with the bat on that night, my dorm mates/friends still took some solid punches to the face and kicks to the body when they were down on the ground from the four or five guys on the other end of their beating. Their faces very clearly showed the damage for a few days afterwards. They didn't want to call the police or go back and "get even" with them, although a group of us had discussed both options at the time.

I wasn't thinking at all about my two friends' recent incident that night until we reached this intersection and I saw the house with its Greek name prominently displayed on the outside. That's when the story of their ass-kickin' came back to me. I knew this was the place it occurred, probably on the same lawn where everyone was now tossing around the Frisbees and footballs.

How do I handle this? What do I do?

It was probably after midnight, and I knew Joe, John Pat, and Ned were kind of bored, and here I was, their "host," their tour guide of sorts for the night. And now I find that I somehow led them toward this frat house where OTHER friends of mine, PSU students from our dorm area, were tuned up pretty good less than two weeks ago. The three guys with me really wanted to check out this party. They liked what they saw and heard, at least from the outside. So, I figured we'd check it out, grab a beer or two, and then leave. I would have fulfilled my hosting/guide duties then and we could call it a night.

The four of us found ourselves walking toward an unguarded back door of this large fraternity house. I followed John Pat, Ned, and Joe in his wheelchair (we had to lift him up a few steps) through the door and into the house. Once inside the doorway, and out of earshot of anyone else, I quickly told the three of them of the incident from a few weeks ago. I felt obligated to do so at this point. They didn't really know the two friends of mine from the dorms who had been assaulted here at the frat house, but I just wanted them to know of that prior incident and that perhaps we should reconsider our visit here, especially as we weren't invited inside. They still wanted to check out the party, but we did agree to stay on guard and watch out for each other's backs. I suppose that would have to work for us.

Although we weren't on the frat house guest list, we still managed to get in to their party as the guest list desk was temporarily and conveniently unmanned upon our arrival. So, upon entry we decided to start making ourselves at home. The four of us did what came very natural to us on a Saturday night at a party; we were drinking some beer and talking to some female guests. We tried to blend right in there, as much as any non-invited guests could, including one in a wheelchair. We would have even contributed a few dollars if they wanted it from us, but no one was collecting money at the door at this point.

It was now closer to 1:00 AM and this seemed like a nice place to visit and end our evening, even if not officially on the guest list. Most of the frat's residents seemed to be outside or down in the basement enjoying themselves on this relatively warm fall night. They were quite loud and seemingly quite drunk and/or high. We were none of the aforementioned, but starting to enjoy ourselves nonetheless.

Joe, as usual, didn't waste any time and was making headway with at least one of the women in the house's large living room. While there, we weren't loud or obnoxious or looking for any trouble. We just wanted to socialize somewhere, even if we weren't specifically invited to this particular somewhere.

After a short time, a few of the frat brothers came in from their Frisbee and football tossing and before long started checking us out visually and making comments. They were loud and clearly drunk, and now inside their own house. We were quiet and not drunk, but inside "their" house, drinking "their" beer, and talking to "their" women. The music was still blaring from the basement as they were busily conversing among themselves while looking in our direction, even though we couldn't really hear what they were saying. There was no doubt that their topic of conversation was about the four of us gatecrashers.

Guys in these situations recognize other guys talking bad about them by how they blade their bodies, look at them up and down, clench and unclench their fists, elbow each other, and manifest the other non-verbal behavior and general demonstrativeness such as this slowly growing group was exhibiting toward us. They didn't know who we were, but they surmised by this time we weren't invited guests. And, they didn't like us drinking their beer or hitting on the women they invited there.

Some less-than-friendly comments toward the four of us were made that we could, in fact, hear after the basement band stopped playing. We also realized within a short time that we were now outnumbered by apparent frat house residents in this large room. Even though John Pat could handle himself quite well, and the rest of us were not exactly slackers in that department (even Joe from his wheelchair, as I was personally aware from a raucous bar visit with him on another recent occasion), there were just too many of them to make it a fair donnybrook, certainly from our perspective. But then, that seemed to be this frat's modus operandi, from what I recalled.

To make matters worse, I looked up at some point and saw a little guy coming down the interior stairs toward the living room. He was apparently one of the frat brothers and as he descended the stairs into the better light I could see he was wearing a Steelers jersey with #12 on it and, oh yeah, he was carrying a baseball bat. This was all coming together just as it did previously with my two dorm friends, except even worse, as we were inside the four walls of the frat house, with no easy egress, and the numbers were growing exponentially even less in our favor. This was not looking good for us as the less-than-friendly comments were getting louder.

Coincidently, and somewhat blessedly as it would turn out, at the exact moment this unfriendly crowd of frat boys peaked inside the house, a police car happened to drive down the street with its overhead red lights on; no siren, just overhead lights. It was clearly noticeable to all of us who stopped and looked out the windows as it lit up the whole interior of the place during its slow drive in front of the place. Perhaps it passed by because of the loud outside party-goers and basement rock band, and perhaps it was an indirect warning for the partiers to quiet things down.

Hmmmm…a chance police car drive-by…a supposed warning to the frat boys…What does this mean? How could this help us in this potentially volatile situation?

The serendipitous presence of this random patrol car made me think of something as the guys inside were clearly eyeing us, being more direct with their comments toward us, and with at least one Terry Bradshaw wannabe menacingly holding that baseball bat and having joined the others. I was thinking of what it was my dad taught me when

going up against that bully those many years before. That is, when in a situation in which you may
be overpowered, outnumbered, or just need an extra advantage of some sort, create a distraction, any
distraction. Do something to throw off your opponent, or in this case, multiple opponents.

In the fight with Carl, the bully from my childhood, I darted my eyes and looked over his shoulder at his friends. That's all the diversion I needed
with him. And, it worked as I landed my first
punch immediately afterwards. Now I needed
something similar, also before any punch would be
thrown, which would hopefully distract these guys.

So, I did. I created a situation that was sure to
distract the frat boys and possibly divert their next
physical actions aimed at the four of us. It was going to be our only hope.

Once the distraction idea came to mind, the rest
of it came to me like a lightning bolt. It was my survival instinct kicking in, thanks to what my dad
imparted upon me in the basement of our Olney
rowhome during my boxing sessions there. I quickly surmised that this idea was worth a try or it
would be my friends and me definitely getting an
ass kicking, with the words "Louisville Slugger"
embedded on one or more of our butts, or more
vulnerable body parts, before it was all over.

As we had earlier noticed a few guys and gals
in the back room of the frat house smoking grass
(an activity of which I did not partake, then, there,
or otherwise), and the frat boys immediately
around us, including the little batboy, getting ready
to pounce, I stepped up and put my distraction attempt in play to the nearest adversary to me.

I very firmly stated, "I don't think you want to be messing with us," nodding toward the police car that just drove by, "especially with your brothers back there smoking dope."

The guy who was sort of their ad hoc leader backed off momentarily and asked what I meant by that statement. I looked at Ned and told him to show this guy his badge. Ned was initially caught off guard, but after a second or two, as if almost right on cue, he pulled it out and flashed it to him.

Ned had a Globe Security Company badge hooked to the inside of his wallet. It wasn't especially official looking, but it was big and a real badge, at least of the security company variety. My friends and I came upon this badge from the same supermarket arm-wrestler who would be responsible for so much other damage (past and yet to come as the reader will learn), and we would pass it around among ourselves when in need. Ned may have even borrowed it from me that weekend, I'm not sure. But, if it was carried by one of us, it was for one reason and one reason only. That is, it could help an under 21 person get into bars. I suppose it did so because the badge made the carrier seem older, more authoritarian, and more official. I suppose. It was real, but like others of us who would carry it occasionally, Ned wasn't, or at least not in terms of him being an actual security officer or any other kind of officer, or 21. But, perception trumps reality in many cases, to include in semi-dark bars. This time, in the semi-dark frat house, with the drunken frat guys at the ready, this perception would hopefully work for us. It had to.

After my comment, which served to associate us in some way with the passing police car, and Ned flashing the badge, which made the association even more real, John Pat took it to the next level. As if on cue himself, he proceeded to state in a loud and very commanding voice, "Everyone, up against the wall! Now! And you, put that bat down," pointing to the diminutive one wearing the #12 jersey.

The eight to ten guys in the living room of the frat house at first hesitated, looked at each other as if to say "What the f**k," but then much to our surprise and relief, slowly and surely started to turn around and put their hands on the long living room wall. The little guy even put his bat down.

In addition, some other people in other parts of the house apparently heard John Pat's officious sounding command, saw the guys lined up against the wall, and someone among them yelled out loud, "Narcs!" It was no doubt one of the people we saw smoking marijuana in the adjacent room. With that magic word being referenced, we next heard the various partiers running out doors and even jumping out of first floor windows. The word was out, something was "going down" in the living room of the house and no one was taking a chance on who we were or who we may have been. The mass exodus of the frat house and the partygoers had now begun. This, no doubt, all underscored by the police car's revolving red lights that had passed by just a minute or so before and perhaps, so they thought, was parked down the street awaiting our commands.

So, here we were. The four of us, Ned and I the only PSU students, me an LEC major no less, John Pat, and Joe in a wheelchair, the latter two visitors to PSU and not even in college at all, managing to convince these pretty drunk and probably smoked-up frat boys that we were cops and/or "narcs." Yet, we never actually said the words "cops" or "narcs" that night. We were too smart and too sober for that, although that was the perception, the distraction, that we apparently created, helped along by the police car with its lights flashing and a security company badge as accompanying visuals. It is interesting the power of suggestion when associated with fear, paranoia, youthfulness, being drunk and/or high, all clearly present in overabundance with these guys in their house.

This was too easy we thought as we looked at each other shrugging our shoulders and grinning behind the frat boys' backs. It wasn't lost on me that night of another contributing factor to their collective reactions. It had recently been publicized that the Pennsylvania State Police had begun working in the PSU area in an attempt to crack down on drug usage, mostly of the smoked variety. There were supposedly undercover cops in the area, and some arrests had already been made both on and off campus, including at some neighboring frat houses, which were in turn temporarily shut down by PSU. We did not go to the frat house that night with this scenario in mind, nor had we ever done anything like this before. Certainly, I hadn't. However, some quick thinking on our combined parts probably saved us from getting the bejesus beaten out of us, especially as it would have occurred in the comfort zone of these frat boys, with the very drunk #12 no doubt swinging away at our heads.

With the four of us now holding about ten frat guys prone up against the wall, and others still gushing out any available back door or window, we were definitely in charge. We started rifling through their pockets pretending we were looking for dope, or at least we told them that. We didn't find anything of value though, nor did we actually want anything from them, as we merely allowed the pocket items, including loose bills and change, to drop to the floor. We just wanted to stall for time and get the hell out of there in one piece.

But, before too long, the fraternity boys were getting reckless when we didn't call for "backup," as the red-lighted police car didn't come back to us, and we really had nothing else to do to "enforce" the law at that point. They started to challenge us too. They were wondering out loud, albeit with their hands still on the wall, what a "cop" was doing in a wheelchair on a "drug bust."

Now it was Joe's turn. He responded quickly and convincingly, not with the wounded vet story this time, but another line. He told them that he was injured "in the line of duty" and what better undercover person could there be? And, he asked them, didn't they ever watch the TV show *Ironside*. They actually agreed with him, that it was a good ploy on his and our part in going "undercover" on a drug bust.

At this point, we were clearly just looking for a way out of the house. Yet, the "detained" subjects continued to doubt us to some degree. The diminutive one then said out loud that he's going to get his bat off the floor, he's had enough of this. I didn't want to see him again with that bat in his hands and I went over and kicked it to the other side of the room. He'd have to get through the four of us now to get his club back, and I assure you, the little one wouldn't have handled a punch from any of us very well running that gauntlet. That's probably why he carried the bat in the first place.

In the midst of this somewhat controlled situation, emphasis on "somewhat," came the moment that changed it all for me. As there was some doubt still manifesting itself among the detained individuals, Joe added for all to hear, "Oh yeah, and we got a probation officer here with us too. Hey, Fitz, show them your ID."

What…!?

While safely back at our dorms earlier that day, I just happened to show Joe the probation/parole business card while recounting my summer internship to him. He was impressed by it, and he remembered it. Unfortunately. This is when a survival situation went from clever to stupid, certainly on my part.

I'm not sure why, but in all the commotion, and still thinking of ways to avoid a possible beating, I pulled out of my wallet my one remaining business card from my summer internship and showed it to erstwhile leader (the one with the biggest mouth) of the frat boys. I even held it up to a dim light so he could read it and see I was "legit." He asked if he could actually hold it to see if it was real. I let him hold it, but with one hand still on the wall. He said out loud, "Yeah, it looks real to me."

Somehow, someway, right afterwards, I got distracted by someone yelling something in one of the back rooms and I failed to take the card back from this guy. Nonetheless, it bought us an extra minute or so. Batboy even stayed with his hands on the wall and did not try to get his bat from across the room.

After several minutes of lecturing the "suspects" on the evils of smoking pot and underage drinking, we figured it was time to get the hell out of there. So, we decided to let them go. We told them they were "un-arrested," we wouldn't call for backup (that they must have thought was the police car that had driven by a few minutes before and maybe parked down the street), and we would slowly exit the place. We advised them as we were leaving that this was a one-time warning and for them to not do it again. We told them other units would be driving by shortly and watching the place. In their drunkenness, they half-heartedly nodded, expressed their sorrow, and we quickly left. It was clear that they didn't know exactly what just happened, but were nevertheless glad it was over. Same here, we agreed to ourselves, as the four of us proceeded to the McDonald's on College Ave. to have a late night, beating-averted snack.

The beating WAS averted that night, but in hindsight, I so wish I took it instead of what later transpired. Or, I certainly wish I hadn't left that business card behind – the one with my name and other information on it. This incident would come back to haunt me only a few weeks later. I'd feel like letting the batboy and his Louisville Slugger swing away at me by that time.

So it was, about a month later, I was home from PSU for the Thanksgiving break. It was the Friday morning after the otherwise restful holiday with my extended family when the phone rang. It was my former supervisor from the Kensington branch office of the PA Probation and Parole Office. I was initially surprised to hear from him and said hello and right away wished him and his a happy Thanksgiving. Upon barely responding to that greeting and in a very stern manner he then asked me to come into the office later that day. I immediately felt the dread coming over me. Something wasn't right. I told him it was kind of short notice and I wasn't sure if I could borrow my parents' car right away, and I had some things to do, etc. But, he strongly insisted upon it. I then agreed and said I'd be there in two hours.

I guessed almost immediately what this was about. It concerned the business card I stupidly gave away while stupidly acting out the beating prevention scenario at the frat house just a few weeks before at PSU. How would I explain this to him, and to my other former colleagues who really seemed to like me at my possible future job? Make that my soon-to-be former possible future job.

I finally arrived at the office. Upon entering the front door, I gave a warm hello to one of the secretaries who just 12 weeks or so before helped plan my surprise going-away party. She said nothing to me in return. She didn't even look up from her desk. I knew this was going to be an awful experience. Probably the worst experience of my life so far up to this time, but I was there and I had to handle it, like a man.

Or, a boy? Which one of those was I now? What do I say to these professionals who had all but offered me a job just a few months ago? How do I frame the details of this ten minute utter act of stupidity from just a few Saturday nights ago?

The office supervisor came out into the little waiting area and brought me back to his office. The second in command was there too. He's the guy I brought home to meet my parents and have dinner with on that not-so-long-ago summer night. They were very serious. They closed the office door. I tried to be friendly and make small talk, but they got right to the point. Did I hand out a probation/parole office business card at PSU and pretend I was an agent? I knew this question was coming ever since their phone call to me, now I had to respond to it.

I didn't want to lie. I tried that with a cop a few years before in Wildwood, NJ, and it didn't work then. Plus, I was not in a habit of lying to people, especially people I genuinely respect. So, why start now?

I told my former bosses that I had lost the card...well, sort of. Yes, I showed the card to some frat kids who were drinking and smoking grass and threatening to beat up my friends and me. Then I actually gave it to one of them and subsequently lost possession of it. Yes, my friends and I just sort of fell into this bizarre scenario by pretending to hold them for the police for drug possession. But, I assured my two former internship supervisors, I never said I was a cop, a narc, and certainly not a probation/parole officer.

I told them that a police car happened to drive by just before then...one of my friends just happened to have a security guard badge on him...the frat guys just assumed who we were...they were smoking pot...it was really a spontaneous thing...we were going to get seriously beaten...one guy had a bat...they had beat up my friends a week before...I showed the card...he took it...I forgot to take it back....

Really, this is, in fact, how it happened. In actuality, I was telling them the truth, but I felt increasingly embarrassed and childish as I was relating the story to them. I put my head down toward the end of it because I couldn't stand looking into their disappointed eyes. As I looked inwardly at that precise moment, I realized that no one in the room was more disappointed than me. Not even close, I'm sure.

How could I have been so stupid while at the frat house? Why did I even choose to go there at all that night, especially as my dorm mates had suffered their own recent beatings at this place? Would we really have gotten beaten up by these guys? Well, probably, as we were outnumbered and outweaponed by them. This is what I was thinking the whole time in the office. I do know that what I was facing now was definitely worse than any physical beating I would have taken that night. And, did I say it was all very stupid on my part? It was, without a doubt.

My two former practicum supervisors seemed to believe me and asked me if I had given out or shown any other business cards and/or did I have any business cards left. I told them "no" to both questions and that was the absolute truth. They said fine, and that was all, and I could go now. They didn't scold me, additionally challenge me, or further confront me. They didn't have to. They heard what they had to hear. I said I was sorry to them and the two men just said simultaneously, "Okay." I walked out of the supervisor's office toward the front door, past one or two of my former summer colleagues, my head literally down, my tail figuratively between legs, with none of them looking up at me. It was very disheartening, and that's putting it mildly.

Bottom-line here, I screwed the pooch. Big-time. I just ruined my first and at that time only chance at the possibility of getting a good job in my field upon graduating from college in about eight months. But, I could now kiss that prospect goodbye. No ifs, ands, or buts about it.

I did a lot of internal soul searching later that afternoon and that weekend. I locked myself in the bedroom of my parents' house and all but cried. I let my PSU partying and yes, sometimes drinking, even at 21 now, cloud my senses and good judgment. I put myself into a situation that I should have avoided all together. The rest of my break was ruined, and I had no one to blame but myself. Cause and effect, I learned, were closely correlated. What happened 200 miles away, three to four weeks before, came back to haunt me now, in Philadelphia. Big-time! What turned into a spontaneous incident one night with friends in which no one was hurt or truly victimized, yet was still very stupid and immature, now caused me to lose a real valuable potential early career connection.

Just as bad, it caused me to lose face and my positive and hard-working reputation with these professionals. It was one that I legitimately earned, albeit over just a short time, but then all too casually threw away. This is the exact opposite of what should result from an internship/practicum.

I had to straighten up and get ready to join the real world. I thought I had, but clearly I had not. It was definitely time to move on to that next level in my life.

My survival-based indiscretion, the distraction/diversion at the frat house, went no further then to my former internship supervisors. No one contacted the local police or my PSU/LEC department heads. My grade of "A" for the summer internship went unchanged. But, I was a changed person. This sort of activity would not happen again to me. Ever!

None did like what happened above, but I had one more issue to address of this general nature. And it wasn't the PA Probation and Parole people the next time. No, it was a much larger agency, and at the federal level.

It was the FBI.

Chapter Seventeen

Yet another incident, or more precisely a series of incidents, were also about to catch up with me. This time it didn't involve being in trouble with just a state agency. No, this time I went right to the top. It was the Federal Bureau of Investigation. Now they wanted to talk to me about...something. This was not a good beginning to my senior year at college. Would it be even worth it for me to graduate, and with a degree in Law Enforcement and Corrections, of all majors? Could I now ever even hope to get a job in this field? Could I survive this second storm, having just barely survived the first? The seas were about to get even rougher for me, but once again, in turbulence all of my own making.

To get to the beginning of this next phase of my burgeoning adulthood, I must go back to the supermarket arm-wrestler, the guy that broke my drug store co-worker Kerry's arm a few years before. Besides arm wrestling and working at the produce department of a large supermarket, he had other ways to make money. Along with security guard badges, he also sold United States Selective Service cards, aka draft cards. They weren't real, of course. He would simply make copies of a real one in which he whited out the name, physical dimensions, and the all-important date-of-birth of the actual person, and sell them. They were sold by him for their eventual buyers to appear to be older than they really were for one simple reason; that is, to purchase alcoholic beverages. They were fake IDs so under-21 males could get served in bars and at liquor stores.

I remembered this guy from the arm wrestling match of a few years ago, knew of his part-time endeavors, and my friends and I looked him up at his store some time later through Big Ed, our significantly older friend and fellow employee of this guy. In the back room of the produce department that afternoon, once again alongside the potatoes, tomatoes, kumquats, etc., he confirmed that he still sold them, but it would take some time for him to take our information, type the cards, and get them back to us. We asked him to just sell us the blank copy and we'd save him the time and effort. He thought about it, all the while washing down various fruits and veggies in a large sink area. He reluctantly said okay, and for a total price that I now forget, my buddies and I were in possession of a good paper copy, front and back, of a draft card. Well, a fake draft card.

All we had to do with it was to make a few quality photocopies and type in our respective names, height, weight, and faux birth date to make us appear over 21. Once the two sides of the card (actually two sheets of paper) were cut down to size and conjoined via laminated plastic, they were good to go. That was our goal and that was what we eventually did.

However, before making my own fake card, with the pseudonym "Jim Andrews," a name choice for reasons still unknown after all these years, I kept one additional blank copy of the draft card for myself. Over the next year or so, from that master copy, I made additional photocopies for some of my other friends and some for the occasional friend of a friend. Some I gave out blank, others I filled out myself with my typewriter, including the requisite year-appropriate biographical info for the potential buyer. As long as the date-of-birth reflected that the person was now over 21, it served its purpose. I would even sign the same name of the local draft board official that was on our REAL draft cards. Of all names, ironically, it was "Sallye Warr." Yes, I even sold a few for the retail sum of $5.00 each. I probably made a few dozen of them over the next year or so, giving some away to friends, and selling the others to people I knew and even some I didn't know at all, through their friends.

It was probably one of those latter people that I didn't know who got caught being underage with a fake draft card in a State College bar one night by the local police. To this day, I don't know who it was, but someone got in trouble and no doubt in an effort to spare himself the full force of the law in such matters, he decided to give up the guy who sold or gave the card to him. Yes, that would be me.

As it was technically a federal offense to copy, alter, or otherwise misuse one of these cards, the investigation of said incidents went to the FBI. This was sort of known to me, and others, as the backside of the card listed this information, including the fact that it was a felony to do any of these things and punishable by imprisonment and/or a steep fine. But, my friends and I weren't violent student radicals out to commit acts of treason or sedition and otherwise overthrow the government of the United States with these cards. It wasn't done for purposes of avoiding the draft. We just wanted to get served in bars and buy beer. We, or certainly my close friends and me, didn't do drugs. At all! So, these warnings, we thought, didn't really apply to us, we were just beer drinkers and liked to do so in nice bars, and not out in the street or in the woods.

But, as I was soon to learn, the federal law actually did apply to me. And I would learn this the hard way.

While home in Philadelphia for a long weekend from PSU in early December of '74, I was out and about on a certain Friday afternoon. When I came home, my parents told me that two FBI agents came to the house looking for me.

I responded with genuine shock and incredulity, as in, "WHAT? For ME?"

They retorted suspiciously, "Yes, Jim, for YOU! Just WHAT the heck is going on here?"

I then asked my parents exactly what the agents said to them.

They told me that the agents didn't tell them anything in detail, but one of them left his business card and he wanted me to call him at his downtown Philadelphia office. Then, my parents asked me again what I thought they wanted to discuss. I told them that I didn't know. Technically, I wasn't lying to my parents, but once again, like with the phone call from my former probationary/parole practicum supervisor (only a few weeks before, no less), I could venture a guess. I couldn't believe this was happening. And again, I had no one to blame but myself.

Geez…my life had to start changing, as in yesterday.

That Monday morning, before driving back to PSU for a few weeks before the Christmas break, I called the Philadelphia FBI office number, which was on the agent's business card. I asked for the agent by name who visited my parents and when he eventually answered I identified myself. He said he wanted to talk to me but wouldn't say specifically why or about what. I told him of my upcoming schedule and that I was heading back to PSU in a few hours as my break was over. He said in that case that I should instead contact Special Agent so-and-so at the State College Resident Agency of the FBI, since the matter is actually being investigated out of that office.

I asked the FBI agent very respectfully, "What is this about, sir?"

He would not provide that information. Either way, I agreed to follow his instructions. Something told me that the fake draft cards were about to come back and hit me, and hit me hard, square in the face.

The very next day, when back at school, I called the agent in the State College FBI office from my Nittany barracks/dorm lobby payphone. After a few missed calls that day, we finally talked and he said he wanted me to come to his office. We set up a time about three days later. The three day buildup to this meeting would now exceed exponentially the queasiness I experienced previously when visiting my former probation/parole practicum supervisor. At least that meeting all began and ended in about three hours. I had butterflies in my stomach the whole time before this latest Jim-you're-in-big-trouble meeting. They (the figurative butterflies) wouldn't let me sleep or eat very well over the next 72 hours or so. I know I lost some weight and looked like crap. I did go to my classes, but my concentration level was severely altered, to say the least.

When the meeting day finally arrived, I purposely got my hair cut relatively short that morning at a barbershop not too far from the FBI Office. I was cleanly shaved, and I dressed at least somewhat adult-like, with a button down shirt to wear over my dress jeans and nice shoes. Not a bad look considering what guys normally wore on college campuses in 1974. I arrived at the FBI office about 20 minutes early. I waited for the agent for a good bit even after the scheduled time had passed. I brought some of my school books with me, including a criminology book, perhaps in an attempt to let the agent know my major and perhaps that one day I too would be working on his side as an officer or investigator and....

Oh, who was I kidding here? He doesn't care about what book I'm carrying or my career aspirations. He wants to know about the draft cards and I better get ready to give it up right away. Then, we'll see what happens to my potential career, if it's even salvageable at all at this point.

The agent finally came out into the waiting room to get me. He was tall, thin, and wearing a starched white shirt with a dark tie under his gray suit, just as I had expected an FBI agent to look. He was the first FBI agent I ever met. I was hoping he would be the last, well at least in a scenario such as this one. He sat me down in a chair and I faced him across a desk. After taking some basic pedigree information from me, such as name, address, birth date, etc., he proceeded to tell me that someone was arrested in State College using a fraudulent Selective Service card, and when asked, that person gave my name as the seller of same. He then asked me if I'd be willing to talk to him about it. I said yes.

The agent replied very stoic-like, "Good," then he proceeded to read me my rights.

Yes, my Miranda warnings. I wasn't expecting this, although through my formal education I should have been. This was truly a first for me. I'd seen it on TV and in the movies, but now I was the one being Mirandized. Does this make me a criminal? If not, I'm at least a suspect. Damn, what have I gotten myself into?

When he was done reading from the form, without really thinking about it, I said I'd waive all my rights and agree to talk to him.

He again said "Good," and I signed the waiver and we began talking.

I proceeded to tell him everything. I told him I got the blank card from a guy who used to work in a supermarket in Philadelphia, but I didn't know his name. I truly wasn't aware of his name. He had a nickname, but that's all I ever knew him by. The agent really didn't seem concerned about this guy. Just in me and what I was doing with these cards. I told him I had made about 15-25 over the last year or so, most of them just for friends. Yes, I charged $5.00 for some of them, but gave away as many. He looked at what appeared to be a fake card in an envelope with the word "Evidence" clearly stamped on it, and said to me, "These aren't very sophisticated copies, are they?"

I agreed with him that they were not. He could plainly see they were just photocopies of a real card that were whited-out and then covered with plastic laminate covers.

After what seemed like five minutes of deafening silence, the whole time while the agent was taking copious notes on a pad of yellow paper, he had me read aloud the back of a copy of an actual Selective Service card he happened to have with him. I read about treasonous activities, acts of sedition, altering/modifying of it, the monetary fines, the prison terms, that it was a felony, etc. I finished reading it and slowly looked up at him afterwards. I assured him in very genuine terms that I had no intention of bringing down the government of the United States, dodging the draft, running off to Canada, committing acts of sedition (I wasn't even exactly sure what that meant at the time), or anything else bad to my country, with my use, or more accurately, misuse, of these fake cards. They were simply being utilized to get served in bars and/or buy alcoholic beverages by under-21 young men.

I further told him I was sorry and would not involve myself anymore in the making of these fake IDs. I so truly meant that statement too. I think he knew it. Plus, I reminded him, I was now 21, so I didn't even need a fake one anymore as I could now drink legally.

Our talk ended after only about 30 minutes. He seemed to understand that what I had done was not any attempt to betray my country or its rightful sovereignty or anything like that. Yet, he reminded me that I could still be in big trouble for what I did.

Then he told me as I was about to leave that it wasn't up to him as to what would eventually happen to me regarding this matter. He would have to present this information, including what I told him, to the U.S Attorney's office in Philadelphia and they would make the ultimate decision as to whether I would be indicted and/or arrested.

Geez, indicted or arrested? Is this really that bad?

It was, at least potentially.

I asked the FBI agent how long this would take. He advised me to call him back in two weeks. I said okay, I would do that. I left his office, once again with my proverbial tail between my legs and head down. I didn't know his fellow office workers, but I felt just as stupid as my unaided "perp" walk at the probation/parole office just a few weeks before.

It took me the full two weeks to find out my legal status. A very long two weeks, coming to a conclusion right before the scheduled PSU Christmas break. I kept this situation to myself, choosing not to share it with anyone; more out of embarrassment than anything else.

After a number of missed calls from the payphone from my dorm lobby to the local State College FBI office, I finally got the news of which I was hoping. The U.S. Attorney's Office in Philadelphia opted to decline to prosecute me for my misdeeds. Upon the agent telling me this news, I let out a breath of relief unlike one ever before. I thanked him and promised him once again this issue was over and done with forever. He strongly advised me that it better be over and done. I assured him once again, it was. And, in fact, that was to be the case. As I did several times before this call, I went again to the PSU chapel afterwards and said several prayers of thanks. I also assured The Man upstairs that this type scenario would never, ever, happen again to me.

My parents asked me over the long Christmas break "whatever happened with that FBI situation." I told them it was now no big deal and that it was a matter about some fake draft cards floating around PSU. They seemed more-or-less satisfied with that answer and asked me no further questions regarding it. Looking back, they probably just didn't want to know the details. They knew I wasn't indicted, arrested, or in jail, I was still going to school, and they just left it at that.

The double-nightmare over those several months during the fall trimester of my senior year at college, that is, contending with two separate criminal justice agencies regarding these thoughtless and immature actions of my recent life, were now in my past. They were each nightmares of my own creation, no question about it. I blamed no one else as I brought these problems on myself. I regretted not just the fact that I was "caught" in both disparate yet somewhat related situations, but that I had engaged in such behavior in the first place. I put everything on the line in doing so, especially with my future career plans. One of these incidents alone could have been a deal breaker for me career-wise. But, fortunately they weren't.

I awakened from these nightmares a different person, a different man.

In the pre-hiring stages of my future law enforcement positions, as a police officer and later as an FBI agent, both agencies were aware of the fake draft card situation and the FBI investigation into it as there was, in fact, a potential violation of the law in that matter, and an investigation that went along with it. Fortunately, when initially interviewed and assessed by representatives of my two future agencies, these blips on my personal radar screen would be discussed with me, but ultimately not a reason that precluded my hiring. And, while I applied for numerous law enforcement-related positions after graduation, I never did attempt to become a Pennsylvania state probation/parole officer. Despite my success and positive experience while at the practicum that summer, the after-effects of that one thoughtless night I felt were too much to overcome. I was not destined to be a probation/parole officer, at least not in Pennsylvania.

As two practicums were required for graduation with a B.S. in LEC from PSU, my next one was the winter trimester of 1975. It was again to be in Philadelphia, this time with the U.S. Bureau of Alcohol, Tobacco, and Firearms (ATF). I lived at home again during this term and went to "work" every day at the U.S. Treasury Building at 2nd and Chestnut Streets in downtown Philly. It was an interesting and edifying experience meeting and working alongside some truly professional federal law enforcement agents. I got to experience a long-planned, large-scale, pre-dawn arrest of a number of outlaw bikers for gun and drug possession and trafficking; stakeouts of some bad guys' homes, bars, and businesses; court hearings in which the agents testified to various aspects of their investigations; court-ordered gun destructions, etc. I wrote a paper afterwards on some related criminal justice issue and attained an overall "A" for the practicum itself.

Most importantly for me, there were no after-the-fact negative ramifications to this endeavor. I did not make any, have any, nor wanted any temporary ATF business cards of any sort in my possession. And I can assure the reader that even if I was somehow forced to take one, it would have not been utilized in any way similar to the fashion in which the previous business card was used only several months prior at PSU. Those days were now over.

I should also add here that I proposed marriage to my long-term girlfriend, Eileen, during the late winter of my senior year. She said "Yes," and we were to be married in a little over a year. I'm sure I loved her. In fact, I know I did. But, looking back, I believe deep down inside at the subconscious level I also knew she was a controlling factor in my life. And I mean that in a good sense, in a positive way. I knew that she, by her mere presence in my life at the time, would help keep me on the straight and narrow path. I felt I had matured, finally, and in no small way thanks to my relationship with her. Oh, and the duress and trauma created by my recent "card" problems of the business and Selective Service variety also added to this new approach of mine toward the world. Life was slowly coming together for me after some very rough patches and extremely bumpy roads.

I went back to the Ogontz/Abington campus for the spring trimester of '75 as I managed to find the four courses there, mostly electives, which I never got around to previously taking. Upon their successful completion, I graduated from PSU with a B.S. degree in LEC that May.

I chose for various reasons to not attend my graduation ceremony at the central Pennsylvania main campus. My primary rationale for this decision was that I attended my high school's graduation ceremony four years earlier at Philadelphia Convention Hall. As there were 1400 or so graduates then and there, with our accompanying family and friends as guests making it around 5,000 people total, another similar large-scale grandiose ceremony just didn't do anything for me, especially at 200 miles away.

My dad and mom were now 71 and 61, respectively by this time, and I just didn't want to drag them on this long and not-necessarily cheap overnight trip just for me to stand in line at PSU's Beaver Stadium along with thousands of others to get my degree. They would have been barely able to even see me anyway, depending on their seats. They would have gladly gone, they said, but I decided against the pomp and circumstance this time.

I should add, my decision not to attend this ceremony was not a reflection of anything negative toward PSU or my experience there during the last few months of the preceding year. It was just time to move on from that place, college life, and start a new life in the real world.

I'll always remember that it cost me $5.00 to NOT attend my graduation ceremony. To this day, I'm not sure why, as there was no fee charged to actually attend it. It may have had something to do with the mailing the diploma itself to me. Either way, it was money I felt well spent, at least for me, at the time.

As it turns out, although I attained two more graduate degrees later in life, my CDHS graduation ceremony in '71 would be the only academic related one I would ever attend of my own. I suppose I'm just not a ceremonious guy, at least when it comes to my own academic degrees.

In closing to this particular phase of my life, specifically relating to what I experienced at the end of '74 involving the two card situations, I'd like to offer just a few more words. No excuses, I promise, but instead context. A person's life and his or her decisions made throughout can only truly be judged in the context in which it was lived. I will try to do that here.

As many are aware, from either having lived it or later heard or read about it, coming-of-age in the U.S. in the late 1960s and the early 1970s was not necessarily an easy time to do so. As I referenced earlier, and it is otherwise well known, these were turbulent times, fraught with great societal change and transition, and much temptation to those in certain age brackets then to undertake new and supposedly fun and "mind-expanding" adventures. Many of these new and fun adventures happened to be illegal too, of course.

Without getting into all of the various clashing cultural issues, I recall at the time one of the biggest challenges to be faced, and one that many a young person then was forced to address, was the ever-increasing use of illegal drugs among our peers.

Drugs of all sorts were ubiquitous in my ever expanding areas of Philadelphia and at the main campus of PSU in State College, PA. They could purportedly enhance a social event or encounter, expand one's consciousness, it was "cool" if one used them, and it could be equally "uncool" if one turned them down from someone at a party, in a club, in someone's car, etc. In view of these issues, there were decisions that each of us had to make back then, and depending on the situation, they were not always easy decisions.

For the record, I tried marijuana about four times in my life. I simply didn't like it, what it did to me or for me, or what it represented to me. Each of these usages was in my early college years and that was it.

I never did any other drugs of any kind at any other time or any other place in my life. Ever! My future police department was advised of these four marijuana related indiscretions, as years later was the FBI. Both still hired me. I was later told by officials in both agencies that to find a qualified candidate who did NOT do drugs back then was growing more and more difficult. They told me that many an otherwise qualified candidate was rejected because of his past drug usage, even if relatively infrequent at the time. Me admitting to just having smoked pot four times, and confirming that statement by passing a mandatory polygraph exam, made me a good candidate (along with hopefully my other attributes) for the jobs to which I was applying.

Sometimes in the application process, drug usage was admitted to by a particular job candidate early on and perhaps he still managed to get hired. Other times, if the illegal usage was instead discovered through his background investigation, the hiring rarely took place because he lied about his drug usage. This issue, however, was not a problem for me.

What I'm trying to relate here is that in the '70s as I was approaching adulthood, my peers and I had lifestyle choices to make. And they were not always easy choices. I had friends from whom I drifted away because they were getting more and more involved in drugs. I was put into situations, several times while driving my dad's car for instance, with a friend or two I knew well who then asked me to pick up one or more new friends of theirs that I didn't necessarily know as well. On a few separate occasions I would do so, and while driving along, they would unceremoniously pull out a joint in the back seat, and without even asking me, they would start to light up. I'd see it in the rearview mirror and/or smell it. I'd then tell them to put it out and stash it.

These friends of friends, who may have been popular and well-liked guys at the time, would then no doubt put me on their unofficial "not cool" list. Not directly, of course, but in a subtle sense. It would hurt because no one at that age wants to be seen as an outsider, afraid to take chances, or worse, a "square" or "unhip." But, I stuck to my guns each time and told my friends to not have their friends put me in that situation again. I eventually stopped hanging out with some of these guys, for obvious reasons. There would be too much to lose in the long run for this fleeting level of alleged popularity.

And for what? Just to get high? To be "cool?"

Another aspect of this hard line personal approach on my part was because I couldn't imagine ever telling my parents I was involved in doing drugs. Or, them getting that phone call, once again from a police officer, that their son was under arrest for drug possession. That call would never be made, of course, because I wasn't ever involved in that type of illegal activity, as I would not even allow the stuff in my/their car.

I suppose it was this general philosophy on my part, if I could call it such, that let me think back then that it's okay to drink, even before 21 years of age. And maybe even do silly, if not stupid, things when drinking, because hey, at least I was not doing drugs. Along with some newer friends, many in LEC at PSU, we were the anti-druggies, un-hippies, non-"heads" ("head" being a common term for a pot smoker in the '70s), by drinking instead of doing drugs, if that makes any sense. Even while making and distributing a couple dozen fake draft cards over a year plus, in my own mind, I was subconsciously saying to myself that "Hey, I'm not promoting drug usage by this activity, just drinking. And that's perfectly legal." Well, if one is over 21 it is, anyway.

While not preachy to friends with these particular newly developed interests, I just believed for numerous short-term and long-term reasons that staying away from the burgeoning drug lifestyle would benefit me greatly then and ultimately again in my later life. I think it did. Make that, I know it did.

Now if only I had avoided some other bad choices....

By the way, back in this time frame, being anti-drug didn't necessarily make me pro-drinking. I wouldn't drink to excess, nor drive drunk, and certainly not drink every night. I was mostly a "weekend-warrior" from that perspective. Besides a few guy-things like fistfights and other related goofy incidents at bars, parties, etc., the worse to come out of my non-drug but drinking years were the business card and draft card(s) incidents as related above.

I suppose, IF I was going to screw up, I might as well do it while young, and not wait until middle-aged like the many politicians, corporate and community leaders, law enforcement officials, et al, making news headlines at any given time for various indiscretions. Then, usually, they make it worse by lying about it. I never went that route.

As it turned out, my youthful screw-ups were non-drug related, non-violence related, and they did not involve directly hurting anyone on any level. They were scenarios which, while still admittedly very stupid, ultimately did no permanent harm to another person, only me. Yet, at the same time, they left a permanent and indelible impression on me for life. Doing them in the first place, and later getting "caught" at them, was immensely cathartic for me. I did learn from my mistakes, that I can assure the reader.

The truly adult portion of my life was now about to begin in earnest. Goodbye young and sometimes immature Jim Fitzgerald. It was time to move on to a slightly older and definitely more mature version of me. He was to be a welcome arrival.

Jim Fitzgerald's Cardinal Dougherty
HS graduation photo, 1971

Jim Fitzgerald's Penn State ID Card, 1974

Rich Davoli   Jim Fitzgerald   Ray Geary

Penn State graduation photos, 1975

Standing, left to right: Tim Klarich, Bill Sena, Jim Fitzgerald
Seated, left to right: Tom Lubas, Big Ed Fehrenbach, Rob McCarthy
(Photo, 1979)

Left to right, John Welsh, Joe Widmeier, Jim Fitzgerald
(Photo 2004)

Jim Fitzgerald with sisters Marilyn, Alma, and Cass
(Photo, 2007)

Chapter Eighteen

For the few months before my (unattended) PSU graduation, I knew it was time to find a job. It was, in reality, the reason I went to college. Well, mostly anyway. The "new" Jim, much more mature now, at least from doing purposefully stupid things again, knew there would be no extended vacations or backpacking through Europe. I wanted to earn some money and start a career...somewhere, somehow. I was also getting married in about a year and I needed a job and money for that next stage of my life too.

So, during my last trimester at school, and the weeks immediately following the receipt of my degree (yes, it eventually came to me through the mail), I spent most mornings searching the *Philadelphia Inquirer* newspaper classified ads for that job. In the afternoons, it was the *Philadelphia Evening Bulletin* which I would scan for potential employment opportunities. The classified headings I would search on a daily basis included "police," "investigative," and "security." Not too many of those positions were listed during this particular time frame. The U.S. economy in the mid-1970s was in a slump and not many agencies/companies seemed to be hiring.

My friends with their business-related degrees were getting interviews, attending job fairs, meeting with professional recruiters, etc., while in their respective last semesters and over that summer. Some of them were actually getting real jobs in their fields, even before they graduated. However, those of us with LEC and related degrees in the social sciences were not so lucky. We were all pretty much relegated to the fact that we would have to start at jobs and in positions perhaps not necessarily where we wanted to be at first.

Quite simply, at this time, my future profession, with some exceptions at the federal level, was not yet overly enthused about taking on college graduates with degrees in this new discipline, one which was actually related to what it is they do, that is, criminal justice/law enforcement. But, I knew this going in. I also knew, at this time, what I wanted to do. What I did not know was where or for whom I would be doing it. But that process was beginning to unfold, even if very slowly for me.

My first official step in this arena took place pre-graduation from PSU. It was the taking of the written test for the position of police officer in Philadelphia. I responded to their newspaper ad in the late winter of '75. It simply read, "Be a Philadelphia Police Officer," the starting salary, the basic requirements, and who to call or write to begin the process. I sent for an application, received it, filled it out, and mailed it back.

Upon completing the Philadelphia PD application, it was somewhat eye-opening to me and my friends who also planned on taking the test that, besides having no felony convictions and being a legal resident of Philadelphia, there were essentially no other requirements to being hired. None! There were no educational requirements listed at all in the application. Not even an elementary school degree, much less a high school or college degree, was needed to apply to be a Philadelphia police officer.

I was nervously hoping at this point that my almost awarded degree wouldn't get in the way of me being hired by them, or other potential agencies down the line. Could I have been over-qualified for this position because of my newly-attained degree?

Regardless of my perceived level of qualification, I took the police officer test on a sunny Saturday morning in May of '75 at Olney High School, coincidently, my mother's alma mater. I could walk there from my home. I'm glad I did as parking was very difficult to find that day. Lots of people evidently wanted to be police officers in Philadelphia that year. The line to take the Philadelphia police officer test wrapped around the school building that morning. There were reportedly almost a thousand people lined up for this entrance exam. And, it was being offered at several public high schools in Philadelphia on that day, not just at Olney HS.

Though the line was mostly comprised of young males, there were a few women scattered throughout. I actually wound up standing next to and conversing with a former schoolmate, Beth Salmon, with whom I graduated from St. Helena School and CDHS. We had lost track of each other since high school and it was nice catching up with her and asking her about, among other things, why she wanted to take the test and maybe become a police officer. She said she wasn't completely sure why as she knew that as a woman she would be one of the few of her sex in the department, certainly as a uniformed officer, and that in and of itself would be fraught with complications for her and her like-gendered peers. However, despite these reservations, she wanted to nonetheless explore her options on this day and at least take the test.

It should be noted that in 1975 the gender-line had, in fact, only been broken a year or so previous for women to apply and be potentially hired as police officers in Philadelphia. This was much to then-Mayor Frank Rizzo's chagrin, as he very publicly protested the notion of women wearing uniforms and badges and (gulp!) even carrying guns. But, lawsuits were filed, courts rendered their decisions, and women were ultimately authorized to apply to various police departments around the U.S. This included the City of Philadelphia, thus breaking the generations-old male-only bastion of the local law enforcement profession.

I recall actively following the media accounts of the day when the matter of women in law enforcement was still a novelty, and with many senior male members of various departments and agencies attempting to keep it that way. Various high-ranking police and city officials in Philadelphia stated publicly that a woman's "monthly cycle" and the accompanying "emotional imbalance" during that time would make it problematic for them in conducting themselves as police officers. It was also publicly commented that women's "protuberances," aka breasts, would "get in the way of an arrest situation," and that women wouldn't fit appropriately into a standard man's police uniform, and their "female figures" would otherwise diminish their role as "authority figures," etc.

Some local women's advocacy groups quickly responded to these publicized comments. They did so by stating that the large bellies of some of the male police officers were, in fact, "protuberances" in their own right, which could also prove problematic, get in the way of arrests, be tough to fit into a uniform, and these "male figures" would in turn lessen them as "authority figures." Candid photos of overweight and out-of-shape male police officers accompanied the women's groups' media responses. Their points were well taken and the "protuberance" argument rapidly lost its muster.

I remember the media coverage of when the first women officers finally graduated from the Philadelphia police academy. That's when the wives of already serving male police officers first publicly had their say. These police wives complained that they felt it was unfair to them to have their husbands riding with a female partner in a car all day long. At least one of these wives made it on to the evening news. While claiming to speak for other police wives, she stated that when her husband left for work in the morning her hair was still in curlers, she had on no makeup, no fancy clothes, and he then would go to work and partner-up with these generally fit, younger women and spend all day sitting next to them in a patrol car. It was simply an unfair edge that these "lady cops" had over the wives who could, in turn, tempt their husbands away from them.

I don't remember if she referenced protuberances of any sort in her protestations.

Despite these various issues, some even brought about by other women, newly sworn female police officers were going on patrol in Philadelphia and all around the U.S. by the mid-1970s. It was about time.

Looking back, women law enforcement officers/investigative agents were there from the earliest days of my career and I essentially never worked without them as partners, colleagues, fellow cops and special agents. In my future agency, the FBI, women would finally enter the ranks of special agent in the early 1970s, coincidently or not, just a year or so after the death of J. Edgar Hoover.

If I would judge any officer/agent at all during my 31-year career, it would invariably be based upon their experience, work ethic, skill set, and perhaps personality, rather than his or her gender or race or some other demographic factor. Today, in Western societies, a woman's place in law enforcement is, of course, a relative non-issue. Not that there aren't still inherent problems related to sexism for some women. That issue still exists, unfortunately in all professions, with law enforcement being no exception. But it's good to know that women officers and agents are here to stay, as they should be, and continue to contribute greatly to the overall profession.

I didn't see Beth Salmon-Kauffman (her subsequent married name) again until my 20th high school reunion in 1991. She told me she scored relatively high in the PPD exam lo those many years ago, but after careful thought and consideration she never did join the department or enter into the law enforcement field. She seemed quite happy with the professional and personal choices she made instead.

It took until mid-summer of '75 for me to learn my results of the Philadelphia police officer test. Through the simple white postcard I received in the mail, I found out that I scored a 99+ (out of a possible 100) on the written test. Not bad, but not good enough. As I was not a military veteran, each of whom was given an automatic ten points added to their raw test scores, my numerical ranking to be hired, or at least to progress to the next step, put me somewhere around number 150 on the list. In other words, any veteran who scored at least a 90 was ranked higher than me on the overall list.

While I would have liked to have been ranked higher, there's not much more I could have done then, especially as I all but aced the written test. And, for the record, I had no issue whatsoever with veterans getting the bonus points added to their test scores. They served their country, with many of these guys in the rice paddies and killing fields of Vietnam, so a bit of a "thanks" to them for doing so in the form of ten additional points on a civil service exam was clearly appropriate and well-deserved in my estimation. I'd have to do very well in any interview and psychological/physical testing follow-ups with them to make up for those added points given to the vets. I felt I could, and I eventually would.

The Philadelphia police officer exam was only one of about four such tests I took that year, one before college graduation and the remainder afterwards. I did relatively well in each of them. Only one agency, the Pennsylvania State Police (PSP), in a pre-test appointment/quasi-physical at the Belmont Barracks in Philadelphia, advised me I was not eligible to be one of their troopers. I was told this literally the day I received my college degree in the mail. The reason, the PSP recruiter told me, was because my uncorrected eyesight was not up to their standards.

Geez, would my LEC degree be for naught if my eyesight wasn't good enough to even be in the criminal justice profession? And here I thought it would be for other recent issues that I may not be hired.

But, my eyesight?

My PSP physical exam, albeit a very basic one, was the first one I had undertaken since before college and it disqualified me right out of the gate, at least with that agency. While I wore glasses on-and-off since my senior year in high school, I didn't need them all the time back then. At least I didn't think so. I didn't need them to read or drive a car. I knew that, as it was not an issue at my driver's license exam. But, now I was being told my eyes weren't good enough to drive a police patrol car. How disconcerting…and frustrating. Was I even physically qualified for this profession? Was this an early omen of bad things to come?

Before I left the PSP barracks that day, the trooper/recruiter (who coincidently was wearing bi-focal glasses) knew I was disappointed by what he had told me. As I was about to exit his office, he said that not all police departments had the same stringent restrictions as did his agency. He advised that I should consider applying to various local police departments as their eyesight qualifications may be less of an issue for me than it was with the PSP. I thanked him, told him I was already doing that, and left his office. It was clear that day that I was not destined to be a PSP trooper.

After graduation, still with no employment prospects, during my daily searches of the Philadelphia newspapers, I recall seeing an ad for the U.S. Army which clearly stated that, upon enlisting, a college graduate would be commissioned as a second lieutenant. With nothing else of any real job potential at this time, I called and spoke to an Army recruiter about my options. He was very professional and we had a nice chat. He described what I could expect, where I could go, for how long, etc., with my commission in the Army. After the initial call, he aggressively called me back a few times, but our discussions did not go much further than that first call.

Despite the negative post-Vietnam War national reputation of the U.S. military (again, over-reported in the media and greatly undeserved in my estimation), I still considered it as a possible career option. Plus, as an extra bonus, I would get those ten extra points in the future on civil service tests, if I was still so interested. But, for very personal reasons, and linked to very specific familial issues, I made my decision.

As my parents were getting older, and the fact that my dad already had a few hospital stays for various health problems over the past two years, I decided against joining the military. I knew it would require me moving away from Philadelphia, for possibly several years or more, and something told me that my parents were not much longer for this world. Quite simply, I wanted to be around them, help them, and even care for them if need be, while they were still alive and as they aged. I didn't see myself in some faraway place for four years, or longer, and being able to address this very personal goal.

I knew I wanted to serve my country, my society, somehow, and I certainly would have joined the military if I had been drafted. I would not have headed to Canada as many of my contemporaries had done to avoid the draft. (I believe I would have enlisted first.) But, as I was not in a compulsory draft situation, and with the Vietnam War being officially over at this time, it would be in some way other than the military. I would serve my country, in some fashion, but it would be as a civilian. How and when and where I would do that was still over a year away from being resolved. There would be one interesting stop first before officially providing that service to my country.

Chapter Nineteen

While still living at home with my parents in Olney in early July of 1975, and still unemployed several weeks after my college graduation, it was my dad who made the "find" for me in the *Inquirer* classified ads early one morning, before I even awoke, that would start me off in my new profession. It read "Security/Store Detective," at the Strawbridge and Clothier (S&C) department store in downtown, aka Center City, Philadelphia. I told my dad initially that morning that I didn't get a B.S. degree to be a security officer at a department store. But, he convinced me that I really didn't have many other options at this point. He was, as usual, correct in his observation.

My friend Rob McCarthy, my earlier lobbing-pennies-at-a-cat co-conspirator, had been a store detective at the Gimbel's Department store right across the street from S&C over the last two years or so. He said it was a fun and interesting job and it prepared him well for his present profession, that being, a rookie Philadelphia police officer. He had taken the entrance exam the year before me and was already on the Philly PD. John Welsh had also worked at the same Gimbel's for a few months before his next career move. He said it was an okay job, too.

So, I called the phone number listed for the store detective position and made an appointment for an interview. The interview a day or so later went well and within a week I was a store detective, carrying a REAL badge for the first time, albeit of the private retail store security variety. (I suppose my eighth grade St. Helena School safety patrol badge was a real one too nine years before; certainly more real than the not-too-long-ago misused Globe Security badge, anyway.)

This new job was definitely a start for me as it was the beginning of the non-academic learning portion of my career, that is, gaining practical experience on top of my previously attained book and classroom attained knowledge.

At the time, S&C was an upscale department store and a Philadelphia retail institution. It was located at 8th and Market Streets. It took up almost an entire downtown city block. It consisted of nine large retail floors, including a dimly-lit "bargain" basement, of goods ranging from quality knick-knacks to high-end furniture, clothes, jewelry, TVs, boutique-style food, and almost anything else one could hope to buy in such a commercial establishment. There was also a warehouse next door which was off-limits to the public. It was essentially a small city composed of nine levels for the public with several floors above those for the administrative offices, and a warehouse adjacent to it. The basement even had a direct exit to a Broad Street Subway platform, specifically, the so-called Ridge Avenue Spur. All the floors and buildings were the responsibility of the S&C security team.

That team now included me.

I would walk almost every square inch of the S&C store and warehouse over the next approximately 14 months. I would get to know many employees and hear much about their lives, some professionally related, some personally related, as time went by. A handful of these employees had been there for decades, some even pre-World War II, and would occasionally share tales from the early days of the local department store giant, to include during the difficult war years. These stories could be very interesting. But, something told me I would not be working there quite as long as some of these career S&C employees.

On my first day at the store, after some basic administrative issues were covered in the office, some equipment provided (including a pair of handcuffs and a very basic limited-range pager), I started my on-the-job training. I simply walked the multiple floors of the large department store with one or more seasoned store detectives, learning the layout and how to spot potential thieves. If the pager went off, I was to pick up one of the many in-house phones, call the security office, and await my orders from the secretary/dispatcher. This type call was usually the result of a salesperson who may have seen something suspicious in their area and requested security to respond. There was also a small speaker on the pager and it if was a true emergency the secretary/dispatcher had a few seconds to blurt out where I should quickly proceed. That kind of call was relatively infrequent, but did occur several times during my tenure there.

There were around ten full-time S&C store detectives, pretty much split evenly between men and women. The ages ranged from me at 22 to folks in their 50s. We were plainclothes detectives, supplemented by a few uniformed security officers. One of our mid-level bosses, Bob Greer, was a fully retired Philadelphia police officer; another was a younger former officer out on a full disability from the Philadelphia police department due to an on-duty injury; and the big boss was a guy who was not a former LEO, but who worked his way up the corporate ladder in the S&C security department.

For me and others hired at the time for this position at this store, there was no initial classroom training, no arrest techniques taught, no rules of evidence, testimony, court procedures, nor any specific legal statutes related to retail theft imparted to my colleagues or me during any time that I was in the employ of S&C. My training consisted of merely professional anecdotes while walking around the large store and learning to identify potential "beats."

A "beat" was not a literary reference to the 1950s writers Ginsberg, Burroughs, Kerouac, et al. It was instead a euphemism, if not regional retail security nomenclature, origin unknown, for retail thieves, aka shoplifters. These beats would keep my co-workers and me very busy during my time at S&C. But, I was to learn, as much if not more of the theft that occurred in retail establishments such as department stores originated internally from their own employees rather than the beats from outside the store. That remains true to this day.

One of my first trainers, and someone with whom I became very friendly at the time, was a part-time employee named John Tierno. He was about 25 years old and a bit different than most of my fellow S&C store detectives. He was the only other college graduate in our crew. In his case, it was a degree in Education from Villanova University, located in the western suburbs of Philadelphia, not too far from where John grew up in Southwest Philadelphia. He also had a Master's Degree from Villanova, and was taking some other grad courses at the same time while working at the store mostly on Saturdays. He even held a black belt in jiu-jitsu. We became close friends back in those days, even going away for a long weekend in the Pennsylvania Pocono Mountains with our respective significant others the following winter.

John would ultimately introduce me to one of his best friends, Bob Yezzi. Bob, too, was a Villanova grad and would come to the store to visit John and grab lunch on several occasions when we happened to be working together. At times the three of us would walk the floor, John and I kiddingly telling Bob that he would be immediately "deputized" if the three of us should come upon a shoplifter. I'm not sure we ever actually made an "arrest" with Bob there, but he was no doubt ready to assist if need be.

I would see Bob and get to know him a little bit better each of the maybe three to five times he visited John during my tenure at S&C. He already had a job of some sort but was considering other career options the same time as me, to include that of a career in law enforcement.

Just a year or so later, post-S&C, while in the next stage of my professional life as a police officer, Bob looked me up and contacted me by telephone at my residence. As an eventual result of that call, I would get much closer to Bob over the next few years, even more so than I had been with our mutual friend John Tierno at S&C, as we would be fellow police officers together.

Ironically, I would only see John one more time after leaving my S&C job. It would be on a very long and sad day, almost four years later, and it involved our mutual friend.

Bob Yezzi will be further discussed in Book II.

As a rookie store detective, I don't recall my actual first arrest at S&C. But, there were lots of them over my 14 months or so there. Technically, as I would learn some time afterwards, I wasn't actually putting anyone under "arrest" when I would confront these people after catching them in the act of stealing something. I would merely "detain" them until the police arrived for them. In essence, we store detectives would be making a "citizen's arrest" each time we detained a shoplifter. If so called, the uniformed Philadelphia police officer would then officially arrest the person upon taking them into custody, based on the information provided to them regarding what the shoplifters were seen doing, the merchandise they attempted to steal, the value of it, etc.

Many offenders were teenage boys trying to steal record albums from the fifth floor music department, or clothes from the second floor men's department, or some quick-grab items, including jewelry, from the first floor. Leather jackets, located very close to one of the main first floor exits, were popular items to steal. They were chained to their respective racks, but wire cutters would be used by the thieves to clip the chains. If their timing was right, dozens of jackets at a time could go out the door. These types of daring, high-value, low-sophistication thefts wouldn't happen very often, but when they did it affected all of us in the security department.

How did we not prevent this type of very visual, embarrassing, and costly theft? This was a question asked by the higher-ups in the store administration. My boss would have to answer this and related questions. The following year's security department's budget would sometimes be threatened based on the number of these type thefts that took place.

I learned hanging out at the men's cologne and hair product booth, directly adjacent to the store's 8th St. entrance and the leather coat racks, would help me catch some of these thieves down the line. I would plant myself there and hold conversations with the two workers assigned to that booth while watching the beats. I learned much from these two guys, and caught some shoplifters at the same time.

The S&C cologne salesmen, what I learned from them, and how it played out in a national headline grabbing police case in which I was involved, will be discussed in Book II.

Very few retail thieves at S&C, I was to learn, were actually stealing items for themselves. Usually they would be stealing merchandise in-bulk, such as the aforementioned leather jackets, and/or as much as they could hide and conceal of some other pricey items, and walk or occasionally run out the door with it. They would then attempt to sell the items later on the street at a greatly reduced price. If the price tags were still intact, which was always their goal, the items could fetch even more money. Intact price tags made the items more valuable on the street as they were then considered brand new and never worn or used. Sometimes, the persons buying these stolen items would in turn come to the store and attempt to "return" them for cash. They would conveniently have forgotten the receipt, of course. If suspicions were aroused, the solution was to take the merchandise from them and ask them for their home address. IF they provided it, a check for the amount of the item MAY be mailed to them. Or not, depending on the advice of the security department if the returner's background and legitimacy couldn't be verified.

I arrested, make that detained and/or had arrested, males, females, old, young, solo individuals, pairs, teams, of all colors, shapes, and sizes. One of my colleagues even arrested an actual nun for shoplifting while I was at S&C. I forgot what she was trying to steal, but her flowing nun habit made it an easy place for her to hide things. Others would use clever bags and boxes with false bottoms, not to mention straps and pockets of various configurations inside their clothing to hide multiple items of value. It was amazing what they could hide in their clothing if done so carefully and surreptitiously.

I remember getting called one time to the first floor jewelry counter because the salesperson was suspicious of the person attempting to use a store credit card. The name on the card had "Dr." in front of it and was arguably of Jewish origin. The bearer of the card that day was a young African-American male, no more than 20 years of age. Something didn't seem quite right, or kosher, with this scenario.

The salesperson who called, who also happened to be African-American, was known to be a good judge of character or the lack thereof, and she had helped us catch other thieves who also tried to steal from her by one means or another in the past. In any event, this young man stuck around, but when he couldn't even spell the last name on the card, or tell us what kind doctor he may be, we detained him. He insisted the whole time, until the police actually took him away, that it was his card and he was, in fact, "Dr. Sol..." whatever last name it was that he couldn't spell or even pronounce. I learned later that there had been a mugging not far from the store just an hour or so before the young man tried to use it. One more case solved.

There was also a former Cardinal Dougherty High School teacher I would see in the store every once in a while. I never had him as one of my teachers while a student there, but I knew he had abruptly quit about halfway through my time at CD for some unknown problem or another.

A rumor that circulated during my school years was that this teacher had "commissioned" one of my then-fellow CD students to get him four new tires of a certain brand and certain size for his car, by any means necessary. Another rumor was that he would also have students shoplift for him from various department stores. He told these students he didn't care where or how they got these items for him, but he would give them a high grade in his class if they completed the various missions. Sometimes he would pay them money, too. It wasn't too long after these rumors spread that the teacher quit or was fired.

Upon recognizing his distinctive look at least six years later in S&C one day, I was convinced that this former CDHS teacher was still a thief and was now attempting to practice his thievery where I was working. Not on my watch, I thought to myself.

The former CD teacher would come into the store with two or three younger men, each carrying bags of some sort, and they would each conspicuously scatter shortly afterwards. I would initially follow him and watch as these kids would come back and quietly advise him regarding something or other, all of them suspiciously turning their heads and looking around for something or someone the whole time. Then, depending on his response to them, they would sometimes scatter again throughout the store. They were of high school age and more likely than not students of his from some other Philadelphia area school where he was employed as a teacher and where they had not yet caught on to his dishonest ways.

I kept my eye on the teacher and his entourage and tried to get my other colleagues to follow his co-conspirators, but of the two times I saw him, he would wind up "making" me or one of my colleagues somehow on each occasion. He may have recognized me from my CDHS days, but it also could have been that it simply wasn't very easy to follow an experienced thief for too long in a department store such as S&C, no matter how good a detective may be in doing so. I don't believe he ever successfully stole anything from the store when I was there, but it's certainly possible he did at other times when I wasn't working or at other times when I simply didn't see him. He would definitely fit the definition of what we would call a beat, whether he actually stole the items himself or commissioned others do it for him.

Shoplifting suspects, once the act was con-firmed and they were confronted, would sometimes want to fight and/or run away, especially if they were close to an exit and could see daylight and if they perceived the ratio of thief-to-security person-nel was in their favor. On more occasions than I care to remember, suspects would start swinging their fists and kicking their feet in an attempt to get out of my/our grip. It was definitely to our ad-vantage to keep the detainment inside the store. Much in the way of control was lost once the "take-down" would occur outside the store, on the side-walk, or on streets of downtown Philadelphia. If time permitted, it was also good to pre-plan the ac-tual confrontation by calling the security office from one of the ubiquitous in-store phones and have them page and send other detectives to the area of the potential shoplifting for back-up. Two is defi-nitely good company and three an even better crowd, of fellow store detectives that is, when un-dertaking an arrest. Then, our goal was to accom-plish it quickly, get the person into handcuffs right away, remove them from the floor (even temporari-ly into a fitting room or nearby storage area if nec-essary until they calm down), make sure to retain the evidence, and eventually walk them to the secu-rity office. That's ideally how it should be done.

Other times, instead of initially fighting, the shoplifters would run if the element of surprise and numbers were not in our favor, but conversely in theirs. I engaged in several mile-plus foot chases along Market Street, running in-between business people, shoppers, tourists, cars and buses, while at-tempting to catch the thief and/or recover the mer-chandise. One such foot chase ended with the arrest right next to the entrance to the Liberty Bell, near 5th and Market Streets. The tourists in line to see one of the great artifacts of U.S. history had an interesting sideshow that day as I tackled a teenager with an armful of record albums, all in their clear view. No "liberty" for this kid for the next few days, I remember thinking while we wrestled on the ground. The record albums were recovered mostly intact. I don't recall which artists the thief preferred. No doubt, they were chosen more for a quick street sale than this kid's own musical tastes.

If in a foot chase, if the one or more suspects running opted to drop the merchandise, it would have to be decided in a split-second as whether to keep chasing them or stop and pick up the stolen item(s). We were instructed to try to recover the merchandise first. If not, then some other thief-of-happenstance in the immediate area would simply pick up the item and walk away with it; a financial loss to S&C either way.

While in an outside foot pursuit, I also learned to identify myself as a police officer to the suspects we were chasing. Since these guys were usually less willing to fight a police officer than a run-of-the-mill, everyday plainclothes security guard, yelling/telling this lie to them while actually chasing them made sense from a self-preservation perspective. Nonetheless, I took a few punches and kicks to the face and body during my short career at S&C. I gave a few back in return too. However, there were no serious injuries sustained, either to me or to the occasional violence-prone beats during my store detective days.

Other shoplifting suspects, if they weren't fighters, would many times attempt to create a public scene by yelling and screaming in an attempt to garner crowd support in their favor. This would usually be on the crowded first floor, near one of the exits, as they were attempting to leave the store with pockets or bags full of stolen merchandise. Sometimes, if they were members of one or more minority groups, they would yell that their "rights" were being violated, or they were being discriminated against, trying to make it appear as if their attempted detention was racially motivated. When my S&C supervisor, Bob Greer, an African-American, and/or one of the other African-American store detectives would arrive on the scene and jump in, it pretty much took the wind out of the shoplifter suspect's sail at that time, at least for this particular ruse.

Other times, the suspect would pretend to faint or have a heart attack in order to gain the sympathy of the crowd in an attempt to somehow be released. It never worked. We'd then bring over one of the many wheelchairs hidden on each floor and roll the person to our basement level security office, in handcuffs, of course. Amazingly, upon being brought to the office, the person was usually "cured" of what ailed them on the floor of the store. Usually....

Another theft-related problem that occurred at S&C, and certainly at other department stores of which I was aware, was that of "till-tappers." These were not shoplifters per se, but men (rarely individual females) who would walk into the store and either through a direct approach, a ruse, or some sort of surreptitiousness, manage to get their hands into the drawer of a cash register and steal the money. Some carried large screwdrivers or small pry-bars with them to facilitate their crime. They would use them on temporarily unattended registers with the hope that there was cash in them. Others would work in teams (these teams would generally be male and female), and while the woman would distract the employee asking about clothing sizes or something like that, the man would somehow get into the drawer, either by prying it or waiting until it was open and grabbing the cash and running away with it in hand. These people worked fast, usually on the first floor near the exits, at high-volume cash registers, and were hard to catch. Their "takes" were never that large, but one or two hundred dollars to some people, especially in the mid-1970s, was not a bad score.

Bottom-line, during my time as a retail store detective, I learned that shoplifters and thieves came in all shapes, sizes, ages, sexes, and colors, and were as different and varied as the rest of our society. What they had in common is that they just liked to steal things from stores, sometimes for themselves, but mostly to sell them for cash.

Chapter Twenty

Besides just looking for ways to prevent retail theft, I had a few ancillary duties at S&C for which I was responsible. One of them was at 5:00PM every weekday, and 3:00PM every Saturday. The specific and rather simplistic task-at-hand was to lock the door on the sixth floor men's room. The reason for this, suffice to say, is because various interpersonal physical engagements between at least two men at a time were known to occur in the stalls in this particular men's room, for some reason usually later in the afternoons. Customers and employees would see or hear of these activities and the complaints would make their way to the security department.

Somehow, this men's room was well known as a meeting place for similarly minded people to engage in certain acts. I was told the location was even publicized in an underground Philadelphia publication as a potential hook-up spot, or whatever contemporary jargon was assigned to this form of meeting back then. It was thusly determined that it made the most sense to simply lock the door after certain times each day, once it was unoccupied, of course. I was relatively diligent about doing it, except for one particular Saturday afternoon, during the late spring of 1976.

I did not perform my door-locking task on that particular afternoon, May 22. I was following a potential shoplifter around in some other part of the store. He eventually left the premises without stealing anything. That happened a lot, of course, and this day was not unusual in that regard. Sometime that day after this potential thief exited the store, around 4:00 or so, I received an urgent call on my pager's mini-speaker that there was a shooting in the sixth floor men's room and I should proceed there immediately. There was only one public men's room on the sixth floor, so I knew where to go. As I was double-stepping upward bound on the store's escalators, one floor at a time, dread descended upon me. This was virtually the one day I did not secure the door, as was our daily protocol, and now this.

Damn!

When I arrived at the sixth floor men's room, within one minute of the original call, I saw that the door was propped open and there were people talking loudly and excitedly around it. One of the employees there recognized me and pointed for me to go in to the bathroom. On my way in, he told me in what can be best described as an unsure and shaky voice, "I think a man has been shot in there."

Damn again!

I entered the men's room. My training at the time, or shall I say lack of training, didn't much tell me what to do next. In fact, it was my prior training from another job in my recent past that may have helped the most in this situation.

I walked into the relatively small men's room, and there half-in and half-out of one of the stalls was a man in business attire, probably in his 50s, lying face-up on the floor, on top of a rapidly expanding pool of blood. I yelled out for someone to call the rescue squad and the police, although I believe that had already been done. I took some paper towels, designed for water absorption, not blood, and nonetheless pressed them onto the spot on the man's cheek from where the blood seemed to be oozing. I tried to talk to him at the same time. He was unresponsive. All I could do was what I learned in the first aid portion of my Red Cross senior life-saving course from a few years before. That was to apply direct pressure to his wound. I was hoping, for his sake, it was his only wound. I again tried to ask him what happened, but with no verbal response at all from him, only strained breathing. He WAS breathing though. Thank goodness!

The rescue squad appeared about five minutes after I had arrived there, followed by some uniformed police officers. I gladly got out of the way and allowed them to take over the scene. The wounded man was eventually taken on a stretcher by elevator down to an awaiting ambulance on the street. The police interviewed me and other customers and employees who were in the area at the time of the shooting.

I later learned that there were apparently two men in the bathroom and a loud bang was heard. Afterwards, a man was seen running from the area and to the down escalator. There were two separate sets of up and down escalators at S&C, in two separate parts of the store. I ran up one toward the sixth floor men's room, but it seems the shooting suspect ran down the other. When the next person entered the men's room, the victim was observed on the floor, bleeding profusely. He exited quickly and told a store employee who then called security.

In the meantime, one of the assistant security department managers, Bob Greer, happened to see a guy running at full speed down the other escalator onto the first floor. As Bob had heard of the 6th floor shooting the same time as me, he followed the guy, who was still moving quickly, into the Gimble's department store across the street. While there, he saw him put a gun into his pocket. Because of this Bob detained him on the scene with the help of another store detective. Upon being searched, the wallet of the men's room shooting victim was found on the suspect. The robbery and attempted homicide suspect was eventually turned over to Philadelphia police officers who then formally arrested him.

In my follow-up talks with the police detective assigned to investigate the attempted homicide, I learned that the shooting victim did not die as a result of his wounds. From what I recall, the man who was shot was not very cooperative with the police about what actually happened in the men's room that afternoon. However, it was not just a traditional armed robbery as I was later told by the detective. Something apparently went very wrong during the "interpersonal engagement" in that stall between the two men, and then the shot rang out.

The suspect who was arrested that day was eventually tried and found guilty of robbery, various weapons offenses, and assault.

Clearly, at the time, it greatly bothered me that I didn't secure the sixth floor men's room on that afternoon. I still think about it to this day and how things could have/should have been different that afternoon. That man would not have been shot if the door had been properly locked by me when it should have been, at 3:00, like I did just about every other day at the designated time. But, I didn't do it that day because of a failed attempt to catch a potential thief, and this poor guy was shot in the face because of it.

I didn't get "in trouble" or disciplined because of this incident. My colleagues knew what I was doing that afternoon, or trying to do, as some of them were helping me follow the possible shoplifter. My three experienced S&C supervisors, at least two of whom were former police officers, with one of them, Bob Greer, actually subduing this guy, each did their best to convince me that if the shooting hadn't happened then and there, it would have surely happened somewhere else, in some form or fashion involving one or both of the men involved. It could have even happened before 3:00 that day, they assured me, when the door would have been unlocked anyway. The victim was also clearly engaging in high-risk behavior in that public men's room and he merely picked the wrong guy, specifically one with a gun, to engage and later somehow upset that day. Perhaps it was about money, perhaps it was about something else, but it was pretty clear that these two men initiated the event by doing something that they perhaps should not have been doing in the public restroom of an upscale urban department store. It then got much worse for at least one of them after that.

On a much, much lighter note during this same general time frame, yet another ancillary duty for which an S&C store detective was responsible (besides catching shoplifters and the occasional robbery/attempted homicide suspect) was providing security for appearances of various authors, celebrities, and even rock-and-rollers.

During the Bicentennial summer of 1976, among other patriotic-themed events at the store that season, the then-very popular singers/rockers, the Bay City Rollers, made a well-advertised promotional appearance there one Saturday afternoon. I believe they had a new record album out at the time. At the store that day, it was a mob scene of hundreds of mostly young teenage girls, and their parents of course, to take in these pop stars du jour.

The band lip-synched three songs in less than 20 minutes at a designated in-store location, signed autographs on just-purchased (and only just-purchased) record album covers, and took some pictures with a few lucky, adoring fans. They then left the store the way they entered, through a warehouse door not accessible to the public.

While escorting them on their way out of the store, I rode an elevator with the five tartan-clad Scotsmen and their small entourage. The band members seemed like nice enough blokes. I got the impression they were a bit frazzled and didn't even know exactly where they were at the time, to include in what city they may be, or exactly where they were going next. Regardless, the S&C security team got them in and out of the store safely and securely to their tinted-windows van, with no young girls or Rollers getting hurt (or stolen or shot) in the process.

They were then free to enjoy their *S-a-t-u-r-d-a-y Night*, wherever that may have been.

Chapter Twenty-one

The first year after college, while working at S&C, I became even more of a newspaper and over-all news buff. For the first time in over a decade and a half, I didn't have everyday forced reading to do, that is, homework, as I had recently completed my formal studies forever (or so I thought). I kept reading, nonetheless. Books, of both the fiction and non-fiction variety, were included in this mix. But, I would also continue to read the *Philadelphia Inquirer*, the daily morning paper, on my bus ride commute to work every morning. On the early evening commute home on the subway or elevated train, I would read the daily *Philadelphia Evening Bulletin* or the *Philadelphia Daily News*. And yes, crime stories were still the mainstay of my reading interest. I couldn't get enough of them. Local, and more and more so, on the national level too.

I was reminded of my year prior mini-hunt for kidnap victim/political radical Patty Hearst when I read of an arrest of yet another '70s radical female, a former college student, bank robber, and cop killer. Her name was Susan Saxe. She was part of the Weather Underground, a left-wing group named after the lyrics in the Bob Dylan song, *Subterranean Homesick Blues*. Her crime oc-curred in Boston in 1970, but her arrest happened

very close to my workplace just a few months before I started at S&C.

While employed at S&C, and after I made a
routine shoplifting apprehension, I called the police
as per our normal protocol. No, the shoplifter
wasn't a wanted radical of any sort, but one of the
arresting uniformed officers who showed up at our
offices that day was, in fact, the officer who had arrested Saxe in March of '75 in downtown Philadelphia. His name had not been publicized in the media, but my bosses knew him and introduced me to
him. It wasn't that he stood out in any noticeable
way from the other uniformed officers I had met
during the course of my time at S&C, but I still
found him interesting and compelling in his own
way in just the short amount of time I spent with
him. He was quiet, polite, professional, matter-of-
fact, unassuming and what I would call even then a
"cop's cop."

I learned from my bosses that back in March of
that year the officer had been routinely shown a
picture of Saxe at roll call at the start of his shift that
day. As fate would have it, while on patrol later in
the day he saw a woman on the street who resem-
bled the wanted person in the picture he saw at roll
call. Despite her demonstrative protestations to the
contrary as to who she was (and who she swore she
wasn't) when he initially stopped her, the officer
very intuitively took her into custody anyway. She
was later positively identified via fingerprints at the
police district and her arrest was formalized.

This officer's powers of observation, visual acu-
ity, intuition, willingness to take a chance, and his
reluctance to not be talked out of his arrest of Saxe

(by her pretending to be someone else) resulted in this greatly sought after fugitive's apprehension.

Saxe subsequently pleaded guilty, albeit reluctantly, to the 1970 bank robbery and co-conspiracy in the death of the Boston police officer. She was sentenced and then served seven years in prison.

Like pro basketball player Bill Bradley's dogged determination and intuition to address something that seemingly wasn't right with the basket height on the hoops court those multiple summers before, this officer saw something that wasn't right, or that his intuition told him had to be addressed. Neither Bradley in his basketball uniform nor this officer in his police uniform knew for sure that what, or who, they were questioning would in fact be an accurate observation on their respective parts. They each took a well-educated hunch that they knew something wasn't right in their immediate surroundings. They were independently proven correct in both cases. No doubt, their individual preparations for each of those moments, the former with years of a steady work ethic, critical observance, and court presence, the latter with years of steady work ethic, critical observance, and street presence, paid off for each. As a result of their actions, their immediate surroundings were made into better places for what it is they do; one a basketball game venue, the other being the streets of the U.S.

Even though I didn't witness this officer make the arrest of Susan Saxe, his story and meeting him several months later clearly reinforced, with much higher stakes of course, what I saw Bill Bradley do some seven years before at a summer-league basketball game. That is, take seriously what it is I do professionally, prepare well for it, and not be afraid to follow through on well-placed intuitions if they're indicative of something being amiss. In doing so in the future, more times than not, I would be right.

It would take me another seven years or so to arrest a highly sought after fugitive. This one was a hit man, a murderer, and an international fugitive wanted by, among other entities, Interpol. He was of a different ilk than Susan Saxe, but still deadly nevertheless.

More on him and his arrest in Book II.

Chapter Twenty-two

As with most arrests and later prosecutions, at some point a law enforcement officer/agent has to testify in open court as to the facts surrounding the apprehension and/or other information relating to the crime or crimes for which the defendant is charged. It can be a daunting experience at any time during one's career, but especially so the very first time, as I was to learn...and yes, the hard way.

My first time testifying was in late 1975, several weeks after the routine arrest of a shoplifter. This guy tried to wear a man's suit out of S&C without paying for it. I observed him go into the second floor men's department fitting room with a relatively expensive three-piece suit and saw him walk out empty handed with his now all-of-a-sudden very tight street clothes over top of the suit. So, I detained him before he left the store without incident, took him to the security department, had him remove his street clothes, thusly exposing the nice, new suit underneath, and subsequently turned him over to the police department for prosecution. The theft and the immediate follow-up to it were so unextraordinary that later I actually forgot some of the facts about it and what occurred when and how. Never a good thing....

I should add here that during my time at S&C I made a fair number of shoplifting arrests and/or assisted my colleagues with their apprehensions. Some of those arrested were formally prosecuted, others were not. Sometimes the various arrest scenarios could blend together and the details could become more or less interchangeable in my mind. That's how I learned early in my career that detailed, accurate, and timely report writing was such a very important habit to develop and the sooner it was done after the arrest/incident, the better.

While the S&C security department did have incident report and arrest forms, my training never put much emphasis in what to actually write on them about any particular incident, crime, or person. The arrest forms would mostly have blocks regarding the value of the merchandise stolen and/or recovered, from where stolen/recovered, its condition, whether it was still sellable, taken by the police as evidence, etc. Oh, and a few blank lines about the arrested person's name, address, and what he/she was observed doing in the store that led to the arrest. We'd also take a Polaroid photograph of each arrested individual and the merchandise stolen, put them into the file, and attach them onto any report that was generated. That could be important for future purposes, to include any subsequent prosecution.

As the S&C security department's annual budget was based to some degree on the value of what it was we recovered every year, the blocks on the arrest form regarding the dollar amount of the merchandise (never the on-sale price, but the higher actual list price) were the most important to fill out. Or, so I was told in the minimalist training session I participated in on my first days at the store. The details of the arrest itself, listed down the page, were almost an afterthought in the form's layout. That section was thusly filled out by me that way at first…as an afterthought.

With this particular otherwise unsophisticated suit stealer, the information I wrote about him and the theft itself in the incident report was not all that detailed. That was the first mistake that came back to haunt me on the day of my initial testimony. My second mistake before the hearing that day was not reviewing the report for longer than just a few minutes. And, not memorizing some important facts (even with the minimal information included therein) just before I testified. I thought I would remember everything I needed to know for what I was told would be a quick and simple hearing. Hey, after all, it was just a routine shoplifting arrest. But, I didn't remember or know some facts, some potentially important facts, and what I did know didn't quite come out right. The defense attorney made me acutely aware of these issues on that day during my relatively brief time on the stand.

I had stayed in contact with the Philadelphia police detective who was assigned to this case. This matter was no big deal for him, and I knew that. It was just a retail theft case, one of many relatively minor cases he was investigating along with some bigger ones that took up more of his time and justifiably so. But, like me, he had to follow through on what we started a few weeks before. He had called me at the store in advance to tell me that I would be receiving a routine subpoena for my appearance in court on that date. I assured him that I would be there. I did, in fact, show up on time that day and awaited our case to be called.

On a related note, when the officers would first pick up the detainees at S&C at the time of the arrest, or sometime later at the police district, they would ask for the home address of the arresting store detective. I was strongly advised by my bosses that I should not give out that personal information and to just provide them with the store address. This was suggested because of the fact that the issued subpoenas for court became a matter of record and the defendant could attain that personal bit of information by just talking to his attorney or reviewing his own legal file.

Since some of these guys we arrested were truly bad-asses with long criminal records, having served prison time, etc., it would not be a good thing for them to have a home address for any of us. Some PPD patrol officers and police detectives would insist upon getting this information because they knew that store detectives would sometimes quit their jobs for various reasons after a short time and they wanted a way to contact them down the line if so needed for court purposes.

Needless to say, when pressed for this personal identifying information being told by the officers that the store address was not good enough, a few digits would invariably be altered on the purported home address and telephone number I would ultimately provide. I hated being less than truthful in this situation as it didn't pay off for me in the past and I was not in the habit of doing so in my everyday life. But, this was different. It once again had to do with self-preservation, and my parents' preservation for that matter, as it was their home address too at this time.

In reality, I had the impression the police officers didn't really care about this matter that much. They knew I worked at S&C and as long as they could fill in the line on their form with some form of alternate contact information, they were okay with it. And, by the way, I made sure through the use of the Cole Cross-Directory Book of Addresses we had in the security office that the address I provided was not a real address, but a non-existing one. Let the bad guy waste his time looking for me at a home address that didn't even exist.

My first testimonial experience was to be at the suit stealing defendant's preliminary hearing. Within six hours or so of an arrest, in the Commonwealth of Pennsylvania, a person charged with a misdemeanor or a felony is to be brought before a district magistrate for his/her preliminary arraignment. That's when they are formally advised of the charges before them and bail is set. A store detective is not necessarily needed for this step in the legal process.

Within ten days of the arrest, the person (now legally "the defendant") is brought before a district magistrate for a hearing to determine whether a prima facie case exists against him or her. That is, does the evidence presented at this hearing, relating to the basic facts of the alleged crime and the subsequent arrest, warrant the matter moving forward in the courts, to an actual trial if he or she so chooses, as opposed to him or her pleading guilty. While other U.S. states may call these proceedings by different legal terms, or the timing of each may differ slightly, the general premise is the same. And, even though the legal statute advises the preliminary hearing is to be within 10 days, in many cases there are court granted continuances (postponements) and it may not occur until a month or more later.

So here I was, about six weeks after the arrest (due to one or more continuances or other reasons) ready to testify at the suit thief's preliminary hearing. At least I thought I was ready.

As I was told that sometimes it was a long wait at the then 75-year-old Philadelphia City Hall building for these types of proceedings, I brought my partially read morning newspaper with me. I wanted to have something to do, to read, to kill the time, while I was waiting for my turn to testify. So, after meeting with the detective in the dark and rather depressing hallway outside of the courtroom, and realizing that we'd probably have an hour or so wait until our case was called, I walked into the courtroom and began watching the mostly routine administrative legal matters unfolding in front of me.

Before too long, the above procedures began to bore me to no end. There were no flamboyant Chippy Patterson-like attorneys in the courtroom that day, nor were there any high-profile murder prosecutions underway. So, in attempting to quench that ongoing and consistent lifelong thirst for information and knowledge, and in an attempt to fight off my boredom, I pulled out the newspaper and began reading it.

Why not? I had nothing else to do while I waited and I certainly wasn't bothering anyone. Right?

Wrong!

About halfway through an interesting article about something or other I heard a loud thud. Hmmmm...it sounded like a hammer hitting something, but with a noticeable reverberation or echo of some sort. That's strange for a courtroom, I thought. And it emanated from the front of the room from the area of the judge's bench. That's strange too. I guess I should look up. I did. Within that second or two, I heard the judge speaking loudly and very distinctly and he was pointing his finger directly at me.

"Put down that newspaper right now or be held in contempt of court!"

Me? Contempt of court? For this? You gotta be kidding!

Actually, he wasn't.

The judge definitely made his issue known to me in no uncertain terms. In view of that, I put the paper on the floor beneath my seat right away, not touching it again that day. In fact, I left it there an hour later when I finally exited the courtroom. Anything that could get me in that much trouble I wanted no further parts of. Not in the courtroom anyway. A police officer sitting on the bench directly in front of me, there apparently for another case, turned around and whispered dismissively, "Kid, you can't read newspapers in a courtroom, especially with this judge. Didn't you see the sign at the entrance?"

No, I hadn't seen it. Later, when exiting, I did see that sign forbidding newspaper reading, talking, gum chewing, etc., in the courtroom. It was prominently displayed at the entrance. Okay, shame on me for missing this advisement when I first entered the room; so much for my alleged powers of observation and use of common sense. Well, at least on that day.

So, within a half hour of my first time ever in a courtroom, the sitting judge threatens me with contempt. And this is before my case was even called. What would happen when it was my turn to testify in front of the same judge who just legally threatened me? I was about to find out.

My case was eventually called, shortly after the police brought in the shoplifter/defendant handcuffed and in his orange jumpsuit. (He was still in custody as a result of a bench warrant for another criminal matter in which he was involved – not for this shoplifting arrest alone.). He was un-cuffed and sat at a long table in the front of the room next to a man in a suit, presumably his lawyer, and they began talking. I watched the defendant at some point turn around and point at me, with his attorney also looking at me and nodding his head at the same time as if in agreement. The attorney then stood up and began talking to another guy in the courtroom, sitting in a row of seats behind his table. This guy was also in an orange jumpsuit and handcuffs, apparently awaiting his name to be called to address his particular legal matter. Maybe this guy was the lawyer's client too. I didn't know nor did I really care at the time.

Shortly thereafter, without any pre-warning or discussion with anyone, the case I was there for was called - something like "the Commonwealth versus..." and the defendant's name. I was then summoned to the witness box by the Assistant District Attorney (ADA). I was sworn in, and after that the ADA asked me to identify myself, spell my name, give my title ("store detective"), and state for whom I worked. That was the easy part. What happened next though was most definitely much more difficult.

(The below testimonial snippets are from memory, not from a formal transcript of the proceedings that day. While certainly not word-for-word, the related Q & A is relatively close to what was verbalized by me, the two attorneys, and the judge, during this preliminary hearing.)

After a few more basic questions, the ADA asked me how I initially came into contact with the defendant. I began my testimony by explaining to the judge (there's no jury at a preliminary hearing) how I received the information that day that eventually led me to detain and then press charges against the individual for shoplifting.

I testified, "Well, I received a page from my security dispatcher, so I called the office from an in-house phone. The secretary then told me to go to...."

"Objection as to hearsay," was then abruptly blurted out by the defense attorney, rudely interrupting me and my train of thought while I was just getting into the gist of my testimony.

"Sustained," said the judge.

Huh? What did I do? What just happened? Before I could even think any more about what I just did or didn't do, the judge responded to the attorney's objection with that one word.

The ADA then advised me to simply state what I next proceeded to do with that information from the phone call.

Oh, okay...I guess. I then reformulated my thoughts for a few seconds and continued with my testimony.

I then picked up with, "I proceeded to the men's suit department on the second floor and up-on arriving there I was called over by one of the salesmen. The salesman told me that a guy...."

"Your Honor, once more, objection as to hearsay!"

Geez, again? This time even louder and more derisively from the opposing attorney, still seated at the long table.

"Sustained," the judge responded, seemingly a bit frustrated this time.

The ADA had to advise me a second time, more pointedly in this rendition, to just relate what it is I saw and what it is I did, and not attempt to repeat what someone else had told me.

Right, okay. Just state what I did and saw, not what they said. I can do this. I hope....

I then couldn't help but think that within my first 90 seconds or so of testifying, ever, in my life, there were already two objections by the defense at-torney, the second time more demonstrative than the first, based on what I was attempting to say, or how I was attempting to say it, with the judge clearly agreeing with him. And, this is shortly after being threatened with contempt of court by the same judge before my case was even called. Man, this is a lot more intense than I thought it would be. Testifying ain't easy, I was learning. It certainly wasn't that day, and I'm barely three minutes into it.

The issue, as I had been legally and officially reminded twice so far that day while on the stand, was that hearsay evidence, that is, testimony relat-ing to what someone else said at a given place and time, even if I heard it and it was part of a conversation I had with that someone else, was inadmissible in a proceeding such as this one. The legal precedent regarding hearsay evidence is based on the fact that there could be no cross-examination of the so-quoted person, no ability to challenge that person about what he or she purportedly witnessed or said, so therefore it is inadmissible as testimony by someone else in open court. I would have to stick to testifying about what I saw and what I said, and what I did, but not what anyone else may have said, even if it made the information I was providing so much more clear and descriptive to the court as to what actually unfolded that day. However, that really didn't matter, I was to learn. I should just state the facts, minus what someone else may have said to me. So, I did, or at least I tried from that point on.

Upon being further questioned by the ADA, I went on to explain, now in as brief terms as possible, how I saw the guy acting suspicious as he was looking at numerous expensive suits, then walking into the fitting room with a suit in hand, and then coming out a few minutes later with no suit in hand, but his street clothes bulging. I further testified that I detained him, saw the suit under his clothes, and took him into custody.

The ADA asked me if the suit was in the courtroom. I replied that I didn't see it anywhere but there was a picture of it in the file. I forgot if I had given the suit to the officer on the day of the arrest for evidence. Sometimes they took the stolen item(s) as evidence, sometimes they didn't and instead just wanted a Polaroid photo of it. He asked me the retail value of the suit. I told him I forgot the exact amount, but it sold for about $150, which wasn't cheap for a suit in the mid-1970s. He lastly asked me if the defendant was in the courtroom and if so to point him out. I told him yes and pointed to the guy sitting at the table in the orange jumpsuit.

The ADA said to the judge, "No further questions of this witness."

Upon hearing that, I stood up to leave the witness box. My job here was done, I thought.

Actually, no, it wasn't. It was far from over.

Upon observing my hasty attempt to exit, the judge abruptly told me to sit down as it was now the defense attorney's turn to ask the questions. Oh, yeah, right, the cross-examination. So, I obediently sat down again.

Now the real fun was to begin.

The defense attorney stood up and walked over to me, pretty much right in my face, and asked me how long I had been a store detective. I told him approximately five months.

He next asked me how many arrests I had made during that time. "Numerous," I replied.

"How many exactly?" He asked more specifically this time.

"I don't know exactly," I advised.

I was told by one of my S&C colleagues who had prior court experience that it was alright on the stand to simply give this sort of reply if, in fact, you didn't know the answer to a specific question. This was clearly the situation here. I did not know exactly how many arrests I had up to this point.

"What do you mean you don't know?" He asked, somewhat indignantly this time.

"Uh, because I don't keep a running count of them," I retorted.

"Can you give me an approximated estimation of how many arrests you've made?"

"I suppose around 15 to 20 or so," I finally guessed/estimated and then testified.

"What was your training for being a security guard?"

Hesitatingly, because I knew of my genuine lack of formal training at S&C, I stated nonetheless factually, "Uh, as a new store detective (a subtle correcting of him as to my actual title), some administrative issues were covered in the office on the first day...I then walked the floor for a few days with some senior and experienced detectives when I was first hired...and I guess that was basically it. Oh, and I also have a college degree from...."

"I didn't ask you about your education, I asked you about your training for your job of arresting alleged shoplifters," he interrupted.

"Oh, okay," I responded and discontinued that immediate line of testimony.

Then he added, "So, you really had no specific, formal training to be a security guard, correct?

I couldn't help but state, "Only what I told you, sir."

Geez, this attorney is a jerk, I was thinking. Why is he talking to me like this? Can't we just have a nice Q and A like I had with the ADA? No, I learned. Not on this day, not with this attorney. I would experience later in my career that rarely on any day with an adversarial attorney during cross-examination would the discourse be less than very challenging, and even arguably combative sometimes, such as this, my very first time on the stand.

The defense attorney then asked me, "Do you recognize this man?"

The attorney was pointing to a guy in an orange jumpsuit, but it wasn't the guy next to him at the long table. It was the other guy sitting behind him on the bench, also in an orange jumpsuit. But it was the guy at the table I had already pointed out was the shoplifter when the ADA had asked me. I hesitated, I was confused. He saw that and he asked the question again, with more emphasis this time.

What was going on here? I was pretty sure that the guy I arrested was the guy at the table next to him, but why would he be pointing to this other guy who's the same general age and the same general description as the guy I thought was the defendant. And, he's not even asking me if this guy is the shoplifter. He's asking me if I recognize this other guy. Why, before this hearing, didn't I look at the Polaroid photo of the shoplifter from the day he was arrested? Did I even bring it with me?

I eventually responded to his question, but no doubt in an unconvincing manner.

"I don't believe I recognize that man," I said, referring to the guy at whom he was still pointing. I was sort of hedging my bets here just in case I was missing something.

"You don't BELIEVE you recognize him? So you're not sure WHO you arrested that day at S&C," the defense attorney emphatically stated.

I replied back with a bit more determination now as I was pretty sure I was correct. I better be.

"Yes, I am sure. But that's not what you asked me. You asked me if I recognized that other man. I don't. But, the shoplifter in this case is the man sitting at the table."

Geez, I hope I'm right here.

The defense attorney was about to ask another question again related to this unknown guy in the back row when the ADA objected, stating aloud that "Your Honor, the defense is trying to purposely confuse this witness by pointing to other people in the courtroom as the defendant."

The judge overruled the objection and stated that my identification of the shoplifter in this case was important and I had to answer the question, even though I had answered it already. I then stuck to my guns and pretty much insisted that the guy at the defense table was, in fact, the guy I had arrested six weeks before. It sure did look like him, at least from what I remember from six weeks or so ago when he was wearing the bulging street clothes.

My cross-examination went on for another ten minutes or so, with seemingly inane and innocuous questions related to store lighting, inside and outside temperatures that day, my precise vantage points in the store, angles and distance from me to the alleged shoplifter at all times, how many racks of clothing, mannequins, support pillars, etc., in between me and the defendant at any given time, precise time measurements of where he was in the store and for how long, and lastly, whether there were price tags still on the suit when I arrested him.

"No, he had pulled the price tags off the suit," I replied to that particular question.

"How did you know that? Were you in the fitting room with him?"

"No, but they weren't on the suit when I stopped him."

"But you didn't see him actually remove the tags from the suit?"

"No, I did not."

"So, if there were no price tags on it, then how did you know that the suit belonged to S&C? Perhaps the defendant just wore the suit into the store that day under his clothing because he liked wearing two sets of clothes. Is that possible, Mr. Fitzpatrick?"

Ok, this was getting stupid, and he called me "Fitzpatrick" on purpose too, I'll bet.

"I suppose it's possible that he just happened to be wearing a brand new suit under his clothes on that warm day, but I have never seen or heard of that before. And, by the way, it's Fitzgerald," I couldn't help but add.

I had to correct him about my name. I was going to turn to the judge and formally object, but I thought I better not press my luck.

I was about to add that one of the salesmen that day told me right away he found the tags from that exact suit on the floor of the fitting room the guy was in just as he exited it and that the suit was a brand sold exclusively in the area by S&C. I could testify to that now, but I knew that would be hearsay if I framed that way. So, I instead phrased my clarifying information in another way.

"Based on a conversation I had with the salesman immediately after the arrest of the shoplifter, I was provided by him with the sales tags from that exact suit. They were found in the dressing room the defendant used, right after leaving it. I independently confirmed later that the tags did belong with that suit which, by the way, is only sold in Philadelphia at the Strawbridge and Clothier store."

No objections this time regarding what I heard and did based on what someone told me.

I answered most of the rest of the defense attorney's questions as accurately as I could, but he nonetheless challenged every response I gave if I couldn't provide exact measurements or very detailed and descriptive accounts of the floor layout and precisely what I saw at any given time. He even asked at one point if I wore glasses. I told him only sometimes and that my overall vision was fine. He then asked me if I had been wearing them during this arrest scenario. I told him no.

(I was hoping he would not call, as a surprise witness, the Pennsylvania State Police trooper who just a few months prior told me my eyesight wasn't good enough to be hired by them. But, I didn't lie. All I said was that my vision was "fine," which it was. I didn't specify anything else about it.)

I did not testify any more as to what anyone else had told me. I think I finally had the hearsay rule down, so learned by me not in a law school class or from a legal book, but having violated it during my first-ever testimonial experience several times that day.

After a few more closing questions from the attorney, with me being compelled to repeat that I never did actually see the man put on the suit and then put his street clothes on top of it, I was eventually excused from the witness stand by those ever so welcome words to any person testifying in a legal case.

"No further questions of this witness, Your Honor."

I didn't move. Not yet. I wanted to make sure I was really done with my testimony this time. And, actually, I wasn't quite done yet. The ADA asked me one more question on redirect examination.

"In summary Mr. Fitzgerald, is it true that the evidence that day strongly suggested to you that the defendant was wearing a new Strawbridge and Clothier suit that he did not pay for and was attempting to leave the store?"

"Yes, that is correct."

"No further questions."

I hesitated again for a bit, but then was pretty sure I was truly done at this point, so I slowly got up out of the witness chair. If I wasn't really done, I didn't want to be moving so fast that I couldn't sit down again right away and make it look like I didn't know what I was doing. But, my testimony was in fact over and I was free to step down out of the box.

The defense attorney delivered a brief closing statement of sorts.

"I would submit to the court that the Commonwealth did not establish prima facie evidence that a crime was committed at S&C on this date. This witness doesn't know the basic rules of law as they pertain to the statute of retail theft, he never saw my client..." do this, do that, and so on.

Now he's insulting me and questioning my knowledge of the laws of Pennsylvania, retail theft, aka shoplifting, etc., right to my face. How dare he? But, in many ways on that day, based on my less than stellar testimonial performance, he was right to do so. Yes, I had a recent college degree in LEC from PSU, but none of my courses there prepared me to testify in a real live court case.

The ADA countered the defense attorney's argument by stating that the Commonwealth did, in fact, establish a prima facie case, etc.

Shortly after the ADA's brief closing remarks, the judge ruled that a prima facie case had, in fact, been established by the Commonwealth and the defendant would be held over for trial. Some bail issues were then discussed, but they did not concern me.

Success, I suppose. Well, for me. Not for the defendant though, who was staying in custody.

This defense attorney's cross-examination of me and his later closing statement directly and negatively referring to me was simply designed to try to confuse me, cross me up, throw me off my game, and challenge my credibility in front of the judge. The ADA was right when he objected, at least about the defendant bait-and-switch attempt in the courtroom that day with the defense attorney pointing to the other man.

To his credit, the defense attorney, after sizing me up early as a rookie witness, partially succeeded in that regard. However, if I had been a bit more prepared, and perhaps coached even a little bit by one of the senior members of the S&C security staff, or even the PPD detective or ADA, some of the problematic issues in my first-ever-testimony experience could have been avoided. However, it was up to me to have been better prepared that day. I did okay as my side "won," but I could have done much better.

In the end that day, even if ineloquently at times, I told the truth, the whole truth, and nothing but the truth, perhaps awkwardly on occasion, and the facts of the case fell into place accordingly. In this preliminary hearing, it was before a judge. In numerous future trials, at the state and federal levels, it would be in front of a judge and a jury.

Based on that early lesson and other experiences in the courts since then, I now find myself almost always over-preparing for any legal proceeding at which I'll be offering testimony. I would suggest that one can rarely have too much preparation in advance of providing legal testimony, of any kind. The critical facts or opinions (the latter only if offering court sanctioned expert testimony) should be well-known, well-rehearsed, and fully supportable.

Regarding actual testimony, it is advisable that in the courtroom the witness should only answer the question asked by an attorney and offer no more or no less. Having information and facts available to be attested to, if need be, is important. But, only providing such information when it is specifically asked is the most prudent and effective. Less lawyerly objections result and fewer cases are ultimately lost that way, no matter for what side the witness may be testifying.

A good chess player always plans well in advance of the next move. A person testifying should always listen carefully to the question asked by the adversarial attorney and should also attempt to determine his or her next move, or next question. The lawyer in many instances is leading into a series of questions to be asked, sometimes seemingly unrelated to the matter at hand, in an attempt at some very specific future question to get a response favorable to his/her side and impeach the credibility of the witness and thereby that to which is being testified. While on the witness stand, one should always be thinking several potential questions ahead when answering the immediate question asked. It's less confusing than it may seem; it just requires some simple planning ahead of each answer. Always tell the truth, of course, but no more information than necessary and try to get a feel of the road the attorney is leading you down.

After court proceedings in which I've participated I still tend to self-critique my testimony. In the later years of my FBI career, and now as a private-sector consultant, my testimonial experiences have mostly been as an expert witness in the field of forensic linguistics; this as opposed to a fact witness, such as my role in the above 1975 shoplifting case and many other criminal cases throughout my earlier career. Even today, upon reviewing the transcripts of some recent testimonial endeavors, I'm not always 100% satisfied with how I may have explained a certain issue, described a concept, discussed a finding, or ultimately provided an opinion.

Without a doubt, the foundational block in my testimonial career in that City Hall courtroom in late 1975 set the stage for the rest of my testimonial career. I'm much better now at providing the triers of the facts, that is, the judge and/or the jury, with accurate, descriptive, and readily explainable information they need to ultimately render their decisions and/or verdicts in either criminal or civil matters as to guilt or innocence, sentence length, civil awards, etc. Of course, and without a second thought, it should always be done so in a truthful manner too. And, if an answer to a question is not known, one should simply testify, "I do not know." Nothing is wrong with that response, as long as it's not given too many times during the course of one's testimony in an area in which the witness should probably know the answers.

As one can read, my initial professional foray into the legal system was a bit bumpy. As with other matters experienced for the very first time in life, whether successfully undertaken or not, one tends to learn from the experience.

The German philosopher Friedrich Nietzsche said, "That which does not kill us makes us stronger."

I applied this above maxim to my life on numerous occasions, some already discussed on these pages, some yet to come. My self-critique of my '75 testimony is not all that praiseworthy. But, it didn't kill me, obviously, so no doubt I'm stronger, or at least better, in that particular area, thanks to that experience. And, the shoplifting case was held over to criminal court, based on my testimony, even if delivered a bit unprofessionally at the time.

I don't know what ever happened to this case and this shoplifter. I quit my S&C job around nine months later and simply don't recall the outcome. Perhaps he plea-bargained and was sentenced to "time served." In any event, I'm sure the police could have contacted me through S&C and advised accordingly. Unless they tried to reach me at the home address and phone number I gave them.

Chapter Twenty-three

Back to my time at S&C, and back to the second floor men's clothing department where a number of detainments/arrests took place. I learned an early lesson of how police officers, whether present or past, tend to take care of each other. I learned of this phenomenon as it applied to a loaded .38 Detective Special found one day in one of the men's dressing rooms.

I responded to a call from our security secretary/dispatcher to proceed immediately to the men's department to recover a found item. When I arrived, the salesman took me in to one of the dressing rooms, which was now blocked off by a few chairs, and showed me what a customer (and fortunately an honest one) found on the interior seat. It was a black holster with a small handgun in it.

Hmmmm…okay, what did my comprehensive S&C training program tell me to do in this situation?

I didn't touch the weapon, as at this point in my life I had never handled a real firearm of any sort and didn't want to endanger anyone in the area, to include myself. I further secured the scene to make sure no one else would touch the weapon. I asked the salesman who he thought could have left it in there. He wasn't sure. Neither were any of the other salespersons on the floor in the department, although at least one salesman was at lunch right then. I called my supervisors and advised them of the situation. They told me not to touch the weapon and that they would be there in a few minutes. I gladly awaited their arrival before doing anything else.

By the time the two supervisors showed up, both former police officers, Bob Greer being one of them, they agreed that it looked like a Philadelphia Police Department-issued weapon and holster. Shortly after they got there the salesman who had been at lunch returned. He was then asked if he knew anything about the gun. He said he did not, but offered to us that he did show a suit to a man just about an hour ago whom he believed to be a police detective. This was right before he went on his lunch break. The man apparently tried on a suit in the fitting room in question, but didn't buy it and left the store shortly thereafter. Nothing unusual about that, the salesman added. As they made a commission with every suit sold, they were each sure to note who bought, who didn't buy, and who could be a potential return customer.

Everyone on the scene agreed that the weapon most likely belonged to the detective, or at least the guy we collectively thought was a detective. While trying on the suit in the dressing room, he must have inadvertently left the gun behind. However, the non-suit-buying customer/possible detective did not leave a name or phone number with the salesman. So, we had a gun that most likely belonged to this officer, but no way of knowing how to directly contact him.

I suggested out loud, in retrospect rather naively, that we simply call the detective division that covers the downtown area, since he was probably assigned there, and tell the supervisor what happened. My two bosses, as former cops and ever empathetic to what could happen administratively to a detective who essentially LOST his gun, collectively and adamantly said "No" to that idea. It'll be handled in another way, they insisted. So, they put the gun in a small yellow S&C bag, and together took it downstairs to the security office. They were now in charge of the lost/misplaced weapon caper. I stayed on the store floor, doing what I usually do, for the rest of the work day.

I was told later that afternoon that although it took my bosses a few hours and multiple discreet phone calls to their PD contacts, they finally somehow managed to track down the detective who lost the gun. He was in court all afternoon a few blocks away at City Hall, and even though he realized he was without his gun at some point that day, he couldn't do anything about it as he was testifying on the witness stand for much of his time there. He later said he was hoping it was where he thought he left it on his lunch break (at S&C) and that someone there found it and secured it for him.

The detective came back to the S&C security offices later that day and was returned his weapon, and no one else was ever the wiser. More importantly, thanks to how it was handled from the very beginning, no one was ever the deader.

I do not know if the detective ever went back to the second floor and bought a suit or not. If so, hopefully he wouldn't leave anything behind in the dressing room on this next occasion.

Very fortunately for the officer, and the public at large, a law-abiding customer found the unattended weapon, turned it over to the sales department, they called the security department, and it was handled accordingly. If it wound up in the wrong hands it would have been very problematic for the detective and possibly much worse for others too. And, in a way, it was nice to see cops, even when retired, take care of other cops. It seemed like a worthwhile fraternity I was looking to enter.

Chapter Twenty-four

By the beginning of 1976, while still doing my everyday job at S&C, I was nonetheless all over the local newspapers for law enforcement employment opportunities in the general Philadelphia area. My store detective job was interesting, it was a positive learning experience, there were some nice people with whom I worked, but it only paid the very basic bills, and I was still living at home with my parents.

At the time, my weekly take-home paycheck was $99.00 for a regular 40-hour work week at S&C. When I started working some 11-hour Wednesdays, when the store was open until 9:00P, with the three extra hours in the evenings at time-and-a-half, my check ballooned to a whopping $120.00 or so for the week. It clearly wasn't enough financially for me, nor was the job meeting my professional goals...however unclearly defined they may have been at the time.

My only real attempts so far to get a job in my field were the taking of the Philadelphia police officer test and stopping by the Pennsylvania State Police barracks one day. I knew the latter agency was a lost cause because of my alleged eyesight issue. Fortunately though, I had just recently been contacted by the Philadelphia PD to take my psychological and physical exams. That was good news. I reached out to the appropriate person as per the instructions in the letter and set up my testing appointment during one of my lunch breaks at S&C.

That day I walked to the Municipal Services Building, which is adjacent to Philadelphia City Hall in Center City, for my scheduled exams. The physical was very routine, with no issues regarding my eyesight or anything else from what I could tell. For whatever reason, the PPD was apparently less stringent in their eyesight requirements, once corrected by glasses, than the PSP. After a total of 30 minutes or so, the physical exam was over and my psychological exam was next. It was to be administered by a psychologist in an adjacent office, and parts of it were definitely not what I had expected.

As instructed by a staff person after my physical, I entered a small, windowless office, and closed the door behind me. The interior walls were devoid of even one painting, poster, or decorative artifact of any sort. The ambience could best be described as early government-esque, with battleship gray being the primary color scheme in the room. Once inside I was advised by the female psychologist to sit on a chair at a standard gray, steel desk, the top of which was completely barren of even a single paper clip. The mid-40s doctor was sitting on the other side of the desk, directly across from my chair, holding a clipboard. My chair was not on wheels. In fact, it was bolted to the floor. There was no opportunity to move a chair in a psych exam, at least not during this one. That was probably by design.

The psychologist initially asked me a few basic questions about why I wanted to become a police officer, my short-term and long-term goals, what did my family think about me becoming a police officer, etc. I answered the best and most honest way that I could. She was nodding her head and taking notes with each response.

I was next given a Rorschach inkblot test. She explained the basic premise of it to me, but I was aware of this sort of test from my psychology courses at Penn State. I knew what to expect, yet I didn't volunteer to her I knew anything about the purpose behind them, how they're scored, etc. I was aware that as long as I didn't describe the various black-and-white images as representing axes splitting human skulls, dismembered arms and legs, genitalia, and/or animal dissections, I was pretty sure I would be okay in her eyes. I believe I told her I mostly saw flowers, clouds, a pretty woman, a lion, and the like in the assorted blots. She again was writing on her clipboard as I turned over each page in the inkblot book. She did her note-taking in a passive and non-emotive manner, so I was convinced I was doing fine so far.

The next part of the psych test was truly odd, or at least I thought it to be, and totally unexpected, at least in the form it took. The psychologist told me she was going to ask me some questions or give me some specific directions, and I should simply respond in the best way I could to each. She asked if I was ready to proceed and I told her I was.

What she next said to me was not a question, but a direction. She requested me to count backwards from 100, by 3s. I no doubt looked at her somewhat quizzically, but with little hesitation otherwise I began by simply counting, "100, 97, 94, 91…."

By the time I arrived at the low eighties, she stopped me by saying "Thank you, that's enough," and wrote something else on her clipboard.

My mind kept going "79, 76, 73...", but it eventually stopped in anticipation of whatever was next.

Next was, in fact, an actual question of me, albeit an unexpected one. The psychologist asked me to tell her the names of the last four U.S. Vice Presidents. Again, immediately upon her request I'm sure I looked at her sort of strangely. But, since I guessed that every one of my responses, to include my overall reactions to the questions themselves, was being quantitatively and qualitatively measured and would figure into her ultimate psychological evaluation of me, I answered the question with minimal delay. So, I said, "Let me see...Rockefeller, Ford, Agnew, and...Humphrey."

Again, she said, "Thank you," while writing down on her clipboard whatever it was she found to be relevant in my verbal responses.

(I should add here, at the time, the above question wasn't necessarily as easy as it may seem. As VP Agnew had resigned in '73, and with President Nixon resigning in '74, with two VPs appointed mid-term as a result of each resignation, it took a bit of recent political/historical knowledge to list them accordingly. Fortunately, I happened to be up on those matters and happened to know how to answer her query.)

Unlike the first two questions which required some degree of thought, and could have been judged as right or wrong by the shrink, the last question to me was clearly of a different nature. Or was it? She quite simply and matter-of-factly asked me what I had eaten for breakfast the day before.

Not today, the day of my exam, but yesterday morning.

I thought for a few seconds and then I told the psychologist. I forget after all these years what I had eaten some 30 hours before this question was asked of me, or if what I told her was even accurate, (it was probably something like eggs and toast or cereal and juice), but I told her whatever I told her and she responded with yet another "Thank you," while writing on her clipboard.

That was it for my psych exam. She told me I was done and I could leave. It lasted less than 20 minutes. I didn't ask her if I passed, as I thought that in and of itself could be a potential evaluative marker. I simply said to her, "Thank you," and I left her office.

Another guy around my age was coming in right after me and I assumed he would go through the same battery of questions; unless maybe he was asked to count backwards by 4s, to list the last four presidents, and asked what he had for lunch the day before...just to mix it up.

I later contemplated the construct and possible meaning of my Philadelphia Police Department psychological exam. I eventually came to the opinion that as far as those three innocuous directions/questions asked of me at the end, what she was evaluating and assessing was less about the answers I provided but more about how I responded to them, and also to her, the question provider. I could have missed a digit or two counting backwards, forgot the names or chronological order of one or more VPs, and even drew a blank on what it is I had for breakfast the day before. But, I was convinced she didn't really care about any of that, nor was the test designed to look for simply the "right" answers to those questions. It was instead about how I would react to answering these seemingly silly and irrelevant questions.

If by the second or third question, I had stated, "Why are you asking me these dumb questions?" or "That's a stupid question," these types of responses could be problematic for me or anyone else taking this test. If I responded as such, and/or if I became visibly angered or overly frustrated at them, or even at her as a result, it could be a potential negative indicator. Her assessment could be that perhaps as a police officer, and when asked questions or given directions by a superior, or in a courtroom by a judge or attorney, or in some other real life scenario, he/she may deem them to be silly, unimportant, or not relevant. The officer could maybe lose his/her cool, question authority, disobey an order, or worse. However, since I answered the questions calmly, with no measurable hesitations or challenges to the psychologist, and with no indications of an anger management issue, it showed me to be a potentially viable candidate as a police officer and not one prone to demonstrability, at least in this particular category.

In fact, I did pass the physical and psychological exam that day as I received a letter in the mail a few weeks later informing me so. Both exams were pass/fail and the results themselves did nothing more to move me up the to-be-hired ladder as I knew a large number of Vietnam-era military veterans were still ahead of me. Unless, of course, some of the vets either failed their physical and/or psychological exams, then I'd move up the list. As far as I knew, I remained where I was on the hire list, but now one step closer to being a Philadelphia police officer. I'd still have to wait for the next step in the process by them, or see if another agency beat them to it.

Then what would I do?

Despite moving that one apparent step closer to employment with the Philadelphia PD, I still had to stay aggressive in searching out jobs and expanding my potential professional horizons as there were no guarantees the PPD would hire me. So, I made a firm new year's resolution as the clock struck midnight at the very end of '75 and the beginning of '76. It was that I would maintain this job-hunting aggressiveness for a good part of the upcoming year. I did, and it would eventually pay off.

Interestingly, and related to my job search, through an ad or maybe it was by word of mouth among my friends and former classmates, I learned that Temple University, located in Philadelphia, was sponsoring a criminal justice job fair on their campus one day. It was one of the first such events in my field in my city of which I was aware. So, along with my friend, Ray Geary, with whom I attended St. Helena grade school, Cardinal Dougherty HS, and Penn State (who was also a fellow LEC graduate as well as a Nittany 8er), I went there and met with representatives of various local, state, and federal law enforcement agencies. It was a worthwhile event and opened my eyes to various potential career and educational opportunities.

While there, I met an assistant district attorney who was representing one of the surrounding Philadelphia counties who actually had the same name as me. He happened to be the first other James Fitzgerald that I had ever met or even knew existed. We were not directly related, as far as we believed, although he too was born and raised in the Philadelphia area. He was a friendly guy and a well accomplished prosecutor. We talked for a while that day about life, school, possible employment opportunities, and related matters.

Initially, I somehow believed that this very unusual same-name advantage may open some potential career doors for me. But, alas, I learned that "same name-ness," in and of itself, would not be enough. This alternate James Fitzgerald, in the on-and-off hour or so I spent with him that day in the large gym at Temple University, was a decent guy who gave of his time to talk to me (and others) and provided some solid advice in the field in which he was already successful, but in which I was just now attempting to gain entry.

Unfortunately, however, no job resulted from the conversation with my "name-alike." I would be reminded afterwards once again that, at least in my life, it wasn't always necessarily who you knew that got you in the door or ahead, even if your name may be identical to that other person's. Yes, knowing people in higher places is a good thing and certainly doesn't hurt, but it's ultimately what you know, and then how hard you're willing to work to prove to those others just what it is you know that will create those professional possibilities for you.

Life's successes, I learned, do not come about by taking shortcuts or going in through back doors in an attempt to substitute for hard work, commitment, and to some degree, taking well-calculated initiatives. Attaining the job, make that career, I wanted would not involve circuitous or back door entries into them. It would be in a direct line, through the front door of whatever and wherever it was I wanted to go, be it the revolving door of a department store, a police car door, or the door to an FBI office.

I managed to get several Saturdays off from S&C and took a few other police officer entrance exams in the winter and spring of '76. One of them was for a small municipality in Montgomery County, PA, about ten miles outside of Philadelphia. There was one opening on their "five-man force."

(Yes, police departments were still referenced as "_#_man force," as when an officer count was specified then. Nowadays, of course, it's the gender-neutral "_#_officer force.")

The test was given in a middle school in their town. There was no residency requirement as a precondition to taking the test, but there was a minimum of a high school degree or GED needed to do so. I suppose this minimal educational requirement was a step in the right direction to begin the process of professionalizing law enforcement. I believe 75 or so candidates showed up that day to take the test. As a non-resident with at least a high school degree, I was one of them.

I scored well in the test and about one month later I was called in for the formal interview. I believe I had a quick physical exam the same day. As with the Philadelphia PD exam, there were no eye-sight issues here either.

The interview itself, like others I would under-go this year, consisted of three uniformed police of-ficers, I believe each a lieutenant or above in rank, with only one of them, the Chief of Police, from the actual hiring department. The other two were from neighboring departments helping out in the process that day.

They introduced themselves to me one at a time. I was told or read somewhere in advance that, in these type of interviews, I should attempt to read the nameplates on their shirts if I can at the distance at which I may be sitting from them, and/or look if there are desk-style nameplates in front of them on the dais, and/or listen carefully to their ranks and names as they introduce them-selves. My use of their individual names when I would respond to their various questions could be very helpful to their overall judgment of me as a candidate for the job. While my answers would most likely carry the most weight, by also begin-ning my response as, "Well, Chief Jones...," or, "Yes, Lieutenant Smith," and as long as I got the rank and name correct, in this type of scenario it could only be a positive thing.

That day, as it turned out, I could not read the names on their shirts and there were no nameplates of the desk variety to be found anywhere near them, so I focused on listening carefully as they in-dividually introduced themselves. Despite being pretty nervous, I did remember each of their ranks and at least two of their names, one of them being the Chief's name of the department for which I was applying. I addressed them accordingly and accurately, or at least I believe so, in my subsequent responses to them. Two with their full rank and name, and the other with just his rank, as it was an uncommon and longish name and I just didn't recall it during the subsequent interview due to my nervousness. If I had mispronounced his name, it could possibly hurt my evaluation by him. At least that's what I thought at the time.

Over the next 30 minutes or so, during the interview itself, they would ask me varied questions about numerous different situations that could possibly present themselves to an on-duty and even off-duty police officer. Some had to do with traffic enforcement issues, others arrest scenarios, others yet dealing with how I would handle matters in my personal life as a police officer, etc.

One of their questions had to do with me giving a traffic ticket to someone and then later one of the town's elected officials contacting me and asking me to "fix" it. How would I handle such a request?

That question surprised me. However, through conversations with other people that I knew who were going through similar type interview processes, I learned that when in doubt regarding a particular question such as this one, to go with the "by-the-book" answer. In other words, to the best of your ability, give the legal and proper protocol-based answer, certainly at first. If challenged, you could then build in some wiggle-room to your subsequent response.

In the ticket fixing scenario, I responded at first that I would not fix the ticket as it was illegal, if not unethical, to do so.

Okay, well how about if your immediate police supervisor later ordered you to do so? Would you disobey his command? The Chief himself asked me these questions.

Hmmmm…now it's a following-orders scenario, and this guy could be my future boss.

I replied that I am not one to disobey lawfully directed orders, but I would need more information in order to do what is being asked of me. One of the other three interviewers then added to the fictitious plotline that the person who had received the ticket from me was an "informant" and providing information to detectives about some criminal activity going on in the town.

Would that matter?

Ok, that changes things a bit…I guess. I acknowledged that this could be a factor in the eventual adjudication of the summary-level traffic ticket. Which, by the way, I had them clarify that this make-believe offense did not involve drunk driving, a vehicular accident, a hit and run, and/or injuries of any sort. They concurred that those issues were not involved. In the end, I stated that the politician could talk to my chief of police; in this case, one of my interviewers. If the chief decided that the ticket outcome could be "plea bargained" to perhaps be turned into a "warning," that would suffice for me to alter the legal outcome of it. They seemed okay with that answer.

In another interview scenario provided to me, I was asked if I was hired by this department and I was off-duty in a stadium or arena at a football game or concert, and the person sitting in front of me was smoking a marijuana cigarette, how I would react. Would I arrest the person? Or allow a lawbreaker to violate Commonwealth of Pennsylvania statutes? What would I do in that situation? They very much wanted to know.

I asked them if this was occurring in my own jurisdiction or some other place in Pennsylvania. It was occurring at the then relatively new Veteran's Stadium in Philadelphia, they added. So, not on my home turf. Ok, that's important to know.

While I would have had arrest powers throughout the state, legally speaking, I advised the three interviewers that considering the large and potential unruly crowd situation, and that there were most likely Philadelphia police officers nearby, as an off-duty officer from another jurisdiction I believe it would be most prudent to instead officially advise the on-duty officers of the pot smoker and let them handle it as they deem appropriate.

One of them then posited, "So, you have the law being broken right in front of you, you're a sworn Pennsylvania police officer, but you would take no action?"

I calmly and respectfully repeated my previous response using almost the same words, throwing in the term "officer's discretion" a few times. That seemed to suffice. Or, at least I was asked no further questions about it.

Does that mean I got it right or wrong? I'd have to wait a few weeks to find out.

Interestingly, I surmised around this time, and had it confirmed later in my career, that it was by design that no matter what answer an interviewee would provide to one of these officers' questions, and no matter how "correct" an initial response may be to it, one of the other interviewers would then challenge the candidate's answer in part or in whole. This was their way of further testing a candidate to see if he/she was strong-willed and adamant in his/her convictions, yet adaptable to some degree if other information was later provided. Of course, the revised response would still have to be an acceptable response to the initial overall scenario as it was presented.

At the end of the interview, the officers from behind the dais asked me if I had any questions of them. It's always good when in an interview in which you want something, that is, a job, a promotion, etc., to have some valid questions to ask of your interviewer(s). I did have a few questions that I had devised beforehand.

I asked the Chief directly, "What are some of the primary crime related issues that plague this community?"

I also inquired as to the size of the department and the backgrounds of the personnel already on board, ratio of officer to civilian staff, what were the future training opportunities, the possibility of being promoted, etc. His answers were suitable for my purposes, and no, I did not then challenge him with various alternate scenarios as they did me. That's their role on this day, not mine.

I did not ask about salary, as that was already listed on a sliding scale in the original ad. Even the bottom of the pay scale at this PD was better than I was presently earning at S&C, so I was fine in regard to that issue.

In terms of my above questions to the panel, it should be noted that this was long before the advent of the Internet where now these types of questions and issues can be readily researched in advance. Issues such as these, quite frankly, are almost expected to be known by a police candidate before he/she even shows up for the interview in today's world.

I should add that before my interview with this PD, I did research in their library regarding the population of the community and related that information to them in passing during my interview. There were also local newspapers in the library and I read some of them and learned of recent events in their town that I also brought up during the interview. I don't believe they were even crime related, but I wanted to let the panel know that I was at least somewhat informed regarding current happenings in the town that was considering hiring me as a police officer.

On the whole, once I left the room, I felt good about my interview that day. Not cocky, but confident. Even parts of it in which I may not have done as well as I would have liked, I figured I would now handle better at the next interview I undergo, for whatever job it is I'm hoping to attain.

I guess I handled the questions from this particular PD panel adequately. The same chief of police who co-interviewed me called my home and offered me the police officer position about two months later. I don't think I was the initial one he offered the job to as he called me during the first week of May that year and he wanted me to start the police academy on May 10. Not much advance notice, I said. He agreed. He advised that I could think about it and call him back in a day or so, but they had to know soon. However, there were a few matters to discuss with him first.

While I knew it was a small department, of only five officers, I wanted to know more about them. I had heard somewhere, subsequent to my panel interview, that there was a bit of nepotism involved at the department. I had to have that issue clarified. Depending on his answer, it would not necessarily be a deal-breaker, but it was something I wanted to know in advance, nevertheless.

I called the chief back the next day. I asked him to further explain the background and the relationship, if any, of his present five-man police force. He told me, of course, he was the chief, he had one lieutenant, one sergeant, and two patrolmen. And without me directly asking he advised that two of the officers were his sons and one was his nephew.

Hmmmmm...so four-fifths of the existing department were blood relatives in some way to one another. I'm not sure where the other officer fit in to the family tree, but I knew if I went there I would be a whole separate tree, and a sapling at that, compared to the rest of them.

On top of this somewhat rushed decision-making process with which I was now faced, and the fact that the present makeup of the department was all but the same family, I had one other issue of my own to address. That is, in about four days, May 8, I was getting married, with a pre-planned week long honeymoon starting the next day.

With all of this added together, including naturally a discussion with my soon-to-be wife, Eileen, I had to make a decision. And I did. I decided to turn down the offer. I was flattered, but for various reasons this PD was just not exactly the right fit for me, certainly not at this time. I called the chief back, advised him of my decision, thanked him, and wished him good luck with his ongoing search. He was polite and wished the best to me too.

It's very possible that I could have enjoyed a long and prosperous career at this small PD. However, for the reasons enumerated above, it just wasn't the right place at the right time for me. Being offered the position at all was a positive step for me and it boosted my confidence to some degree. I guess I was doing something right.

But the job search must continue. And, it did.

Chapter Twenty-five

Back at Strawbridge & Clothier…along with my part-time fellow store detective and friend John Tierno, in the fall of '75 another individual joined our ranks full-time in the security department. He became a good friend of mine too, albeit in his relatively short time there. His name was Chuck Boyle.

Chuck graduated the same year as me from Bishop McDevitt High School, a suburban Philadelphia rival, at least in the sports realm, of my Cardinal Dougherty HS. We didn't let that scholastic rivalry get in the way of our blooming friendship as we got to know each other during our daily "patrols" of the nine retail floors at S&C. I was assigned as his "training detective" and we walked the floor for days on end while I imparted upon him, to the best of my abilities, everything I knew about retail security, the detainment/arrest process, the store layout, the regular "beats" who would visit us, suspicious employees, the better bathrooms (and when to religiously lock the door on at least one of them each day), reasonably priced nearby restaurants for lunch, etc.

Chuck was smart, a quick study, and we made some good arrests together early on. He could also handle himself physically on the few occasions that we met up with a confrontational shoplifter and he wasn't afraid to tackle, wrestle, and/or duke it out with the ones who thought they could escape us or fight us. It was nice to have a partner with whom I could walk the floor and build a friendship at the same time. As it wasn't too long until I was getting married, and he had an Irish-born girlfriend with whom he was very serious, we would compare notes about dating women of Irish ancestry. These conversations went long and far and were edifying to both of us, to say the least.

After Chuck was at S&C just a few months, and after catching our fair share of shoplifters together, as well as occasionally drinking a few beers together at a local pub after work, he called me at home one Sunday in November. He told me he had an offer of a much better paying job doing construction work, and it actually started the very next day. In view of that, he was going to call our boss at his home and quit the store detective job right then and there. He didn't like leaving S&C on this short notice, but he really didn't have much of a choice. I told him I was disappointed in no longer having him as a store detective partner, but I was happy for him if the new job was what was best for him. He reciprocated with similar congenial words to me. We stayed in touch by phone over the next year or so, but eventually we lost track of one another.

I learned in those few months working with Chuck Boyle, as I had on a part-time basis with John Tierno, that there's something about a security or law enforcement related job in which you have a partner who, well, "has your back." Things could get nasty during a shoplifting arrest sometimes, and it definitely made a difference to have a guy or gal working with you that wasn't hesitant to join in the ruckus if, in fact, it developed into one. This notion was reinforced on many levels when I eventually joined the ranks of law enforcement as a police officer and later as an FBI agent.

When kicking in a bad guy's door, conducting a felony car stop, or undertaking an arrest of a violent person anywhere, there's no better feeling than to know that the person you're with, perhaps the one you would consider your work partner, is there to protect you and cover you if things go bad, just as you would do the same for him or her. Every police officer and state or federal agent, and for that matter store detective too, knows this feeling. Through experience, through training, through conversations, through actions, when taking that ultimate step as an officer/agent at any level, that is, when legally depriving a known or suspected lawbreaking individual of his immediate freedom, if you're fortunate to have alongside you a partner that you trust implicitly, one who will work with you and protect you in any situation, as you of course would do for him or her, it's a very good feeling. It's a bond that lasts a long time and can transcend many other personal and professional issues.

John Tierno and Chuck Boyle were two guys I trusted implicitly in my days at S&C and I gladly and proudly put both of them into the category of "partner," in a law enforcement/security sense. I would like to believe that they would say the same about me.

In 1998, as a criminal profiler assigned to the FBI Academy in Quantico, Virginia, I received a phone call at my office one day. It was from a Detective Boyle of the Philadelphia Police Department, Homicide Division. We started talking and soon realized we had each worked at S&C in the mid-70s. Yes, it didn't take the trained profiler or seasoned detective too long on the phone that day to figure out our mutually shared past. After Chuck's S&C stint, and a short time with a job in the construction field, he joined the PPD. As it turns out, he was now a homicide detective, a much heralded and sought-after position within the department. In that conversation, we caught up briefly on our personal and professional lives as we hadn't been in contact since early 1976. As it turned out, however, that wasn't the reason he called.

Chuck had been assigned as the lead detective in what the local media came to call "The Center City Rapist Case." This violent criminal had raped various women in downtown Philadelphia over the course of a year, and in his most recent attack, he silently killed his victim as two uniformed police officers were knocking at her apartment door. The city was very much on edge.

Chuck and I would be working together again, on this investigation. Only the stakes were clearly much higher this time. It wasn't just trying to catch a shoplifter like in the old days, now it was trying to catch a rapist and killer who showed no signs of stopping.

Fortunately, our teamwork paid off. The rapist was eventually identified after he left Philadelphia and moved to Ft. Collins, Colorado, where he continued his raping ways.

Chuck Boyle and I have stayed in touch since this case and arrest. We're not "partners" anymore in the law enforcement sense, but remain good friends, without a doubt.

More on the Center City Rapist case in Book III.

As referenced earlier, my other internship/ practicum in college, with the Bureau of Alcohol, Tobacco, and Firearms in the winter of '75 was a very good one, with only positive things resulting from it. I learned during my time there that the first step to gaining employment in the ATF was to take what was known then as the Professional and Administrative Career Examination, aka the PACE test. It was an exam designed for entry level to at least 118 different U.S. federal government jobs. The ATF was one of the many federal agencies that used it to hire its future special agents.

So, after signing up for it months in advance, on a Saturday morning in early '76, I took the PACE test at a federal building in downtown Philadelphia. I forget exactly how the process worked then, but I think when signing up one would designate on the application the specific agency or agencies to which the results were to be sent. I, of course, listed the ATF.

The test itself was similar in design to the SAT test everyone took to get into college. It consisted of math, vocabulary, and reading comprehension components. Several of my fellow LECers from PSU, including Ray Geary and Larry Morrissey, took the test that day too. We all met afterwards and had lunch and discussed how we thought we did. I didn't have a great feeling about it.

I rarely fared very well in these types of standardized tests. I'd pass them, but not necessarily do stellar. There were books one could buy, and courses one could take, to possibly improve the chances of getting a higher score in these tests. As it so happens, I never took advantage of either. Perhaps I should have done so with this and other similar tests, but I didn't. Give me a blue book exam, a term paper to write, or even an oral presentation to provide, and I do just fine, in fact, even exceptional at times as I've been told. But, in standardized tests, the math sections tended to pull down my overall score and I would suffer the results. I'm clearly a verbal guy, not a math guy. I learned that early on in my life at among other places my 70-student St. Helena grade school classrooms.

A month or so later, I received the postcard in the mail. I scored an 84.5 on the PACE test. I received a letter shortly thereafter from the ATF advising me that I didn't score high enough on the test to be further considered for employment. Oh well, another job opportunity down the drain. However, I did hear that my good friend from Cardinal Dougherty and later Penn State, Larry Morrissey, who was also an LEC grad and one of my Nittany 8 dorm co-inhabitants, scored an exact 85 on the test that same day. He had also listed the ATF as his agency-of-interest and in turn got a letter from them around the same time as me. It said that his score was passing and he was being further considered as a special agent applicant. He eventually went through the interview process and background checks and before 1976 was over, he was in training at their academy in Glynco, Georgia, on his way to becoming an ATF agent.

I was very happy for my friend Larry and also perhaps a little bit envious. But I was mostly mad at myself for not having answered just a few more questions correctly and reaching the "passing" score of 85 to have also been considered for a position within this agency. Alas, it wasn't meant to be.

Larry Morrissey went on to have a successful career in the ATF, albeit one tragically cut short. As a young agent he received specialized training in arson and explosion investigations. He was on the ATF's National Response Team for bombings and arsons. As a result, he and his team responded to the first World Trade Center bombing in New York City in 1993 and the Atlanta Olympics bombing in 1996, along with many other bombing and arson scenes throughout his career.

During the timeframe Larry and his team were responding to these crime scenes, some still smoldering and with microscopic toxic materials permeating the air he and his colleagues were breathing, hazmat protective gear was at a minimum for the agents who did this kind of work. Larry paid the ultimate price for this as in the late 1990s he was diagnosed with cancer. It is believed the cancer developed as a result of his exposure to these hazardous materials and the lack of special equipment to protect him. He died in October 2000 in North Carolina.

Larry is not the only ATF agent suspected to have died or become very sick as a result of exposure to these infectious crime scenes and their devastating effects on the unprotected investigators assigned to assess them. A class action lawsuit has been filed against the ATF and the federal government by the families of the deceased and the sick agents themselves regarding these numerous and potentially linked deaths. Let's hope justice is served in these civil actions' eventual outcome.

Larry was at my wedding and I was at his when he married Betsy, a very nice young woman that I indirectly introduced to him through my girlfriend/future wife, Eileen. His death at age 46 was a tragic loss to the law enforcement community, to his friends, and of course most importantly, to his wife and three children.

Larry is gone much too soon and very much missed by all who knew him.

I can't help but wonder sometimes…but for the difference of one half-point, higher or lower, on that PACE test…for me and/or for Larry….

Chapter Twenty-six

Sometime in the late winter or early spring of 1976, yet another ad was placed in one of the Philadelphia newspapers for a test for police officer positions. Fortunately, I saw it and applied accordingly.

The ad was for the Bensalem Police Department (BPD), in Bucks County, Pennsylvania, a suburban community directly north of Philadelphia. I didn't really know the area all that well, except having visited the Neshaminy Mall on Rt. 1 on various occasions over the last few years. Almost directly across the street from the mall was the Trevose Barracks of the Pennsylvania State Police. It was there in 1969, at their driving course, that I first attained my driver's license. Other than trips to Bensalem for those reasons, I knew virtually nothing else about this town. As it turned out, I would get to know the Neshaminy Mall and its environs very well over the next few years and not from shopping there.

After calling the PD and getting an application mailed to me, it was off to Bensalem High School one Saturday morning where I took the test. It was probably the fourth police entrance exam I had taken in the last year or so. They were becoming almost a quarterly routine in my life. At this point, there was no real prepping for these type exams. Simply getting eight hours or so of sleep the night before was the best I could do to now prepare for them.

Upon my arrival at the exam site, there were several hundred people there, including lifelong friend Ray Geary and my S&C friend-of-a-friend Bob Yezzi. It was again mostly men, but I noticed there were some women there too, more than at the last few exams I had taken. We were then assigned to various classrooms in alphabetical order, given some basic instructions, and told to open our examination booklets. I opened mine, took the test, turned it in upon completion, and went home.

I don't recall it being a particularly difficult or a particularly easy test. Somewhere in the middle, I suppose, when compared to the other tests I had already taken. Like most local police entrance exams at the time, if there was a math component, it was pretty basic and I did fine with it. Not like the federal government PACE test.

This was the last of these tests that I took during this time frame because not only did I attain a high score on it, but after passing the subsequent medical test (no vision issues) and psych test (no inkblots, backwards counting, vice president, or meal related questioning), background checks, a polygraph exam, and the oral interview over the subsequent few months, I knew it was a very good possibility that I would get hired by the BPD. It was just a matter of time.

That time came as I was walking the floor at S&C one Friday morning in mid-August of '76 when I received a page from our secretary. Expecting to be sent to an area of the store where there was some suspicious character trying to steal something, I called down to the office. However, instead of a possible shoplifting in progress, she told me I had a message to call someone at a certain phone number. The person simply gave his name to her and a contact number and asked if I could call him back. He didn't include a title or mention his company or agency by name. When she gave me the message, though, I immediately recognized who it was.

As I knew there wasn't much space in the relatively small security office to make a private phone call, I decided to return the call from one of the few phones on the retail floors that I knew to have direct outside line capabilities. The one to which I was nearest, and which I knew offered a modicum of privacy and quietness, happened to be in the ladies' accessories department on the third floor. So, in and around racks and stacks of handbags, purses, scarves, etc., with a nod of my head to a nearby saleswoman with whom I was friendly and who was assisting two young female customers, I went behind the sales counter and quietly dialed the requisite phone number.

I knew, of course, that the name and number was that of Sergeant Bob Hughes at the BPD. He was the administrative supervisor facilitating the testing and the hiring of numerous future police officers at his agency. After the police dispatcher put me on hold, a length of time which seemed to go on forever, the news Sgt. Hughes gave me right away was very good. He told me I was next on the list to be hired at the Bensalem PD. If still interested, I was to be sworn in two weeks from now on August 27, and start the Municipal Police Officers' Training

Course at the Pennsylvania State Police Academy on the following Monday, August 30.

Geez, an information overload and I still haven't even grasped the reality of it all yet. I think I went silent for longer than I should have as I was writing things down at the same time on a scrap of paper I happened to find next to the cash register.

Sgt. Hughes eventually said, "Fitzgerald, are you still there?"

"Oh, yes sir...sorry," I replied.

"Well, are you still interested in the position?"

I gave him an emphatic "YES," and thanked him profusely for all he did to bring me to this point.

He said, "No problem, it's my job."

Hughes then told me to be at the BPD at 10:00AM on Friday, the 27th, in suit and tie, to be sworn in, to have my police ID photo taken, and to handle other various administrative-related matters. The sergeant further told me in the next day or two I would receive a letter in the mail to my residence confirming all of this. I thanked him again, and said goodbye.

Ironically, this phone call with Sgt. Hughes would turn out to be pretty much the high-point of our professional relationship during the next 11-plus years. It would slowly spiral downwards before too long, certainly as my police officer career was progressing.

But, let's not digress just yet from this very happy moment for me. My relationship with the later bully-like Hughes, and his various similarly minded BPD management cohorts, and how I ultimately fought back, will be further discussed in Book II.

After ending my semi-secret phone call on the retail floor of S&C, I instinctively walked over and hugged the nearest person to me, that being the friendly ladies' accessories saleswoman, who was still dealing with her customers. I simply told her out loud that I got some really good news and I'd be back to tell her more about it later. I even went over and half-hugged the two customers who were standing right next to her and who were in the process of comparing various purses to their newly bought high-heeled shoes. They had big smiles on their faces when they saw me in such an ebullient and demonstrative mood after the phone call and my hug of the saleswoman. So, I guess instinctively, I embraced the both of them too. They were kind of cute, after all, so why not?

As I was leaving the ladies' accessories area, I quickly pointed to some purses and suggested to the two shoppers that they, in fact, would look great with their shoes. They laughed and thanked me as I walked away. I never saw them again, but I was told a few days later by the saleswoman that they actually bought the purses that I suggested. What a great day for the soon-to-be police officer, the S&C accessories department, and no doubt those two purse shopping women with whom I shared my good mood and also offered valuable fashion advice.

Next that morning I called the now Mrs. Eileen Fitzgerald at her job and told her the good news. Shortly after, I called my parents and told them. They were all happy for me, or at least it seemed so. I knew I had to next tell my boss, but my dad, ever the pragmatist, told me to wait until I had the actual letter in-hand from the BPD before I told my employer I was going to quit, just to make sure it was official and that I had the offer in writing. He was right. So I stayed quiet about this for the next two work days. It wasn't easy.

I did, in fact, get the official letter of acceptance at my residence by the following Monday, and the next morning, with nine working days' notice, I told my S&C supervisors that I was leaving the job. It wasn't a complete surprise to them, as there had been some background checking of me, job confirmation calls, and things like that over the last few months from a few different PDs. They were also happy for me.

One of my store detective colleagues, a guy a few years older than me and with whom I never really did get that friendly, heard of my quitting S&C to become a police officer. He sarcastically said, in our office in front of some of our others colleagues, "So, you're gonna be a cop, eh? Good luck with that. You know they shoot real bullets out there, don't ya?"

Hmmmm…Thanks for the nice send off, Charlie. No wonder we never made too many arrests together.

My last week-plus in the store was relatively uneventful. While still helping my colleagues undertake a few arrests/detainments, I made the rounds to various departments and said goodbye to the people I got to know and like over the last almost 14 months. It was sad in some ways, but I was certainly happy to be finally taking the next step in my chosen career.

My last official work shift at S&C was on Thursday, August 26, as I was being sworn in as a

BPD police officer the next day. The assistant security department manager with whom I was probably closest on the job, Bob Greer, privately gave me a gift at an impromptu "goodbye" lunch my colleagues put together for me on that day. He surprised me with it as we were walking out the door of the restaurant that day. As he took the initially unrecognizable item out of his pocket, he told me he carried it "on-the-job" for most of his police career. There was no fancy gift wrap on it, just the item itself.

It was a "blackjack." This particular gift had nothing to do with a card game or the number "21." A blackjack was a small non-lethal weapon that police officers were issued in those days. It was about 10" long, black, and all leather. It consisted of a handle, wrapped in leather, which was actually an interior spring of which on the end was the heavy metal "club," or jack part, also covered in leather. It was designed to hit non-compliant bad guys on tender parts of their bodies in order to make them, well, comply with an arrest.

My later issued uniform police pants even had a special narrow pocket for it at the mid-thigh level. My official blackjack that was issued to me in a few months by the BPD was of the flat-shaped variety. My newly acquired gift blackjack club was of a cylindrical shape. Most of the newer varieties were of the flat style. This older style had a more effective stopping effect, Bob assured me.

Bob stated upon giving it to me that he had modified it somewhat years ago. He had cut the leather strap on one end so it was less of a handle, but now free flying, at least one end of it. He told when he was a cop, he would use the heavy club head to strike the real bad guys who were fighting him tooth-and-nail. But he would use the loose, free-flying strap to manage punk kids, or "knuckle-heads" as he used to like to say, who just needed to be taught some manners and/or to get them off of a street corner somewhere.

I thanked Bob for his thoughtful gift.

Later, in my police career I did, in fact, have occasion to use it. Sparingly, but I did employ it at times, both the club-end for the heavy hitters and the strap-end for the occasional "punk" who had to be reminded to move along from where he was loitering after a few warnings. I can assure here, each recipient earned its usage at the time. And amazingly, once the blackjack was either seen or felt, these guys would become almost immediately compliant in whatever legal situation I was enforcing.

Blackjacks became illegal for police officers to carry sometime in the 1990s as a result of numerous police brutality lawsuits. Officers are not issued blackjacks anymore, of the flat-head or cylindrical-head variety. Nonetheless, I still have that well-worn gift from Bob Greer.

And, no, I haven't used it on anyone in a few decades now.

Of course, this whole new situation was not without a downside to it, at least a small one. I now knew I was going to be living away from home for the next 12 weeks as the PSP Academy in Hershey was about two hours by car from my then-residence in Philadelphia. I could come home on Friday nights, but had to be back to the PSP Academy in Hershey by 9PM on Sunday nights. I was only married three months at the time, and now I was going to spend early September through late November away from my new apartment and, yes, my new bride. Some extended honeymoon. Well, except for the weekends, I suppose.

Some other good news I learned just a few days after my career-altering phone call was that Ray Geary, my friend from Olney with whom I shared so many other school experiences, received an identical call from the BPD on the same day. Since graduation from PSU, he had been a correctional officer at Graterford State Prison in suburban Philadelphia. He couldn't wait to leave that state penal institution and be a cop, he would later tell me. He said working in prison for eight hours a day was like being a prisoner himself during each shift.

It was interesting and coincidental that Ray and I would start this journey into the next stage of our professional lives together, after having begun first grade at the same time and travelling together all the way through high school and college graduation and now into the police academy. It would be nice to have a guy with whom I was friendly to share the various challenges that police academy life would surely bring us, not to mention then becoming rookie cops together afterwards.

Despite all the years Ray and I spent together, certainly in various academic settings, while still good friends we nonetheless moved around in somewhat different social circles. But, they were interwoven circles as virtually all of our friends knew each other from either our Olney neighborhood and/or schools. In view of this, Ray and I made plans to meet in a local bar to celebrate the attainment of our new jobs. We set it up with our collective friends for a night the week before we were to start the Academy. Around a dozen or so of our friends showed up that evening. Among them was Joe Widmeier in his wheelchair, Ned Graham without the security guard badge this time, Jim Coyle, a great friend since freshman year in high school and the Best Man at my wedding (and later me at his), now Philadelphia PD Officer Rob McCarthy, now-firefighter John Welsh, and Gary Farrell, the latter another Olney guy who was a very close friend of Ray's.

Along with the ongoing socializing among everyone, John Welsh and I had an edifying side-talk at the bar that night, away from the other guys for a while. He had just recently completed the Philadelphia Fire Department Training Academy and was assigned to a ladder company in West Philadelphia, a very busy urban firehouse. Interestingly, even though it was John who told me about the Law Enforcement and Corrections major at PSU, as it was his major at the time, he didn't follow through in that field as his career. He changed his mind at some point and wanted to be a firefighter. He took their entrance exam and the next battery of tests, did very well in them all, was hired as a cadet, subsequently graduated the fire academy, and officially joined the ranks of the PFD as a firefighter.

Among other joint celebratory conversational topics that evening, John and I half-kiddingly yet half-seriously discussed our recent career developments. Somewhere in that conversation, we agreed that both of us had strong positive rationales for our respective public service career choices. When comparing our two chosen professions that night, I told John that I didn't think I could do what he was doing as I really did not like fire, at least anything larger than a warm and cozy fireplace. I confessed that the concept of dealing with an out-of-control fire, and especially the thought of running into a fully engulfed building in an effort to save it or someone trapped inside, genuinely scared me. I further advised John that I felt much more equipped to deal with human beings, even the violent criminal-types, than with the wrath of nature as in a burning house or multi-story factory building.

John laughed at my contention and said that while he greatly respected nature's force as manifested in a fully developed and spreading fire, what really concerned him was being seriously wounded, or worse, by a gunshot. He thought he'd have a much better chance with his training to fight a fire rather than a felon with a loaded gun. We eventually realized that evening that we were discussing issues both esoteric and simplistic at the same time, all while under the influence of a few beers in a bar.

So...a blazing building fire versus a criminal with a loaded gun....

Is one really easier to deal with than the other?

John and I kiddingly agreed that the worst case scenario for both of us would be a crazed gunman inside a burning house shooting at us. Upon making that seemingly silly observation, we each downed the remainder of our respective mugs of beer and decided to rejoin the rest of our friends in the ongoing frivolity.

Neither of us knew at the time how truly prophetic that last observation would become for John in less than two years.

Later that evening, as I got around to talk to Ray's good friend, Gary Farrell, I learned that he had taken the same Philadelphia Police Department entrance exam as Ray and me circa 14 months ago and was also on the list to become an officer. None of us knew it at the time, but he was one year away from being hired. Gary was very anxiously awaiting his appointment. He had two brothers already on the force and his soon-to-be wife would join the PPD too around the same time as him. Because of his brothers, he knew what it was like to be a cop. He shared some brother-related cop stories with us that night and we were each pumping the other up about our future careers in law enforcement.

As it turned out, within a little over four years, in separate incidents, two of the aforementioned people in the bar that night would be shot. For one of them, it would prove fatal.

These men were only two of the people I knew who would be later shot and/or killed in the performance of their first responder duties. Unfortunately and very sadly, others I knew would follow.

Charlie from my Strawbridge & Clothier department store days, in his own ignominious and snarky way just a few days before, was right. They did shoot real bullets out there in my new job, and those bullets could kill.

Chapter Twenty-seven

It was on a hot and steamy Friday morning, August 27, 1976, that I officially entered the law enforcement profession. Well, sort of. I still had to graduate the police academy. That was another 12 weeks away. However, I figured with confidence (again, not cockiness), I could handle that assignment. First on the agenda was getting officially sworn in by the chief of the Bensalem Police Department.

I arrived at the BPD Headquarters by 9:30 that morning for the 10:00 swearing in. My friend, Ray Geary, arrived there shortly thereafter. Ray and I commented again how strange it was for us to be starting yet another stage of our lives together, this after beginning, and completing, grade school, high school, and college together. Here we were again, two kids from the Olney neighborhood of Philadelphia, growing up about six blocks from each other, now out in the 'burbs, about to start yet another stage together, this time becoming police officers. We talked about all those Law Enforcement and Corrections courses we took together at Penn State University. Now, it would be applying them and our other life skills to the hopefully not too mean streets of Bensalem, Pennsylvania.

Would we complete this stage together too? Would we go all the way to retirement in this new profession? Neither of us was 100 % sure about that possibility, but we were at least at the starting gate together. What was next for us neither of us could truly know at this time.

There were six others with Ray and me that day also set to be sworn in. One of the others with us had been a BPD dispatcher for a few years, but the rest of us were all outsiders to the department, with only two others even living in Bensalem itself. Most of us came from Philadelphia or its other nearby suburbs. As we learned, we were the second phase of hires at the BPD that year. There were 15 or so who were sworn in a few months before and they were about to be assigned their squads in the next month or so, after they graduate from their police academy class which had already started and was near completion.

I also found out that morning that we were essentially being hired thanks to a federal grant bestowed upon the BPD by the Law Enforcement Assistance Administration (LEAA). The LEAA was part of the U.S. Department of Justice and it was one of the agencies created under the Omnibus Crime Control and Safe Streets Act of 1968. Interestingly, in 1973, as one of the LEAA's many requirements for police departments to receive the potentially generous federal funding for personnel, equipment, cars, education, etc., it was decreed that any agency receiving such grants had to abolish height requirements for potential police officers. This, of course, opened the doors for females (and smaller males) to apply for the position of officer. The bottom-line was that if an agency wanted the federal money to grow and otherwise enhance itself, each had to play by the federal rules. Most did. BPD was one that did, and of the 30 new police officers hired that year, one of them was a woman. And, a few of the male rookie officers were definitely under the height of 5'8", that being the former minimum vertical requirement at the BPD. (No, I wasn't one of them. I've been an even 6' my entire adult life.)

As a result of applying for and receiving this LEAA grant, my new department was going to almost double in size, from about 40 sworn officers to 75, by late-1977. The grant money would pay our full salaries and benefits, provide us our uniforms and weaponry, and cover the other necessary and related costs for the next three years. At that point, the funding would incrementally decrease over the following few years to where Bensalem Township taxpayers would then have to eventually start footing the bill for its enhanced police force. The township was growing with both a residential and commercial building boom and no one in control there felt it would be a problem paying for the new officers in the years to come. They were correct about that.

On an individual basis, from the late '60s through the early '80s, the LEAA also paid for many police officers to go to college and earn their degrees. Most did it part-time, while working around their various rotating shifts. Their majors, of course, had to be law enforcement related, such as criminal justice, sociology, psychology, etc. Not many officers had a problem choosing a major related to police work, especially as the tuition was free. Of course, various universities and colleges in the U.S. knew of these LEAA grants, so many started their own criminal justice departments. Everyone was benefitting from these monies. This would include the taxpayers and citizens of this country too as they were getting a better trained and more educated police officer as a result. A win-win for everyone back in the '70s was the general consensus in this regard.

However, most good government programs seem eventually to come to a bureaucratic demise before long. Unfortunately, this agency ceased to exist after 1982. Police departments and officers would have to find other ways to attain funding for hiring and advancing themselves from that point on. I know I did.

Back at the BPD headquarters, after meeting with various BPD officers and administrators over coffee and doughnuts (yes, the cop/doughnut stereotype was reinforced for me there and then, on my very first day), we had our ID card photos taken, we filled out some insurance forms, next-of-kin (gulp!) forms, got measured for uniforms, holsters, etc., and took care of other related administrative matters.

Lieutenant Jack Robinson, who would become an early mentor of mine, led us around the police headquarters that morning. He gave us a brief tour and showed us the pertinent parts of the building, from the detective division to the holding cells, to the dispatcher room, to the officers' locker room, to the roll-call room. It wasn't a large or particularly modern two story building. The exterior measured approximately 200' x 150', with the police department housed entirely on the first floor. The township administrative offices and a mid-sized conference room were on the second floor. However, this place would be the professional home for the foreseeable future for me and the other rookies there that day. Actually, it would be much more so AFTER we graduated from the academy, of course. We weren't home yet.

As we were all being sent to the Pennsylvania State Police Academy in Hershey, PA, Lt. Robinson advised us that the PSP was now the agency the BPD used to train its rookie officers. Most of the existing officers in the department attended the Philadelphia Police Academy where they mixed in with the Philadelphia police officer cadets. But, for mostly financially related reasons, the PSP Training Academy was where BPD was now sending its cadets.

The group of 15 other BPD officer cadets ahead of us was already in the PSP regional Academy in Downingtown, PA, a not-too-far away suburb of Philadelphia. There's was a commuting-academy, meaning that those officers-to-be could come home every night. As the Downingtown PSP Academy was full for its next class, our group of eight, hired when we were, would be staying in the "barracks" at the main Hershey PSP Academy, and only able to come home on weekends. I already knew this information, but wasn't crazy to hear it again.

Hershey? For 12 whole weeks? And with a roommate?

Geez, I thought I was done with living in dorms. Or barracks. Or whatever they called them. I guess not.

Hmmmm...if only I had been hired in that first batch, I wouldn't be spending these 12 weeks away from home. If only I answered one or two more questions on the entrance exam correctly....

No! I must stop thinking like this. Things such as this happen for a reason. I should have known that by then. Just accept it. In less than 72 hours, I would be at the PSP Academy in Hershey. At least I had my friend Ray there to make being away a bit easier. Not that he was crazy about the notion of being away that long either – and he was still single.

We agreed it probably wouldn't be too bad. Would it?

We'd be finding out soon enough.

Before the swearing in that morning, the BPD Chief, Larry Michaels, gave us a little geography and history lesson as it pertained to Bensalem Township and the police department itself. He pointed to a large wall map of Bensalem Township and reminded us that three of the busiest highways on the East Coast, they being U.S. Route 1, the Pennsylvania Turnpike, and Interstate 95, all passed through and/or intersected in the township. And with those size highways, the Chief said, came crime.

Perhaps related to that, and what I remembered most of the rest of his talk before our swearing in, was what occurred in the last year alone in Bensalem Township. That included one of the police sergeants walking in on a bank robbery and being taken hostage; another officer in a shootout with yet another bank robber; a mass killing of six people in their home, including five members of a family and one of their young friends; and last but certainly not least, the murder of BPD officer James Armstrong while attempting to arrest an armed robbery suspect.

This place may have formerly been a sleepy suburb of Philadelphia, but not anymore. It was growing in leaps and bounds, and obviously in the violent crime category, too. Maybe Chief Michaels was providing us these informal geography and history lessons to give us one last chance to change our minds before being sworn in and going off to the police academy.

It didn't work. Not with the eight of us, anyway.

By noon that Friday, we went upstairs to the Township Manager's office, met her, and then went to the adjacent conference room. There, with our right hands raised, and our left hands on a bible, the eight of us were formally sworn in as Bensalem police officers by Chief Michaels and Township Manager Marge Strange. In doing so, we affirmed, under oath, that we would uphold the Constitution of the United States, the laws of the Commonwealth of Pennsylvania, conduct ourselves in a professional, moral, and ethical manner, etc., ending it all with "...so help me God."

That was it. It was now official. Chief Michaels shook all of our hands and we were given temporary ID cards, but with no individual photos on them. The real ID cards, along with our badges, would have to wait until we graduated from the Academy in late November. I suppose that was fair. In the meantime, we had a lot of work to do, but none of it here, in this building. Instead, it would be in a much larger building and complex in Chocolate

Town, U.S.A., aka Hershey, Pennsylvania, about 60 miles due west from where we were now standing.

Before heading off to Hershey, I would have to accomplish one more important task. That was to get another haircut. I was reminded of this by Lt. Robinson as I was leaving the township building on Friday after the swearing in. While my hair wasn't by any means long, it did touch the top of my ears. My then hair style was actually probably pretty conservative for the mid-'70s in the U.S. But, after Lt. Robinson told me that the PSP troopers will send back any cadet whose hair is too long, I decided it was time for yet another haircut.

I would argue that much more so than in the early 2000s, a young man's hairstyle was a very important part of his image back in the late '60 and throughout most of the '70s. Even if wearing hip clothes, driving a cool car, good-looking and with a great personality, if your hair was really short back then you were assumed to be either a cop, fireman, the military, or a dork. And, these were not the most popular professions (or personality classifications) of which to be a member in those somewhat post-radical times.

Members of each of these three professional entities (though not dorks, as far as I know) sued in various courts to argue that men should be allowed to wear their hair consistent with the existing cultural norms in the country. Each time the suits were dismissed, even at the appellate levels. The argument became even more convoluted as women were authorized to serve in these various agencies, yet their hair was allowed to remain long, even if worn in a bun while on-duty. A clear double-standard was now present, which added to the on-going arguments at this point.

It was all for naught. By the time some lawsuits regarding hair length were eventually won in favor of the police officers, the style was changing back to shorter hair for men. New York City Police Department (NYPD) officers legally challenged the long hair rules and after several levels of appeal, eventually won in the courts.

I recall seeing pictures and video of long-haired and even bearded uniformed officers of the NYPD. Even though I was on their side philosophically, I have to admit these uber-hairy uniformed cops did, indeed, look kind of strange back then.

Regarding my personal hairstyle in the mid-'70s, it had been long-ish since I started college. It was never hippie-style, for example, down my back, or anywhere near that length, but it rested comfortably over my shirt collar and completely covered my ears. When I graduated college and started at the department store, I had it trimmed a bit shorter, but not by that much since my bosses there didn't care. It helped me blend in better with the shoppers and not look so much like store security to the potential shoplifters.

I pretty much had a five year run of long hair through the early to mid-'70s, more or less like almost every other under-40, non-public servant I knew. But, it now had to come off. And, it did.

Although I moved out of my Olney neighborhood to the Northeast section of Philadelphia in May of '76, after I married, I would still travel back to the old neighborhood to visit my parents on an almost weekly basis. In doing so, I simply kept the same local barber that I had for the last few years. When I went to the 5th St. shop that day, located just north of Lowell schoolyard (of basketball playing days) and a bit south of the Modern Pharmacy (of cat/penny throwing arrest scenario), the barber said as usual, "Just a regular trim?"

I almost choked, but still managed to say, "No, not this time. I'm starting the police academy on Monday. Cut it short, cop-short, please."

He knew what I meant and he obediently did so, as I knew he had other police officer customers who required the same follicular styling.

It wasn't easy looking at the mirror in front of me and seeing my hair being systematically chopped off. This had been me, what I looked like, who I was, through good times and bad, since the summer I graduated high school, all throughout my college years, and even during the course of my first real full-time job. But in one to two inch lengths, one scissors snip at a time, there it went, onto the barber's tile floor, all because of this next job of mine. When he was done, I looked in the mirror, not instantly recognizing the person who was staring back at me, and quietly just shook my head back and forth.

The barber then said, "Is that OK? You want it shorter?"

I told him no, that I think he's done plenty of damage already. He looked at me quizzically but then smiled.

He said, "You'll get used to it. They all do."

I hoped he was right, at least as it pertained to me.

Upon walking back inside my 3rd St. parents' home, they told me they actually liked the cut. No surprise there. When Eileen saw it she told me I looked like I did when she first met me back in high school. I wasn't sure if that was a compliment or an insult. But, either way, it would be my hairstyle of choice - no, make that my hairstyle by mandate - for the immediate future. Hopefully the state troopers in Chocolate Town would approve of it when they saw me on Monday morning.

Chapter Twenty-eight

Ray Geary picked me up around 7:00AM on Monday morning, August 30, 1976, and off we drove the two hours westbound on the Pennsylvania Turnpike toward the PSP Academy in Hershey. Over the last few years, in travelling to both the PSU Berks campus, and later to the PSU Main Campus in State College, I found myself driving in the same direction on the same highway, sometimes even with Ray to State College. My early adult life, and the educational and now professional pursuits associated with it, seemed inextricably linked to this particular stretch of the PA Turnpike. Later in my professional life it would be the New Jersey Turnpike, then later still, Interstate 95. But, for now, I'd be getting very used to riding the PA Turnpike, on 12 consecutive Sunday and Friday evenings, with my friend and fellow police cadet at the wheel of his car.

Upon arriving at the Academy that morning, we were ushered into the large auditorium in the northeast corner of the multi-acre complex. The entrance to the auditorium was the closest one to the distinctive red-and-white checkered water tower, which stood tall (and still does) over the sprawling grounds of this renowned law enforcement training facility. Ray and I recognized the six other Bensalem cadets there and we all sort of hung out together waiting for the procedures to begin. There were about 50 of us in the room that day. We were comprised of all white males of varying ages and sizes, with the exception of one mid-20s female. She was a cadet from the State College Police Department, the same town where PSU was located, and where I had spent the last few years of my life, on and off.

As we were told to do so in advance, everyone was wearing a suit or sport jacket and tie. Well, except the one female cadet who was nonetheless dressed appropriately in her business suit. This garb, for any of us, would not last long though. Before the day was over, we would all be issued our two pairs of khaki pants and five matching long-sleeved shirts and a snap-on black tie. That would be our uniform for the entire time we were at the Academy. No exceptions, except on Wednesday nights, the one night during the week we were authorized to leave the Academy grounds and go into exciting downtown Hershey for a few hours.

That first morning, around 10:00, the major who ran the PSP Academy opened the proceedings. He advised us that we were being trained under the relatively new Act 120, aka the Pennsylvania Municipal Police Officers Training Act. It was officially put into law in 1974, and it was now a requirement in Pennsylvania that all police officers successfully attend and complete this 12-week training academy, run by the PSP. This included not just brand new hires like me and the other officers-to-be, but experienced and usually older officers who had never received any formal training prior to this as, quite simply, the law in PA had not required it in the past. That explained the presence of at least ten of my new classmates seemingly 40 years of age or older, who quite frankly, did not appear to be in the best of overall physical condition. How would they make it through the physical training part? We'd all soon find out.

I got to know some of these older officers as our training progressed. Yes, they were actual police officers working at various Pennsylvania departments, some with 20+ years of experience already. They told me that in "the old days," it was much different for them and their police colleagues. Virtually to a man (yes, they were all men back then), they advised that when they were hired, they were simply given a gun, a badge, and a uniform, maybe drove around in a patrol car for a week or so with a senior officer, and they were then let loose on the job. There was no formal training at all for them.

The exception to this lack-of-training would be PSP troopers, and the larger departments in PA, such as Philadelphia, Pittsburgh, and a few other municipalities. I later learned that this policy was not very different throughout the rest of the U.S. at the time.

After the older and somewhat friendly-sounding major gave us his relatively brief welcome talk, it was next the turn of a younger, well-built, chiseled-face, officious-sounding corporal who would read us in no uncertain terms the rules and regulations of his home, and our new home, the PSP Academy. He would remind us up front that he knew we were not troopers-in-training, so the Academy rules would be a bit less imposing on us, as opposed to the rules with their own rookie trooper cadets. But, nonetheless, as "guests" of the Academy we were to adhere to and follow the rules to a man (and one woman), without exception. Any violation would result in a "gig."

A what? I'm sorry, say that again, please.

This corporal, who told us he was also an attorney, continued over the next 45 minutes or so to read to us from a checklist every violation possible that could occur there. Some of which I never even thought of until he actually mentioned them, for example, tampering with the horses in the PSP stable, skipping out on KP duties, having non-polished shoes, just to name a few. The general violations went from not making our beds properly each morning, to leaving our dorm rooms messy, to cursing, fighting, not shaving, or God-forbid, having sex on the Academy grounds. He specifically looked at the one female cadet in the class as he was advising of this particular potential breach of conduct. If such a violation was to occur he would state after each one, "That's a gig."

He added at the end of his checklist, "Too many gigs, and you're out of here."

Okay, again...just what the hell is this "gig" thing?

As one of the corporal's first listed gig-sanctioned violations was talking in class or during auditorium presentations, we didn't dare ask anyone around us what it may be or represent for fear of getting one of these things that we didn't know what they were. He never did actually define it to us.

I silently motioned to Ray, who was sitting next to me, for the answer. In doing so, I used nothing by facial expressions and hand movements, as so far these were not known to be gig-able offenses. So far. Ray responded, also silently with face and hand gestures, that he didn't know either. Yet we both knew we did NOT want to get one…whatever it was.

It remained during this longish morning session a nebulous word that I found could be used as a noun, a verb, and an adjective. That is, "You will receive a gig (noun) if you…;" or "You'll be gigged (verb) if you…;" or "It is a gig-able (adjective) offense if you…."

Then, after adamantly advising us that we did NOT want to see him again, especially in his office as a result of attaining too many gigs, the corporal wished us a good day and abruptly turned left and exited the stage. I came to an early conclusion that morning that I did not ever want to see him again, gig-related or not gig-related. And I still didn't know what a gig was.

I actually did see "Corporal Gig" again, but only at our graduation three months later. He seemed to be a more affable fellow at that time. He was so much less gig-focused then.

At lunch that first day, upon talking to some of our fellow classmates who had been in the military, we learned that a gig was simply a negative mark put on your permanent record if you did something wrong. If too many gigs added up here at the Academy, you would get in trouble, maybe a warning, maybe a suspension, maybe worse. And, your individual department would be notified too. That would not be a good thing.

I learned early on to avoid these now somewhat loosely-defined gigs at all costs. And, I'm happy to report, I managed to go gig-free my whole time while in the training academy. In retrospect, I'll always be appreciative of the officious corporal for his pep talk that morning. It scared me, and the others in the room, straight.

We would also learn during our morning introduction session that we would each assume KP duties during our stay there. Yes, even though we weren't actual PSP troopers-in-training, but instead "guests" of the Academy, we'd still have to take turns working in the kitchen before, during, and after our three meals each day. For each of us, this would be for two of the total of twelve weeks we were assigned there. Just like in a military mess hall, we cleaned food scraps off plates, washed dishes, and otherwise handled all the cleanup chores associated with a large institutional-style kitchen. At least we were spared from cleaning out the horse stables while assigned there. The trooper-cadets, we learned, had that duty also as part of their daily routines.

Thank goodness, no horse s**t assignments for the municipal officers-in-training. In numerous ways, that would come later in my police career.

Our next trooper-speaker that day, after lunch, was the Academy's course curriculum supervisor. He told us about our classes and what was expected of us in order to graduate. The 50 of us would be divided alphabetically into two separate sections. Our respective sections would meet every Monday through Friday from 0800 hours until 1700 hours. (This was my first exposure to military time; translated it means 8:00AM until 5:00PM. I'd be getting used to it over the next 11 years.) There were no exceptions to this schedule. There were no upcoming holidays off except for the Labor Day holiday which was the following weekend. Our training would mostly take place in the Academy classrooms, but sometimes also in the auditorium, in the gym, and on the outdoor firing range. The academic-oriented courses would include Pennsylvania Criminal Law, Pennsylvania Motor Vehicle Law, the Pennsylvania court system, and the U.S. Constitution as it pertains to search-and-seizure, arrests, interview/interrogation, various drugs and their classifications, and other relevant legal issues as they relate to the duties, obligations, and responsibilities of a police officer. The classes were to begin on the very next morning, at 0800 hours. We'd all be there, or be gigged.

And so the classes began. It was about 60 weekdays in a row of educational stimulation and knowledge attainment. But, these classes were different. That's for sure. During one interesting early classroom session on drugs, the trooper/instructor brought in some marijuana to show us. He wanted us to see it and smell it, both in its natural state and when burning. After walking up and down the aisles showing us the equivalent of a nickel bag of pot, he then lit it in a large ashtray and walked the same course again among us. He wanted the class to know officially the odor and aromatic features of marijuana, in both forms.

This pot exposure was necessary because, if in our future law enforcement duties we would make an arrest based on the detection of someone smoking pot as our probable cause, we could then later testify in court that we were familiar with that smell because of our training at the PSP Academy. This way, there were no embarrassing responses by the arresting officer during potential cross-examinations by a defense attorney alleging that either the officer doesn't know what marijuana smells like, or if he/she does know, it's possibly because he/she uses it themselves in their private lives. That would not be good for the officer, so the burning of it for a few minutes in our class was a valuable learning experience.

And, no, none of us got high that day breathing in the essence of the burning marijuana. The trooper walked too fast for it and extinguished it within minutes. He also told us that he had to sign in and sign out for the specimens he brought into class each new training session. So, it wasn't from his personal stash, either.

Our physical defense and tactics training was at least three days per week, if not more. There, a burly but in otherwise excellent shape corporal would have us run outside during each of our classes, and do sit-ups, push-ups, etc., afterwards in the gym. He wouldn't drive us too hard, because he was apparently concerned about the ten older guys in our class. Quite simply, he didn't want them to die on him. Apparently, that exact scenario had occurred in one of their classes a year or so ago to an older trainee. Since we were all "locals" (as opposed to their own trooper cadets), the physical training aspect wasn't pushed too hard on us. Some of us younger guys kept up with the corporal in all he did, and the other, mostly older ones who couldn't, just did their best. It was fine as long as when we were practicing handcuffing techniques, weapon retention, and basic self-defense, everyone could pass the muster. We did, and these experienced officers actually taught us a few things, from a self-defense and arrest-making perspective, that the corporal didn't cover in his classes.

The firearms training also occurred around three times per week. Our primary range instructor was an older trooper who had more target shooting awards himself than did the entirety of many smaller police departments. As it was the first time I had ever shot a firearm of any kind in my life, it was good to have an experienced instructor such as this man to teach me the right way to do it, from hitting the target to safely securing the weapon.

Those of us in the Bensalem PD were each issued Smith & Wesson .357 Magnums, as that was the official weapon of our department. (The weapons had been separately dropped off at the PSP Academy by a Bensalem officer. The eight of us were not to be trusted, yet, with the weapons in our personal possession. They were stored in secure gun lockers at the range.) Other cadets from other departments were shooting smaller .38 caliber weapons. I don't recall anyone in our firearms training classes shooting a semi-automatic pistol. Not many cops carried them during this time frame, certainly not in Pennsylvania. It was the revolver with which I would become initially proficient, with the relatively new-fangled "speedloaders" to help hasten my re-loading and shooting time.

Speedloaders were round plastic devices that would be pre-loaded with six bullets. Gravity then became your friend. When you had fired off your first six rounds, you would simply flip open the gun's round cylinder, point the barrel upwards, and empty it of the six spent casings down onto the ground. You would then quickly point the barrel downwards, and reload the cylinder with fresh rounds by a quick turn of the knob on the speedloader device which allowed the new bullets to fall into place in their individual chambers. It was certainly faster than loading one bullet at a time into each chamber of the weapon, as was done for a hundred years-plus before this ingenious device was invented.

I always carried two speedloaders on my leather holster when I was in uniform and on patrol. That would have been 18 rounds at my disposal right away, including the six already in the cylinder of the .357. Oh, and yes, another six rounds in my backup .38 I carried in my ankle holster, oh, and also a fully loaded shotgun alongside of me in my patrol car. There were extra boxes of bullets and shotgun shells in the glove department of each patrol car too – just in case. If I couldn't handle a real-life situation with 24 bullets and at least five shotgun rounds at my disposal, not to mention the extra ammo boxes for each, I suppose I would be in deep doo-doo at that point. Hopefully, if it came to that, the reinforcements wouldn't be far behind. Fortunately, it never came to that for me.

Later, in my FBI career, when I switched over to a semi-automatic pistol, I would carry two ammo magazines with me, along with the one in the weapon. That was approximately 40 rounds at my immediate disposal, oh, and a fully loaded MP-5 shoulder weapon in my trunk, with extra magazines and ammo boxes for it. Fortunately, once again, it never came to me needing this much weaponry in any tactical situation.

I made it through the first month or so of the Academy without any injuries of which to speak, certainly not from our defensive training. I was in pretty good physical shape at the time, so the running and other calisthenics were not a problem to me. However, at least three different parts of my body suffered to some degree as they were simply not used to what was happening to them, or at least not to the frequency to which these body parts were accustomed. That is, my too-tight shirt collar with the metal clasp of the cheap snap-on tie was digging into my Adam's Apple; the brand new black cordovan shoes, which were very rigid and stiff, irritated my heels so much that I had to buy and wear thick gauze bandages under my socks on each heel; and, for the first time in my life, I was shaving five days a week and, quite frankly, my face hurt.

I know, I'm coming across like a whiner here. But, these individual body parts were bothering me, each at the same time, and it would take a while for them to heal or get used to my new wardrobe pieces and at least one new everyday bodily function. While I didn't complain to anyone about these relatively minor maladies, it created a level of discomfort and distraction for me up until about halfway through my time at the Academy. After that, thanks to strategically based bandages and just toughening-up, I simply got used to them.

I don't expect any sympathy for withstanding these relatively mundane ailments at the time, but anyone preparing to enter the military or a law enforcement academy should be aware of these possible issues, along with everything else the staff is going to throw at you.

Our training at the PSP Academy continued day-in and day-out through the fall of '76. It was edifying and useful information that we were absorbing, or at least trying to absorb. Some of what we would learn, besides routine criminal violations and motor vehicle weight and speed restrictions, would hopefully also save our lives too, if ever confronted with such a situation. One example of how to not be shot during a "routine" car-stop was exemplified in a 16mm movie clip we were shown one day.

Although VCRs and videotapes were commercially available during the mid-'70s, the PSP did not choose to utilize such electronic equipment at their Academy, at least when my class was there. So, every few days, a movie projector and screen were brought into our classroom and with the clickety-clack of the old Bell and Howell droning on in the background, we would watch movies of what to do, and what NOT to do, during car-stops and other arrest situations.

I recall one of several car-stop scenario films in which the camera lens represented the eyes of the officer who pulls a car over. In other words, his point-of-view (POV) was exactly what we were seeing on the screen in the front of the classroom. The film began with the lone officer observing a speeder and then properly turning on the patrol car's red lights and siren and advising the dispatcher via his police radio of the make, model, year, and tag of the car he's pulling over and the highway where he's stopping it. The officer then gets out of the car and walks up to the driver side of the car that he has stopped. All executed very well, so far.

Through the officer's POV, behind the wheel, in what today would be seen as an anachronistic and sexist representation, is a 30 or so years of age, full-figured, blonde woman in a low-cut top. As the filmed car-stop scenario continues, the woman is observed now turning her body toward the officer, resting her arms on the opened-windowed car door, looking up at him from the driver's seat and talking to him in a very friendly and flirtatious manner. The POV of the officer clearly focuses on this woman and her very obvious and over the top personality traits and physical features, but not much else. This somewhat playful discourse, certainly on her part, not to mention the overly glamorized visual images of this woman, go on for 45 seconds or so.

The officer, again through his POV, does not seem to be doing anything wrong at all at this point. The scene, as it's playing out, is actually boring with the somewhat friendly, yet professional, conversation between the officer and the woman as he is attempting to attain her license and registration information.

After class, many of us away-from-home cadets admitted that we were focusing on the charms of this seemingly very friendly and attractive woman in her loose fitting and revealing shirt top. It was only natural. Well, for most of us in the class anyway.

But suddenly, this blissful and enticing picture changed for us, and not in a good way for the officer conducting the car stop. All of a sudden, a hairy and tattooed male right arm was observed ever so quickly extending itself from the other side of the front seat, over her chest, in the hand of which was a firearm. It was then fired from point-blank range at the officer. As the now-shot officer's POV is slowly falling downward, toward the ground alongside the stopped car, we see that a man was lying on the seat next to the woman, ostensibly the whole time, partially covered by a blanket or long coat of some sort. Remember, cars tended to be larger during the '70s, with uninterrupted front bench seats almost six feet long in some cases, explaining why, along with the female distractor, the officer and his POV never noticed the man.

As the officer was clearly distracted by the female driver (as truth-be-known, so were many of my classmates), he (and we) failed to visually inspect the rest of the car as he approached it. Because of that misjudgment, he was shot in this fictitious scenario. That is not a good thing at a car stop. Ever!

My PSP Academy class would view many similar type 16mm films during our training, although this was the only one in which an attractive female-turned-gun-moll played such a role. We also practiced car stops in real police cars, in the large back parking lot of the Academy. We undertook these exercises during the daytime as well as evening hours. Darkness, I would learn then and later, brings a whole different dimension to police work, from car stops, to shooting, to bad guys, and to some potentially attractive but inherently dangerous women.

I later asked the one female cadet in our class, Diane Conrad, if the buxom-woman-as-a-car-stop-distraction scenario bothered her. She said it didn't, that she was relatively used to such examples in her embryonic law enforcement career, and even in other academic and police training pursuits before the PSP Academy. Diane further stated that knowing she was somewhat outnumbered, what with 49 male classmates and an all-male faculty, she didn't have all that much choice with these type teaching techniques. Nonetheless, she managed her 12-week stay there very well and conducted herself as a true professional. She became, "one of the guys," and I mean that in a very positive sense.

Diane, our lone female cadet classmate, was assigned to a single room in another wing of the Academy, away from the men, with her very own bathroom and shower. What a deal! I was jealous, as I heard slamming dorm doors all night long and had no privacy whatsoever in our shared men's bathroom and showers.

I admired the spirit and intensity Diane brought to our training experience. I later learned she was one of the first female cadets to graduate from the PSP Academy, as either a "local" cop or trooper. Diane did excellent in our training class and later I learned she had a great career at the State College PD.

As difficult as it may have been for the one female cadet in our otherwise all male Academy class, it wasn't always that smooth of a ride for the rest of us either while there for those 12 weeks, and not just in the classroom. In other words, besides the pressure of the everyday training regimen, in-class exams, physical training testing, etc., individual personalities could clash too. Near the end of our Academy training, I found myself engaged in one such clash, and ironically it was with one of the other seven Bensalem PD cadets.

The incident itself was relatively minor, and occurred outside in the parking lot of the Academy while we were training in how to conduct felony car stops, removing potentially violent suspects from their cars, and the like. As we were trained, once the car was stopped and pulled over, lots of firm, command-style yelling at the "suspects" in their cars, such as "Put your hands out the window, NOW!" and "Down on the ground, arms and legs spread, NOW!", was necessary to gain lawful control of the potentially dangerous guys. So, adrenalin and testosterone were clearly pumping in over-abundance during these so-designed emotional training sessions.

In the midst of this controlled yelling and screaming, something was said, a flashlight was misused, handcuffs squeezed closed too tight, or something like that, and my fellow future BPD officer made some now long-forgotten but nonetheless snide remarks at me. It was out of earshot and view of our two PSP instructors who were on the other side of the Academy training lot, and I felt free to remark in kind back to this guy. He then proceeded to walk over to me, got in my face, said something else I didn't like, and motioned as if he was possibly going to punch me. I had heard and seen enough at this point and I beat him to the punch, literally, perhaps.

Before my classmate could follow through with a punch, instead of me striking him, I simply pushed him hard with both hands on his upper chest. As a result, he stumbled backwards and fell squarely on his butt. He said something else nasty to me while getting up on his feet as he moved quickly back at me, and I assumed the pugilist position to be ready for anything from him. But, fortunately for both of us, other cadets intervened and stepped in between us, effectively ending the skirmish before it really even started. We would definitely have been gigged for this physical altercation if it had been observed by the troopers. But, no gigs resulted, luckily for both of us.

Eventually, the two of us became civil again to each other again before graduation, but just barely. Neither of us apologized to the other and we never became friendly in any way, shape, or form through the rest of the Academy training or even later when we started working together as street cops. There was just something about the guy that rubbed me the wrong way. I saw it during our Academy training and observed it again in him when we were both cops, especially in how he would treat civilians with whom he would come into contact. He could be very rude, very authoritative, and even semi-violent, when none of these reactions was necessary at the time.

This same cop clearly rubbed some other people the wrong way too about five years later, to include a former girlfriend and other Bensalem police officers. He decided one day for whatever reason to burglarize the home of this ex-girlfriend. When she later discovered her missing items, she called our police department and provided the facts and the evidence. The officer/ex-boyfriend/alleged burglar was interviewed. His story didn't make sense. So, he was arrested and eventually fired from his job. He pleaded guilty later to some lesser theft-related offenses and received probation. He did not come back to the BPD and I believe his law enforcement career was effectively over at that point. At least I hoped so.

Chapter Twenty-nine

Nearing the end of our training, when our class was about three weeks from our mid-November graduation day, we were advised that there would be two class speakers chosen by the faculty to represent our graduating class. This was precedent at every graduation from the PSP Academy, whether that of their own troopers or these relatively new municipal classes. We learned that one of us would speak at the formal ceremonial dinner the night before graduation and the other one would speak at the next day's graduation itself. Each of the cadets was then compelled to write a three minute speech and present it individually, one at a time, to a panel of three troopers.

Since I had to undergo this "audition," I resurrected a semi-humorous speech I gave in one of my last year college courses at Penn State, modified it to some degree to make it applicable to a law enforcement group, and just casually presented it to the panel when it was my turn. I forgot all about it shortly afterwards as I had no true burning desire to give a speech at either ceremony.

To my great surprise, however, several days later, our class was told that I was selected to give the ceremonial dinner speech. Interestingly, Ray Geary was separately chosen to give the graduation speech the next day. It was impressive, looking back at it, that out of 50 potential candidates, both speech givers were from the Bensalem PD, who coincidently were also friends going back to first grade at St. Helena School and all the way through high school and college.

It was something in the "wooder" we drank in Olney, I suppose.

As there were no dropouts, flunkouts, or debilitating injuries in our Academy class (yes, I eventually got over my face, neck, and heel soreness), each one of us who started on August 30, 1976, graduated on the scheduled date of November 19, 1976. My wife, Eileen, drove to Hershey, accompanied by both my parents, and we stayed overnight in rooms at a local Hershey hotel. The formal, ceremonial dinner was only for graduates and spouses or dates, so my parents had to wait behind in their hotel room while my wife and I attended the dinner. I always regret that my parents didn't get to see me deliver my speech.

My talk to my soon-to-be fellow grads, their significant others, and the attending PSP faculty members went well that night. I wrote it and delivered it to be a bit on the personal side and with an attempt at humor, as the evening was designed for us to let our hair down a bit and celebrate with loved ones the end of 12 weeks of sometimes intense and difficult training. During my talk, I managed to elicit a few laughs from the attendees, although no doubt with some of my class and dorm-related anecdotes going over the heads of the invited guests and perhaps even the instructors in attendance.